The Story of
Palo Duro Canyon

Palo Duro Canyon with view of the Lighthouse in the distance, early twentieth century. Note lack of cedar, mesquite, and other vegetation dominant now. Photo courtesy of Panhandle Plains Historical Museum, Canyon, Texas.

The Story of Palo Duro Canyon

Edited by
Duane F. Guy

New introduction by
Frederick W. Rathjen

Texas Tech University Press

Cover design by Bryce Burton

Library of Congress Cataloging-in-Publication Data
The story of Palo Duro Canyon / edited by Duane F. Guy ; new introduction by Frederick W. Rathjen.
     p. cm. — (Double mountain books—classic reissues of the American West)
Originally published: Canyon, Tex. : Panhandle Plains Historical Society, 1979.
Includes bibliographical references and index.
     ISBN 0-89672-453-0 (pbk. : alk. paper)
     1. Palo Duro Canyon (Tex.)—History. 2. Palo Duro State Park (Tex.)—History. I. Guy, Duane F. II. Series.

F 392.P16 S86 2001
976.4'833—dc21   00-066324

01 02 03 04 05 06 07 08 09 / 9 8 7 6 5 4 3 2 1

Texas Tech University Press
Box 41037
Lubbock, Texas 79409-1037 USA

1-800-832-4042
ttup@ttu.edu
http://www.ttup.ttu.edu

CONTENTS

INTRODUCTION

Most people who live in the Texas Panhandle agree that it is a nice place to live. It is droughty, of course, and occasional high winds are irksome, but elevation and a typical Great Plains environment provide a relatively cool, dry climate rarely extreme in either heat or cold. Travelers racing through on I-40, as well as residents indifferent to their surroundings, usually perceive little, if any, of the subtle beauty of the Panhandle-Plains. After all, *apparently* endless sameness of landscape and big sky reveal themselves less dramatically than, say, the front range of the Rockies as viewed from I-25. Traveling on northward from I-40, one encounters the breaks of the Canadian River where the more obvious contours of riverine erosion relieve the flatness of the plains and create pleasing views of the wide river valley.

Then there is Palo Duro Canyon. One of several canyons that cut into the eastern escarpment of the Staked Plains, the Palo Duro excites the imagination as few others do. Even veteran canyoneers experience some sense of pleasurable surprise as they approach the rim and find the earth opening up before them. Sharing that experience with a first-time visitor is both fun and a satisfying joy. The newcomer doubtlessly has heard of "the Canyon" and probably seen pictures of the iconic Lighthouse formation, but the thrill of discovery comes when the newcomer approaches the rim and, without forewarning, the Staked Plains open into the geological and ecological wonder that is Palo Duro Canyon. For the local escort the satisfaction is two-fold: his or her own rekindled wonderment and observing the surprised, awestruck gasp-response of the guest.

However many times one visits Palo Duro Canyon, active curiosity contemplates a variety of questions: How did the canyon get here? What caused the varicolor of the walls and formations? Why do some formations stand completely separated from the canyon walls? Did the little stream running along the canyon floor form this canyon all by itself? Who were the first people to find this canyon and how did they react? Imagination goes to work on this last question and contemplates what ancient people must have felt when they, even less aware than we, stumbled upon the chasm rim and quickly realized that they had found a bonanza, an immense concentration of water, wood, game, and protection—all they needed to sustain life.

The canyon's archeological and ethnological treasures suggest about twelve thousand years of human habitation, rising and waning as climate varied among periods of abundant moisture, aridity, and sometimes fearfully severe drought which all but destroyed the resources that had to be immediately available to sustain the lives of preindustrial people.

To experience fully the rewards of Palo Duro Canyon, we should spend a few nights camping within earshot of rustling cottonwoods, get out of the twenty-first century culture which envelops us, and allow romantic imagination to run a little wild. We camp in places like Palo Duro Canyon to simplify our lives and get some perspective on our life situations. Who knows but what the family of some ancient chieftain or historic Comanche or Kiowa family pondered their situation by a teepee fire on the same spot where we pitch our tents and, despite sharp cultural differences in modes of expression, respond to the Palo Duro ambience much as did the people of time long past.

Any discussion of Palo Duro Canyon necessarily centers on Palo Duro Canyon State Park. For practical purposes, the park and the canyon are more or less synonymous since only the park is state owned and therefore publicly accessible. The park's birthing pains were severe and its survival far less than certain. Probably neither birth nor survival would have been possible except for the near-militant devotion of private citizens who caught a vision of what could be, believed in the cause, and despite the economic stringency of the Great Depression, resolved to see Palo Duro Canyon State Park become a reality. As events turned out, the hard times of the 1930s brought unexpected aid when the Civilian Conservation Corps, a major component of President Franklin Roosevelt's New Deal, provided the manpower to construct automobile access to the canyon floor and to build basic facilities for public accommodation.

The public responded to the park despite the fact that, for many years, Palo Duro was the only Texas state park requiring entrance fees. After World War II, visitor numbers increased yearly and the adequacy of Depression-era improvements correspondingly deteriorated while park administration, maintenance, and personnel remained underfunded and deficient.

For true park lovers there was an advantage: one could find and keep quiet about private hideaways, pitch one's camp, and at least seem to be entirely isolated from the rest of the world. As one would expect, there were abuses, much to the dismay of responsible campers who carefully subordinated their activities to the park's well-being and cleaned up after those who did not.

In the 1970s, better organized campgrounds and sanitary facilities were constructed which, on the whole, benefited users and mitigated harmful impact. Time, use, and occasional flooding have made many of these improvements obsolete and, in some cases, useless. As the millennium turns, Palo Duro Canyon State Park faces the same crises confronting state and national parks throughout the United States.

Visitor impact exceeds carrying capacity of both park environment and funding. Park managers find themselves dealing with the demands of conflicting constituencies (campers, hikers, bikers, and horsemen) who often look upon parks as their playgrounds, sometimes get contentious over whose activity takes precedence, and often, though by no means always, are indifferent to impact which induces erosion or other damage. Then there are casual visitors who simply do not understand that the Palo Duro environment is fragile. *Fragile?* The appearance of harsh ruggedness may cause one to wonder, "How could you possibly damage a place like this?" How? Quickly, easily, and permanently. Disturbed areas of well developed soils and generous moisture can recover fairly quickly. Recovery is slow or even non-existent in semi-arid, desert-like terrain where soils are thin, friable, and exposed, and annual precipitation averages about twenty inches. That is why Palo Duro Canyon is fragile and requires users' conscientious restraint.

Add to these problems and physiographic realities the demands of economic interests who value a park primarily for the tourist dollars it brings to surrounding communities. For them, the number of visitors is the criterion of park success, and the well-being of the park in question is of little concern.

Obviously, funding alone cannot guarantee the integrity of any park; but just as obviously, integrity cannot be achieved without funding. On this point, despite its wealth, Texas had little to brag about. In 1998, Texas observed the seventy-fifth anniversary of the establishment of the state's first park. Among the publicity accompanying that event, the Texas Parks and Wildlife Department published these startling, hardly celebratory, figures: In per capita funding for state park operating budgets, Texas ranked forty-ninth among the states, or $1.79 as compared to a national average of $4.81; in per capita spending for all parks and recreation, Texas ranked forty-eighth, or $3.00 as compared to a national average of $13.00; in park staffing, Texas ranked forty-eighth, employing .5 persons per ten thousand per capita, as compared to a national average of 2.5 employees. These data leave Texans with little to be proud of, especially when the 2000–2001 *Texas Almanac* chortles, "If Texas were still an independent nation, it would be the eleventh largest economy in the world" (577).

The greater a park's distinctiveness, the greater its attraction, and therein lies the problem with many of our national and state treasures. How do we protect the qualities which elevate mere places to treasures and also make them available for the enjoyment of our people? In some national parks, stringent measures are implemented. One would hope that anticipatory action prior to crisis would protect Texas' state parks and keep them accessible. If not already here, crisis is a forthcoming reality, especially if a projected Texas population of thirty-four million people by 2030 actually materializes.

A part of the solution lies in grassroots citizen volunteer participation in park maintenance, including even some of those citizens resident in that stolid Anglo-Saxon institution, the county jail. In the case of Palo Duro Canyon State Park, generously given citizen expertise, materials, and labor provide improvements such as trail building and maintenance and relieve pressure on the park budget and professional personnel. But funding is still a problem.

To compensate for legislative parsimony, the Texas Parks and Wildlife Department developed Lone Star Legacy, a program designed to endow each of the state's parks and wildlife areas through a vast system of foundations, one for each unit, funded from private sources. Fortunately for Palo Duro Canyon State Park, a local support organization, Partners in Palo Duro Foundation, Inc., is well established, thanks largely to a handful of dedicated people who acted in the tradition of the citizens of the 1930s.

The Partners' long term goal is to build the Palo Duro Canyon State Park Legacy Fund through the Texas Parks and Wildlife Foundation. Meanwhile, though far from ready to fund the park fully, the Partners provide critical support from their own funds, including basic law enforcement equipment essential to effective enforcement and to the safety of law enforcement personnel.

Undoubtedly, much of Palo Duro Canyon's magnetic attraction comes from its sharp contrast with the surrounding terrain. Although its presence is scientifically explainable in terms understandable to an interested layman, the sense that it just, somehow, ought not to be there must enhance its dramatic impact upon the observer. Most observers enjoy the scenery and come away mentally impressed and emotionally refreshed. For others, Palo Duro Canyon inspires a creative and perhaps even a spiritual response. Extant rock art certainly suggests such an inspiration through all the ages of Native American presence.

In 1853, Captain Randolph B. Marcy approached the canyon from the east under orders to find the headwaters of Red River. From a point south of present Fort Sill, Marcy ascended the Red and Prairie Dog Town Fork, the little stream flowing through the canyon floor. Eventually the Captain reached a spring bursting from the base of a cliff in Palo Duro Canyon. This spring, he was sure, was the headspring of the great Red River, but he was not very precise in identifying the spring's location. No matter, at least for the purpose of this essay. It does matter that Marcy described a biosystem which included black bear, mountain lions, and wolves, all long extirpated. With almost boyish awe, Marcy responded to the canyonlands as observed from down-canyon, and his journals reflect his reaction with a vividness of imagery that is delightful, but not as helpful as precise scholarship would like. To put it in a positive way, Captain Marcy came, saw, and described with a more artistic sensitivity than one would expect from a presumably hard-bitten frontier infantryman. Assessment of Marcy's journal as "artistic" may seem a bit extravagant, but he anticipates a distinguished array of creative spirits who were similarly inspired.

Georgia O'Keeffe's biographers report that she had virtually given up on a career as an artist until she came to Amarillo, and two years later to Canyon, to teach. Here, in the vastness of the

High Plains and the grandeur of Palo Duro Canyon, she found the stimuli that revived her artistic creativity and set her on the path to becoming one of America's most honored artists. Since O'Keeffe's time, three generations of artists and photographers have found similar inspiration, and their canyonscapes rest among the prized possessions of countless art and Palo Duro Canyon lovers.

Similarly, Samuel Jones's *Symphony No. 3, Palo Duro Canyon* evokes for the auditory sense what artists and photographers evoke for the visual sense. All three go beyond the intellect to edify and amplify the spirit.

Early on in this essay, I suggested a few questions likely to occur to a thoughtful visitor. *The Story of Palo Duro Canyon* addresses those questions and many more, and stimulates and directs inquisitive minds to formulate others. None of the authors would argue that all has been said; all agree that ample challenge remains to command the inquiries of present and future scholars, both academic and non-academic. These authors have resisted the temptation to write to impress other specialists. Professional as they are, they wrote for curious, perceptive observers motivated by impulses characteristic of the great American naturalists such as John Muir, Aldo Leopold, or Texas's own Roy Bedichek who, more's the pity, appears not to have found Palo Duro Canyon.

Contrary to the contrived, hubristic images of "rugged individualism," civilizations in the semi-arid plains have survived through cooperation between individuals and among groups. So publication of this new edition of *The Story of Palo Duro Canyon* is historically appropriate. Its publication is possible because of the cooperation of the Panhandle-Plains Historical Society, the original publisher (in the 1978 issue of the *Panhandle-Plains Historical Review*), and Texas Tech University Press, both products of High Plains and canyonlands culture and active agents for its literary expression and preservation.

Frederick W. Rathjen

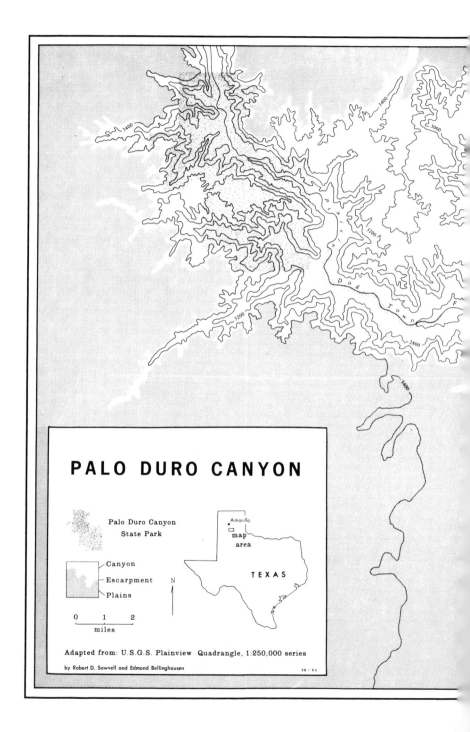

PALO DURO CANYON

Palo Duro Canyon
State Park

Canyon
Escarpment
Plains

0   1   2
miles

Amarillo
map
area

N

TEXAS

Adapted from: U.S.G.S. Plainview Quadrangle, 1:250,000 series

by Robert D. Sawvell and Edmond Bellinghausen

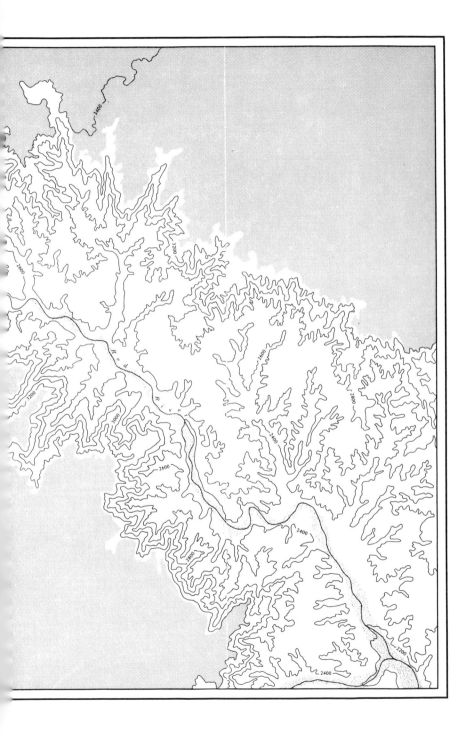

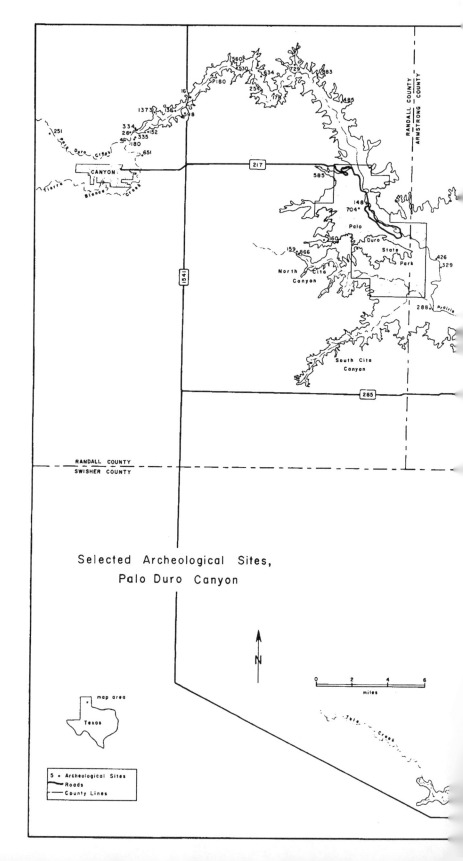

Selected Archeological Sites,
Palo Duro Canyon

RANDALL COUNTY
ARMSTRONG COUNTY

RANDALL COUNTY
SWISHER COUNTY

Palo
Duro
State
Park

North Cita
Canyon

South Cita
Canyon

Prairie

CANYON

Palo Duro Creek

Tierra Blanca Creek

map area
Texas

N

0   2   4   6
miles

Tule Creek

5 • Archeological Sites
Roads
County Lines

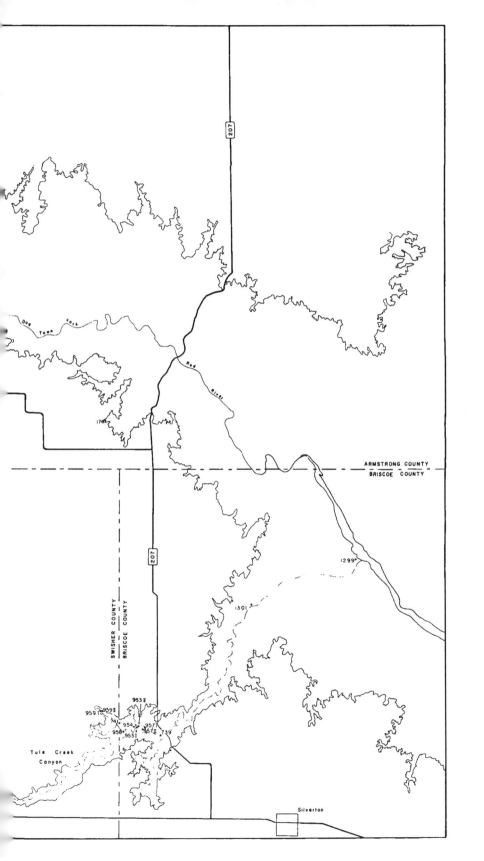

207

Dog Town Fork

Red River

1745

141

ARMSTRONG COUNTY
BRISCOE COUNTY

207

1299°

1301

SWISHER COUNTY
BRISCOE COUNTY

953 II
959 I 959 II
141° 954° 957 I
958° 957 II 739°
953 I

Tule Creek
Canyon

Silverton

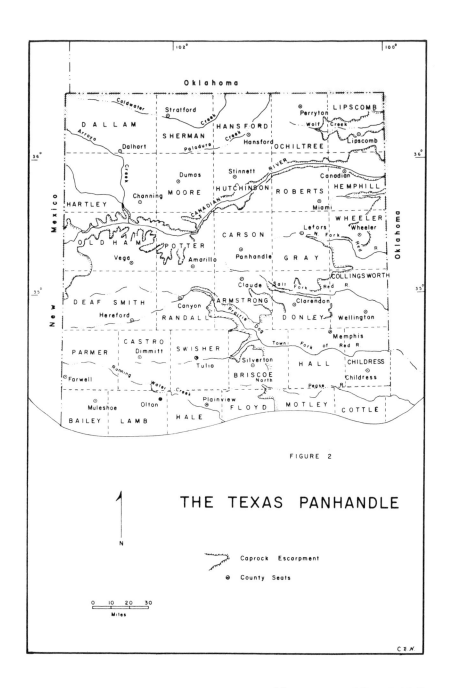

FIGURE 2

THE TEXAS PANHANDLE

N

‌ Caprock Escarpment

‌ County Seats

0 10 20 30
Miles

C E N

Map courtesy of Gary L. Nall.

INTRODUCTION

Palo Duro Canyon, the most striking, spectacular and unexpected feature of the Panhandle of Texas, is the site of the largest state park in Texas. The park itself compromises only a relatively small portion of the approximately one hundred and fifty mile long canyon. The canyon begins inauspiciously at the headwaters of Palo Duro Creek, a stream which is virtually nonexistent, and indistinguishable most of the year. This small and insignificant stream, in conjunction with the most prevalent natural resource of the area—wind, has been constantly at work for millions of years cutting the great gash in the plains of the Panhandle.

This slow but inexorable process has revealed a geological, paleontological and anthropological record which has attracted the attention of scientists, both professional and amateur, to the canyon to explore, study, record, and preserve the millions of years of the earth's history.

Historians have also become aware of the historical significance of the canyon in relation to the plains area surrounding it. Having access to the archeological, anthropological and, since the middle of the sixteenth century, written records, historians have been able to piece together the history of the canyon from the time the first European viewed it to the present.

This volume of the *Panhandle-Plains Historical Review* is devoted entirely to the pre-history and history of the canyon. Each contributing author to the volume is knowledgeable about his field of expertise because of his personal contact and research, having devoted countless hours in the canyon examining and researching his subject area. The articles in this volume are, for the most part, based on original research.

Even though this issue is devoted to Palo Duro Canyon, the contributing authors represent a wide range of interests and specializations. Each is a professional in his area of expertise and is devoted to maintaining the standards of his profession. The careful reader will soon become aware of what appears to be inconsistencies in the style of writing, footnotes, and bibliographical entries. The reason for the apparent inconsistencies is that each of the disciplines represented in this volume has developed its own style to meet its own needs. Rather than having each author deviate from the form he knows and is accustomed to using, it was decided to forego consistency in style of writing in favor of having each author maintain the standards of his own profession.

Several of the authors, artists and cartographers received financial assistance from the Organized Research Committee of West Texas State University. This assistance is gratefully acknowledged and appreciated.

Duane F. Guy
Editor

GEOLOGY OF PALO DURO CANYON

H. Charles Hood
Geologist, Tuthill and Barbee
Amarillo, Texas

James R. Underwood, Jr.
Kansas State University
Manhattan, Kansas

One of the memorable experiences of the traveller making his way across the broad, almost level expanse of the High Plains of the Texas Panhandle, whether it was Coronado in 1541 or the visitor of today, is arriving abruptly at the rim of Palo Duro Canyon. The canyon, a winding re-entrant into the "caprock" escarpment of the eastern High Plains, begins in northeastern Randall County and extends southeast for some 60 miles through Armstrong and Briscoe counties. Cut by the Prairie Dog Town Fork of the Red River, this magnificent example of nature's painstakingly slow sculpturing of the Earth's surface reveals in the canyon walls 600-800 feet of orange-red, lavender, gray, brown, and yellow rocks. Viewed especially in the warm light of early morning or late afternoon, the scene truly is striking.

The colorful setting immediately calls to mind the Grand Canyon of the Colorado and, interestingly, the geologic record exposed in Palo Duro is a stratigraphic and chronological extension of that recorded in the Grand Canyon, i.e. the age of the rocks at the rim of the Grand Canyon, a mile above its floor, is approximately the same as the age of the rocks exposed in the floor of Palo Duro. The rock record in Palo Duro extends upward another 600-800 feet and represents much of the last 230 million years of geologic history.

In neither Palo Duro Canyon nor in the Grand Canyon of Arizona, however, is the rock record complete. Ancient buried surfaces of erosion or non-deposition, known as unconformities, represent long periods when rocks either were being eroded or were not being deposited. Although much of geologic time is not represented by layers of rock in Palo Duro, the rock that is there has recorded faithfully a fascinating interplay of a long-vanished sea, rivers, floodplains, lakes, and swamps. The work of early geologists laid the foundation for our present understanding of the geology of Palo Duro Canyon.

EARLY GEOLOGIC STUDIES

Several early expeditions traversed the Texas Panhandle area following the initial Coronado expedition of 1541, which marked the beginning of the historical era of the Southern High Plains. The first such expedition was that of Captain Randolph B. Marcy in 1852. Professor George G. Shumard was acting geologist of the party which passed along the eastern Caprock Escarpment and in part explored Palo Duro Canyon to its headwaters. Shumard misidentified the strata of the High Plains as Cretaceous. In 1858 he joined his brother, Benjamin F. Shumard, in establishing the first Geological Survey of Texas. In 1853 Lieutenant A. W. Whipple of the Corps of Topographical Engineers led an expedition near the 35th parallel to search for a good railroad route across the region. Professor Jules Marcou was the geologist with the party which passed along the northern escarpment near the Canadian River. Marcou identified what he thought to be Jurassic rocks in the northern High Plains region.

More detailed geologic work began in 1890 with the first of a series of expeditions headed by W. F. Cummins of the second Geological Survey of Texas (the Dumble Survey). Cummins identified Triassic rocks in the Texas Panhandle and eastern New Mexico and assigned these to the Upper Triassic Dockum Group. Shortly thereafter, N. F. Drake (1891) subdivided the Triassic deposits of northwest Texas and eastern New Mexico into three separate units.

Professor E. D. Cope (1893) published the first paper on Triassic vertebrates of the southern High Plains, and in 1899-1901 J. W. Gidley of the American Museum of Natural History, New York, led a series of expeditions through the Texas Panhandle to study Cenozoic rocks and collect vertebrate fossils (Gidley, 1903).

Charles N. Gould of the U. S. Geological Survey headed a series of expeditions across the area in an effort to understand better the Permian and Triassic "red beds" of northwestern Texas (Gould, 1905). Gould subdivided the Dockum Group of Cummins into an upper unit of sandstone and conglomerate (Trujillo Formation) and a lower unit of shale and clay (Tecovas Formation). It was Gould who suggested the drill site for the 1918 discovery well of the great Panhandle Field.

In recent years a number of articles concerning both general and specialized work in the Palo Duro Canyon area have been written. These include a number of guidebooks by the West Texas State University Geological Society beginning in 1959, and a guidebook on Palo Duro Canyon published by the Bureau of Economic Geology (Matthews, 1969). Asquith and others (1973) prepared a guidebook to the Upper Triassic sandstone of the Texas High Plains.

Several unpublished Master's theses dealing with aspects of the geology of Palo Duro Canyon have been prepared for area institutions. Among these are theses by Cramer (1973), Massingill (1975), Hood (1977), and Boone (1977). A regional study of the Triassic by Green (1954) included the Palo Duro Canyon area.

Generalized geologic maps appear in most of the guidebooks. The only other published geologic map of the Palo Duro Canyon area is the Plainview Sheet of the Geologic Atlas of Texas, scale 1:250,000 (Barnes and Eifler, 1968).

In addition to the contributions to Panhandle geology mentioned above, perhaps the most intensive study of the Palo Duro Canyon area has been in the field of Cenozoic paleontology. Several vertebrate fossil sites have yielded abundant material which has been described in numerous publications, e.g. Cope (1893), Johnston (1938, 1939), Johnston and Savage (1955), and Savage (1955, 1960).

SEQUENCE OF ROCKS

Insight to the complex geologic history of the area is obtained by close examination of the strata exposed in the canyon walls, from the oldest rocks exposed on the canyon floor to the youngest rocks exposed at the canyon rim. Rocks representing a time span of some 240 million years crop out in the walls and on the floor of the canyon (see chart, page 7; map, page 8). The Upper Permian Quartermaster Formation is the oldest widely exposed rock formation in Palo Duro Canyon, although in limited areas the underlying (and consequently older) Cloud Chief Gypsum also crops out. The Quartermaster is overlain by the Upper Triassic Tecovas and Trujillo formations, which form the bulk of the rocks exposed and compose many of the spectacular rock shapes in the canyon. Capping the rock record and forming the steep rim around the upper reaches of the canyon is the late Tertiary Ogallala Formation. Much of the water used for cities and for irrigation on the High Plains comes from the Ogallala. Windblown "cover sand" and playa lake deposits dot the present High Plains surface.

PERMIAN SYSTEM

Cloud Chief Gypsum

The oldest rocks exposed in the central Panhandle area are those of the Upper Permian Cloud Chief Gypsum; this formation crops out in the upper reaches of Palo Duro Canyon directly beneath strata of locally uplifted Quartermaster Formation, also Upper Permian in age.

The Cloud Chief Gypsum originally was designated the Greer Formation by Gould (1906) for exposures along Elm Fork of the Prairie Dog Town Fork of the Red River, Greer County, Oklahoma. Later, Gould and Lewis (1926) revised the classification and changed the Greer to the Cloud Chief Formation. The type locality has from 150 to 200 feet of brick red clay, shale, and interbedded massive gypsum with some limestone and dolomite. Locally steep dips are common.

The only known exposures of Cloud Chief Gypsum in Palo Duro State Park occur in, and immediately adjacent to, an area known as Velloso Dome, located 0.1 mile west of the junction of Sunday Creek with the Prairie Dog Town Fork of the Red River. There, some 15 feet of massive gypsum of the uppermost Cloud Chief are exposed in a five-acre area. The gypsum is characterized by complex minor folds and faults (see Photograph A). Massive gypsum occurs in beds ranging in thickness from one inch to two feet, with interbedded mudstone lenses up to one inch thick.

Velloso Dome is believed to be the result of hydration of anhydrite to gypsum (Fandrich, 1966). The process of hydration, or the adding of water, results in a volume increase of the rock of 30 to 50 percent. The expansive force created a small dome together with complex folds. During folding, numerous small faults, with displacement seldom exceeding one foot, also developed.

A smaller exposure of Cloud Chief is found 0.3 miles south of Velloso Dome on the west side of the Prairie Dog Town Fork of the Red River. There a local anticline (up fold), characteristic of the Permian of the Palo Duro area, has exposed 15 feet of massive gypsum over a distance of 30 yards along the river.

Quartermaster Formation

The Quartermaster is composed predominantly of orange-red to dark-red claystone and some sandstone (see chart, page 7) and

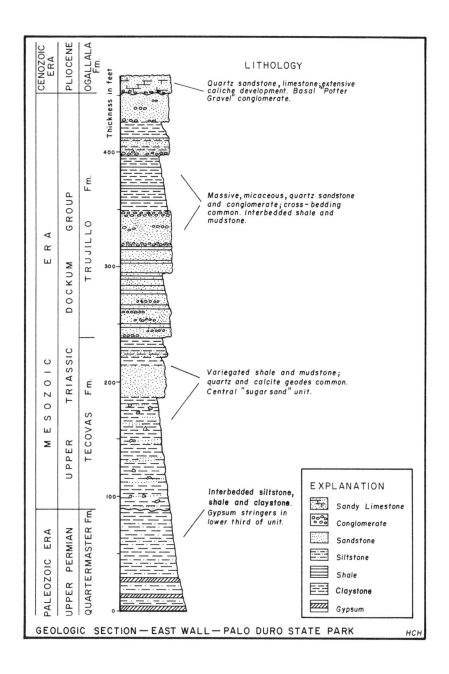

LITHOLOGY

Quartz sandstone, limestone; extensive caliche development. Basal "Potter Gravel" conglomerate.

Massive, micaceous, quartz sandstone and conglomerate; cross-bedding common. Interbedded shale and mudstone.

Variegated shale and mudstone; quartz and calcite geodes common. Central "sugar sand" unit.

Interbedded siltstone, shale and claystone. Gypsum stringers in lower third of unit.

EXPLANATION

Sandy Limestone

Conglomerate

Sandstone

Siltstone

Shale

Claystone

Gypsum

GEOLOGIC SECTION — EAST WALL — PALO DURO STATE PARK   HCH

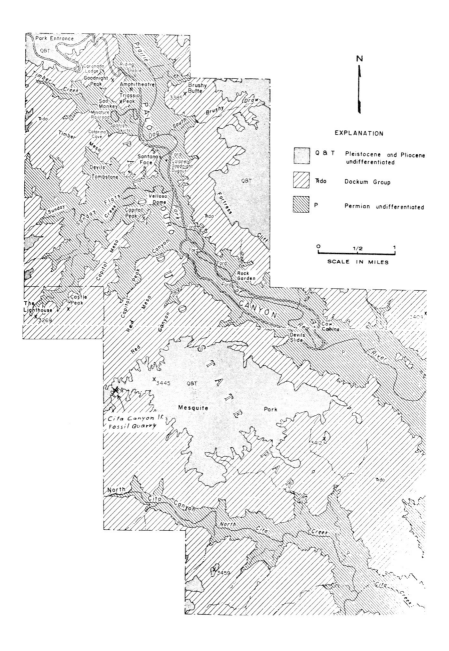

Generalized geologic map of Palo Duro Canyon State Park. (After Matthews, 1969, p. 14, 15.)

forms the lower slopes and much of the valley floor in Palo Duro Canyon. The lower part of the formation is characterized by abundant crosscutting seams of satin spar and selenite gypsum. Most of the thicker siltstone units also occur in the lower part of the exposed Quartermaster. All of the gypsum and most of the siltstone is absent in the upper half of the formation, giving way to massive claystone.

Numerous interesting sedimentary structures are found in Quartermaster siltstone. Symmetrical wave ripple marks associated with shallow marine deposition are locally abundant. Asymmetrical ripple marks and cross beds indicative of continental stream deposits are found interbedded in the shallow marine deposits. Pseudomorphs, or "false forms," of halite (rock salt) are present on the underside of some of the siltstone layers. "Flame structures" produced by interpenetration of silt and clay are found in some of the basal siltstone layers (see Photograph B). Also common are reduction halos, gray-green circular areas of varied size that are in striking contrast with the orange siltstone within which they occur. They represent areas where ferric iron oxide has been altered to ferrous iron oxide. Irregularly shaped reduction zones occur as well.

Rocks of the Quartermaster Formation are unfossiliferous in the Palo Duro Canyon area. Farther to the east, local lenses of dolomite, thought to be in the basal Quartermaster, in places produce a variety of poorly-preserved marine clams and snails (Roth, Newell, and Burma, 1941). No fossil amphibian or reptile remains, so typical of the older Permian formations in Oklahoma and central Texas, have been found in the Panhandle area.

The thickness of Quartermaster rocks in the Panhandle area varies from 200 to 350 feet. A maximum exposed thickness of 155 feet occurs above Water Crossing 2 in Palo Duro Canyon State Park. Farther to the east along the eastern Caprock Escarpment the entire Quartermaster is exposed.

The part-continental, part-marine sediments of the Quartermaster Formation were laid down during a series of marine transgressions and regressions, or times of alternating rise and fall of sea level (Matthews, 1969). Deposition in a landlocked arm of the brackish Permian sea was responsible for the interbedded claystone and siltstone. A gradual southwestward retreat of the Late Permian sea brought the Permian Period, and thus the Paleozoic Era, to a close.

TRIASSIC SYSTEM

Rocks of the Upper Triassic Dockum Group, established by Cummins in 1890, unconformably overlie Permian strata in all parts of the southern High Plains. The Dockum is represented by a lower unit of variegated mudstone and some sandstone called the Tecovas Formation, and an upper unit of massive sandstone, conglomerate and some mudstone called the Trujillo Formation (see chart, page 7; map, page 8). Both the Tecovas and Trujillo were named by Gould (1907), the Tecovas for exposures along Tecovas Creek in Potter County, Texas, and the Trujillo for exposures along Trujillo Creek in Oldham County, Texas.

Tecovas Formation

The contact of the Tecovas with the underlying Quartermaster is very conspicuous and occurs where the brick-red claystone of the Quartermaster gives way to the yellow, gray, or lavender mudstone of the Tecovas. Quartermaster and Tecovas sediments are, in many places, sandier near the contact; in rare instances, intermittent lenses of "Tecovas Flint" or chert are visible within a few feet of the contact.

The lower third of the Tecovas is composed of a series of multi-colored mudstone beds. These gray, yellow, maroon or lavender, orange, and red mudstone layers, together with the underlying Quartermaster deposits, form the striking "Spanish Skirts" visible in many areas along the lower slopes in Palo Duro Canyon. These lower mudstone units in places contain irregularly shaped concretions of hematite (iron oxide) and psilomelane (manganese oxide), together with quartz- and calcite-lined geodes.

Overlying the variegated mudstone and shale is a ledge of massive, white, calcareous "sugar sand" up to 40 feet thick. Above this middle sand member is a varied thickness of reddish-orange mudstone which continues to the Tecovas-Trujillo contact. Thickness of the Tecovas varies, but averages 120 feet in the Palo Duro Canyon area.

Of particular interest to area, as well as national, institutions is the local abundance of a variety of Late Triassic reptile, amphibian, and rare fish remains. A number of locally rich pockets containing abundant teeth, coprolites (fossilized excrement), and bone fragments have been recorded by the Panhandle-Plains Historical Museum and West Texas State University. Near-complete skulls and other skeletal material of several kinds of phytosaurs (Cope, 1893; Gregory, 1962), metoposaurs (=*"Buettneria"*), and desmatosuchians have been recovered, together with fish remains of the lungfish *Ceratodus* and the coelacanth *Chinlea* (Schaeffer and Gregory, 1961; Schaeffer, 1967). The lower variegated mudstone units are the predominant horizons which produce these fossil vertebrates. Mineralized wood also is common in Tecovas strata.

The Tecovas deposits are believed to be entirely continental, having been deposited by low-energy streams flowing northwestward into broad, shallow inland basins. Trauger and others (1972) believed the Tecovas sediments to be fluviatile and tidal-flat deposits, laid down during conditions similar to those currently existing in the Amazon River basin. Much of the sediment was derived locally by erosion of the Permian red beds. The probability of more distant sediment sources, such as the Ouachita-Marathon tectonic belt to the south and east, are indicated by analyses of cross beds and heavy minerals and by occurrence, in outcrops to the south of well-rounded pebbles of vein quartz.

Trujillo Formation

Overlying the Tecovas sediments, with apparent conformity in most areas, are the coarse, massive conglomerate, sandstone, and mudstone of the Trujillo Formation (see chart, page 7; map, page 8). The contact between the Tecovas and Trujillo occurs just below the first thick, massive sandstone and conglomerate above the Tecovas Formation.

Typical Trujillo in the Palo Duro Canyon area consists of a series of three massive sandstone and conglomerate ledges, each up to 60 feet thick, with interbedded red and gray mudstone and siltstone. The massive sandstone units are composed of medium- to coarse-grained, micaceous quartz sandstone with a calcareous matrix. Lenses of calcareous clay-ball conglomerate are present in all units. Various types of cross-stratification, together with channel-bar, channel-lag, and channel-fill deposits, identify the Trujillo as a fluvial deposit.

The massive sandstone and interbedded mudstone units of the Trujillo are much less fossiliferous than the underlying Tecovas. The clam *Unio* is known from many areas. Amphibian and reptile remains are known but are not nearly as abundant. The controversial palm-like angiosperm, (flowering plant) *Sanmiguelia*, has recently been reported from upper Trujillo deposits

in Palo Duro Canyon (Ash, 1976). Silicified and sometimes lignitic wood occurring in the sand and conglomerate units are the
most abundant fossil remains found. Fossil wood remains are
sometimes associated with uranium-bearing minerals; these
minerals recently have become the subject of considerable regional investigation.

The Trujillo Formation forms the upper steep valley slopes of
Palo Duro Canyon and its major tributaries. Thickness varies
considerably, although 200 feet is average for Palo Duro Canyon.
A considerably thicker section of Trujillo is present a few miles to
the south. By contrast, the massive sandstone and conglomerate
layers are virtually nonexistent 20 miles to the north.

The continental Trujillo sediments were deposited in a braided
stream environment. Sedimentologic studies have indicated a
source area to the south and east, with sediment transport to the
north and west (Asquith, and others, 1973). In addition, some of
the material was derived from erosion of local deposits.

TERTIARY SYSTEM

Ogallala Formation

The Trujillo is unconformably overlain in most areas of the
southern High Plains by sand, silt, clay, and limestone of the
Ogallala Formation (see chart, page 7; map, page 8), named by
Darton (1899) for exposures of calcareous claystone, sandstone,
and limestone of late Tertiary age in western Nebraska. Extensive calcium carbonate (caliche) development in the upper part of
the Ogallala has formed the most conspicuous part of the formation, the resistant "cap" or "caprock" of the High Plains.

The Ogallala is composed of a lower unit of calcareous, medium-
and coarse-grained sandstone and an upper unit, the caliche caprock. Brown (1956) noted the occurrence of two separate caliche
caprocks cropping out along the eastern Caprock Escarpment,
some distance to the east. Beginning in the northern reaches of
Palo Duro Canyon and continuing to the north, a local upper
sandstone unit overlies the caliche caprock.

A basal sandy conglomerate, locally known as the "Potter
Gravel," occurs in most areas and consists of round igneous,
metamorphic, and sedimentary pebbles and cobbles, most of
which were transported from the west. Waterworn fossil oyster
shells (*Gryphaea* sp.) probably derived from Cretaceous rocks to
the west, also are present. The "Potter Gravel," whose thickness

reaches five feet in some parts of the canyon, rests unconformably on Trujillo conglomerate, sandstone, or mudstone.

The caliche caprock is composed of dense, finely-laminated sandy limestone and is thought to have originated from downward percolation of calcium-rich water, followed by exposure and desiccation (Reeves, 1970). A lens of low-grade opal occurs in some places at the base of the caliche cap. Opaline cement in small vugs or cavities is present throughout the formation, giving the caliche an "agatized" appearance.

Of great interest is the presence of vertebrate fossils in the Ogallala at several area localities. An important site in the Palo Duro Canyon area is that of the Axtel local fauna, which produced a variety of late Hemphillian vertebrates several million years old (Johnston, 1939; Johnston and Savage, 1955).

The Ogallala, the major High Plains aquifer, forms the High Plains rim around Palo Duro Canyon and its major tributaries. The formation is 20 to 40 feet thick in the Palo Duro area, but at other places in the southern High Plains, the Ogallala is as thick as 700 feet.

Ogallala sediments were deposited by streams originating in the eastern Rocky Mountains. Sediments were laid down as a vast alluvial blanket on the undulating pre-Ogallala surface (Frye and Leonard, 1957 a, b).

PLIO-PLEISTOCENE AND HOLOCENE DEPOSITS

Resting on the Ogallala surface and forming much of the topography we see today are a variety of Pleistocene and younger deposits (see map, page 8). Eoalian, lacustrine, and fluvial sediments are represented in varied proportions over much of the area.

Most of the High Plains surface has a blanket of eolian "coversand" modified by sheet wash. This is the most extensive and characteristic deposit of the High Plains. Occurring in some basin deposits are several volcanic ashes, of which Pearlette Type O, dated at 600,000 years B.P. (Wilcox and others, 1970), is present in the Palo Duro Canyon area.

Dotting the High Plains surface are thousands of shallow upland basins, or playas. These occur in a variety of shapes and sizes, depending on their age and location. Wind deflation is thought to have been responsible for the formation of many of them. Lacustrine and eolian sediments are visible in the headward areas of some of the tributaries of Palo Duro Canyon and represent "dissected" playas. One such deposit is found at the beginning of the steep descent of Park Road 5 into the canyon. In the Panhandle area, dissected playa sediments have yielded an abundance of fossil mollusks and a few fossil vertebrates, including microvertebrate assemblages. Of particular importance is the Plio-Pleistocene (Blancan and Irvingtonian in age) succession in North Cita and Sunday canyons, described by Johnston (1938) and by Johnston and Savage (1955).

A succession of Pleistocene fluvial terrace deposits is found along the floodplains of major rivers, streams, and their tributaries. Extensive terrace development occurs along the Canadian River and its major tributaries. Rather minor terrace development occurs along the Prairie Dog Town Fork of the Red River in Palo Duro Canyon, although floodplain deposits are quite extensive.

ECONOMIC ASPECTS OF THE GEOLOGY

The economic and cultural growth of the Panhandle can be correlated with the economic geology of the area. The two most important natural resources—water and soil—are geological resources vital to the area's economy. The area's water resources are summarized in Gould (1905, 1906, 1907) and in Baker (1915). Soil types and distribution are described in Jacquot and others (1970).

The Ogallala Formation is the major High Plains aquifer, which supplies municipal and industrial, as well as agricultural, needs. Most of the Ogallala water comes from the basal sand and gravel and is generally pure and soft. Rainfall and resultant infiltration is the principal source of Ogallala recharge (Baker, 1915), which unfortunately is only a small fraction of consumption. The Ogallala is a classic example of an aquifer whose water is being mined, i.e. an aquifer whose recharge is negligible compared to consumption.

Highly-mineralized water from the Permian and, in lesser quantities from the Triassic, also is present. The town of Canyon, located 10 miles to the west of Palo Duro Canyon, is currently (1977) studying the feasibility of using water from the Triassic for domestic use. Intermittent springs flow from the Permian, Triassic, and Ogallala in the heads of many Palo Duro Canyon tributaries.

Another factor vital to the area's economy is soil, which is the main ingredient in one of the nation's leading farming and ranching regions. Upland soils, ranging from clay to sandy loams, support a variety of agricultural crops as well as grazing and cover grasses. Soils on the lowlands and on broken land in Palo Duro Canyon also support a variety of native grasses and shrubs suitable for domestic and wild animals (Jacquot and others, 1970).

A variety of rocks and minerals are present in the Palo Duro Canyon area and have a minor economic influence on the region. Open-pit quarrying of caliche and gravel at several localities in the Canyon-Amarillo area provide a source of road topping and concrete additives. The massive Trujillo sandstone has been a source of building stone for many of the buildings in Palo Duro Canyon State Park and elsewhere in the region. Mineralized wood also has been used in lesser quantities as a building stone, most notably in some of the older buildings on the campus of West Texas State University.

The occurrence of uranium-bearing minerals in Upper Triassic rocks throughout the Southwestern United States is being studied intensively. Although some radioactive minerals, e.g. jarosite and tyuyamunite, are known to exist in Palo Duro Canyon, economic quantities have not yet been discovered there. Several exploration companies are devoting an increasing amount of time and money in the search for uranium from the Upper Triassic of Texas. A recent report by Dickson and others (1977) cites potential uranium-bearing Triassic rocks some distance south of the project area. Spectrographic analysis of Upper Triassic rocks in the Palo Duro Canyon area yielded little evidence of the presence of radioactive elements.

Several other minerals, although present in many localities, are not abundant or of a sufficiently high grade to be important economically. The iron oxides hematite and limonite are present as nodules or as a secondary cement and grain coating in sandstone. The manganese mineral psilomelane occurs as high-grade nodules or as secondary cement in sandstone. Azurite and malachite, both copper carbonates, have been found as stain in sandstone and mudstone and as replacement in mineralized wood. Celestite, a strontium sulphate, in places fills veins in the lower part of the Quartermaster.

Occurrences of opal in the Ogallala are common in basal caliche caprock layers. Although the opal does fluoresce and is sometimes near-gem quality, extensive fractures and impurities render it useless for most lapidary work.

Possible limited vein occurrences of nickel in interbedded upper

Tecovas mudstone and sandstone have been noted over the years in Palo Duro Canyon. A rather extensive occurrence was found along Park Road 5 where it descends into Palo Duro Canyon. Thin, interfingering veins of nickel up to several feet long and characteristically associated with carbonized plant remains occur in the Tecovas "sugar sand" and interbedded mudstone lenses.

Potash, a salt found in Permian rocks in the Southwestern United States, has possible future economic importance in the Palo Duro area. A study by Udden (1915) of well samples throughout the Texas Panhandle noted the greatest abundance of potash from two wells in the Potter-Randall county area. The potash occurred from 800 to 1700 feet below the surface, a major drawback for the technology at the time of the study. Apparently no follow-up work has been done.

Petroleum has yet to be discovered in the Palo Duro Basin, a sedimentary and structural subsurface basin that underlies much of the southern half of the Texas Panhandle. The density of wells drilled thus far is about one well per 100 or more square miles. The basin still is considered to be a petroleum frontier.

FORMATION OF PALO DURO CANYON

When the gravel, sand, silt, and clay of the Ogallala were first deposited by eastward and southeastward flowing streams draining the rapidly eroding Rocky Mountains to the west, the debris extended much farther east and southeast than it does today. Erosion of the Ogallala has resulted in the eastern and southern margins of the formation retreating northward and westward. During this prolonged period of erosion, caliche development in the soil of the Ogallala resulted in the formation of the hard, resistant "caprock." Simultaneously, drainage on the Ogallala surface was eroding downward and headward and major reentrants into the caprock escarpment slowly developed; one of the largest of these is Palo Duro Canyon.

To appreciate fully the development of the canyon, we must recognize the role played by a variety of processes. Although the Prairie Dog Town Fork of the Red River made a significant erosional contribution in developing the canyon, the primary contribution of the stream has been the removal of material supplied to it by the gravitationally motivated processes of creep, debris flow, slump, and rockslide. Piping, especially, is an effective process in the arid southwest. This process enhances slope retreat by downward transport of material by percolating water moving through vertical to near-vertical desiccation fissures or rock openings in fine grained, unconsolidated material. Undercutting occurs at the base of slopes when the water emerges through ever-enlarging openings. Wind erosion also has played a continual but relatively minor role throughout.

The picture of canyon development that emerges, then, is one of canyon lengthening, widening, and deepening by stream erosion, by mass movement of material downslope to the channel of the Prairie Dog Town Fork of the Red River, and by transportation of the material downstream. These processes continue today.

A well-dated volcanic ash bed, the 600,000-year-old Pearlette Type O whose source was the Yellowstone volcanic center, clearly has been cut by vertical erosion that produced Palo Duro Canyon. At the site of the ash bed, therefore, the canyon is at least 600,000 years old. Up on the High Plains surface where the stream channels of some of the tributary canyons are just beginning to form, the canyon system is as young as the last heavy rain.

It is proper to think of Palo Duro Canyon as being much older southeastward toward its mouth and younger in its headward reaches to the northwest. Although rocks as old as 230 million years are exposed in the canyon, the canyon itself is less than one million years old.

GEOLOGIC HIGHLIGHTS

Buttes and Mesas

The characteristic landforms in the canyon are flattopped hills known as buttes and mesas. In Palo Duro, many of the buttes and mesas are capped by resistant sandstone of the Trujillo Formation (see Photograph C). Flattopped hills of restricted surface area are buttes, and very areally restricted tower-like erosional remnants are pinnacles. There is a gradation, in areal extent, smallest to largest, from pinnacle to butte to mesa to plateau. The High Plains surface is, in fact, a plateau.

Differential erosion, brought about by the variation in erosional resistance of the different rock layers and by variation in the effectiveness of erosional processes in different parts of the canyon and in different orientations, has created a "balcony or three-level" topography. The lowest level is the relatively broad and flat floodplain flanking the Prairie Dog Town Fork of the Red River. Because of the protection offered by the resistant sand-

stone of the upper Trujillo, the Tecovas and Quartermaster slopes
below are relatively steep. In like manner, the caliche "caprock"
of the Ogallala protects the underlying softer beds of the Ogallala and uppermost Trujillo, and in most places these soft rocks
form steep slopes. Thus the three-level effect is created by the
High Plains surface supported by the caprock, by the interior and
lower mesas and buttes of the Canyon supported by the resistant
sandstone of the upper Trujillo, and by the still-lower floodplain
bordering the Prairie Dog Town Fork.

The Lighthouse

This erosional pinnacle is the "trademark" of Palo Duro
Canyon (see Photograph E; map, page 8). Located about three
miles up Little Sunday Canyon from its juncture with Palo Duro,
the pinnacle is composed of the uppermost Tecovas and the Trujillo formations. The resistant sandstone of the upper Trujillo
caps the Lighthouse and protected it while erosion, concentrated
along vertical fractures (joints), removed unprotected rock
around it. The Lighthouse rises almost 300 feet above the nearby
canyon floor.

Pedestal Rocks

There are many of these distinctive forms, also called balanced
rocks or hoodoos, scattered throughout the canyon and superfi-
cially they resemble the tall, erosional remnants called pinnacles.
In pinnacles, however, the rock composing them is in normal
stratigraphic sequence and has not been disturbed. In most pedestal rocks the resistant capstone has moved downslope from its
original position. Because in Palo Duro, blocks of the resistant
sandstone of the Upper Trujillo commonly come to rest on the
softer mudstone of the Trujillo and Tecovas below, erosion lowers
the surface around the resistant boulder but does not attack as
vigorously the softer rock beneath it. Thus as erosion progresses,
the surface of the surrounding slope drops farther and farther
below the resistant rock or capstone, which typically is tilted at
the angle of the original surface of the slope. The Devil's Tomb-
stone (see map, page 8), 1.2 miles west of a point on Park Road 5
midway between Water Crossing 1 and 2, is an outstanding example of a pedestal rock.

Catarina Cave

Accessible by a half-mile long trail leading west from Park Road 5 about 0.2 mile south of Triassic Peak, this cave (Photograph D; map, page 8) was produced not by solution as are most caves but was formed in a landslide mass by the process of piping, or grain-by-grain removal of rock by percolating water. Surface water infiltrates through vertical or near-vertical root openings and desiccation fissures and percolates downward, enlarging those openings by removal of grains of sand, silt, and clay. The water emerges at the foot of the slope through openings that are gradually enlarged. As the sometimes tortuous channels enlarge, they may merge with other nearby piping systems to form a complex of underground cavities. At Catarina Cave and in the area of Devil's Slide, these kinds of caves are unusually well developed.

Velloso Dome

Most of the rock layers in the Panhandle area are horizontal or nearly so; the strata in Velloso Dome are unique in that they are tightly folded (see Photograph F; map, page 8). Velloso Dome, about a thousand feet up Sunday Creek from its confluence with the Prairie Dog Town Fork, is not a topographic feature but a structural one, i.e. it is not a rounded hill but rather a roughly circular area of several acres where rock normally hidden beneath the surface has been uplifted locally several tens of feet and exposed. The uplift of, and the intense folds in, the Cloud Chief Gypsum that composes the dome, are the result of the expansion of anhydrite as it converted to gypsum through hydration, rather than the result of a regional compressive stress regime.

Triassic Peak

This prominent landmark (see Photograph C; map, page 8) derives its name from the age of the rocks that compose the upper two-thirds of the peak. The south end of the prominent block of Trujillo sandstone that caps Triassic Peak, when viewed from Park Road 5 in suitable light, resembles the face of a frowning, or sad, monkey. It is this rock for which the Sad Monkey Railroad was named.

The annual summer production of the musical "TEXAS" is staged with the east flank of Triassic Peak as a natural backdrop. The colorful sandstone, siltstone, and claystone of the Permian

Quartermaster and the Triassic Tecovas, and Trujillo formations have been viewed over the years by the million or more people who have seen the musical drama. Triassic Peak rises more than 300 feet above the adjacent floodplain.

Capitol Peak

About half a mile west of Park Road 5, in the vicinity of Water Crossings 2 and 3, is Capitol Peak (see Photograph G; map, page 8), a pointed domical hill that is composed of the Quartermaster and Tecovas formations. It is more than 200 feet high and in profile reminds one of the traditional dome-topped capitol buildings common in the United States.

Fortress Cliff

This prominent landmark (see Photograph H; map, page 8), which dominates the skyline along the east flank of Palo Duro, is a verticle to near-verticle cliff more than 200 feet high in which are well displayed the lateral and vertical changes in lithology of the Trujillo and the Ogallala formations. The caliche caprock of the Ogallala has retarded retreat of the upper part of the cliff and allowed the slope beneath to steepen. This, together with slumping of huge blocks, has produced the precipitous wall.

Rock Garden

This name is aptly applied to an area along the left flank of the canyon just south of Water Crossing 5 where unusually large sandstone blocks of the upper Trujillo have moved downslope. Some of these blocks (see Photograph I; map, page 8) are as large as small houses; these and other such blocks of the Trujillo throughout the canyon may show well developed cross beds, i.e. beds inclined at an angle to primary bedding planes. Where the rocks are in place, these cross beds are used to determine the current direction of the transporting medium, in this case rivers and streams. The downslope direction of the cross beds is the direction of transport of sediments by the ancient current; for the Trujillo Formation this direction, on average, is northwest.

Devil's Slide

Extending out from the southwest wall of the canyon about 0.8

mile west-northwest of the turnaround is a spur of claystone and sandstone of the Quartermaster and Tecovas formations (see Photograph J; map, page 8). The steep slopes of the spur form the Devil's Slide, a dangerous area for the unwary. Because the claystone that makes up most of the slide has a deceptively hard surface created by deposition of a thin film of calcite, the material is difficult to stand on without sliding. Once a person begins to slide, it is difficult or impossible to gain a foothold or handhold. The serious and fatal accidents that have occurred there have prompted the name Devil's Slide for this feature.

Unconformities

Unconformities are geologically ancient, areally extensive buried surfaces of erosion or non-deposition. They represent missing rock and they have, therefore, a time or temporal significance. In Palo Duro Canyon, there are several unconformities: (1) the Late Permian-Late Triassic unconformity separating the Quartermaster and the overlying Tecovas (see Photograph C); (2) a possible Late Triassic unconformity between the Tecovas and Trujillo formations (see Photograph C); and (3) the Late Triassic-Pliocene unconformity between the Trujillo and the Ogallala (see Photograph H). These unconformities, where beds above and below are essentially parallel, are properly designated disconformities. On a regional basis, there may be angular discordance, i.e. the beds above truncate those below: such unconformities are termed angular unconformities.

Concretions

Concretions are generally spherical masses made of the same material as the rock in which they occur, but they are slightly harder and therefore weather out of the country rock. Their hardness derives from their being formed by a local concentration of cementing material. In Palo Duro, calcareous concretions are common in the resistant sandstone of the Trujillo. In most cases they are oblate spheroids and average one inch in diameter, although they may range in diameter up to two or three inches. In the Tecovas, distinctive septarian concretions are common. These are concretions that have fractured while still in place, and the fractures have filled with calcite or quartz. When the concretions weather out of the strata, the quartz or calcite veins weather more slowly than the mudstone of the concretions, and the polygonal pattern of veins, rising slightly above the surface of the concretions, gives them the gross appearance of a turtle shell. Many who find septarian concretions are convinced that they have, in fact, recovered the shell of a fossilized turtle.

Geodes

Geodes, spherical masses that commonly are partially filled with crystals of quartz or calcite, occur in the basal Ogallala and in the Tecovas Formation. Most geodes have a hollow center in toward which near-perfect crystals of quartz or calcite have grown. In some geodes the original cavity has been completely filled by secondary mineralization.

The development of geodes is somewhat complex. It has been suggested (Pettijohn, 1975, p. 474-475) that the cavity in rock produced originally by the decay of organic material is filled with groundwater. Eventually, a layer of silica gel will line the cavity, which probably has enlarged somewhat since the decay of the organism. When the water inside the cavity becomes more saline than the fresher groundwater outside, osmotic pressure directed outward may cause further enlargement of the cavity. When the salinity inside and outside the cavity is equalized, osmosis ceases. The cavity lining of silica gel eventually crystallizes as chalcedony; later, as cracks develop in the chalcedony, groundwater once again enters the cavity. When saturation, temperature, and pressure are suitable, minerals such as quartz or calcite begin to precipitate and to grow inward from the chalcedony-lined walls of the cavity. Because the crystals are not crowded, characteristically they will develop perfect to near-perfect forms.

Cross Beds

These distinctive inclined beds are common in the resistant sandstone of the Trujillo Formation. As sediments such as silt, sand, and gravel are deposited, they accumulate in layers that are horizontal, and thus the associated bedding planes also are horizontal. Within these horizontal layers there may be smaller-scale inclined beds, or cross beds, which were formed by currents moving in the direction in which the beds slope downward. These cross beds commonly are referred to as paleocurrent structures, i.e. they are sedimentary structures from which it is possible to determine the direction of flow of the stream or river that deposited the sediment millions or hundreds of millions of years ago.

SELECTED REFERENCES

Adams, J. E., 1929, Triassic of West Texas: Am. Assoc. Petroleum Geologists Bull., v. 13, no. 8, p. 1045-1055.

Alexander, W. H., Jr., and J. H. Dante, 1946, Ground-water resources of the area southwest of Amarillo, Texas: Texas Board Water Engineers, 45 p.

Ash, S. R., 1976, Occurrence of the controversial plant fossil *Sanmiguelia* in the Upper Triassic of Texas: Jour. Paleontology, v. 50, no. 5, p. 799-804.

Asquith, G. B., S. L. Cramer, and R. M. Winn, 1973, Sedimentology of the Upper Triassic sandstones of the Texas High Plains: West Texas State University Dept. Geol. and Geol. Soc., Fall Field Trip, Canyon, Texas, 29 p.

Asquith, G. B., and S. L. Cramer, 1975, Transverse braid bars in the Upper Triassic Trujillo sandstone of the Texas Panhandle: Jour. Geology, v. 83, no. 5, p. 657-661.

Baker, C. L., 1915, Geology and underground waters of the northern Llano Estacado: Univ. Texas Bur. Econ. Geology and Technology Bull. 57, 225 p.

Barnes, V. E., and G. K. Eifler, Jr., 1968, Geologic Atlas of Texas, Plainview Sheet: Univ. Texas Bur. Econ. Geology.

Boone, J. L., 1977, Lacustrine depositional systems of Triassic Dockum Group in Tule Canyon, Texas Panhandle: MS thesis (in prep.), Univ. Texas at Austin.

Buckthal, J. R., and J. R. Underwood, Jr., 1977, Review of the Ogallala aquifer of the Southern High Plains, Texas, *in* Underwood, James R., Jr., and Hood, H. Charles, eds., Geology of Palo Duro Canyon and vicinity, Randall County, Texas: Field Trip Guidebook, Mid-Continent Regional Meeting of Am. Assoc. Petroleum Geologists, Amarillo, Texas, September 11, 1977, p. 52-70.

Cazeau, C. J., 1960, Cross-bedding directions in Upper Triassic sandstones of West Texas: Jour. Sed. Petrology, v. 30, no. 3, p. 459-465.

_____, 1963, Detrital heavy minerals of Upper Triassic sandstones of West Texas: Am. Assoc. Petroleum Geologists Bull., v. 47, no. 2, p. 352.

Christian, W. G., and L. C. Smyers, 1938, Records of wells and springs, drillers' logs, and water analyses, and map showing location of wells and springs in Randall County, Texas: Texas Board Water Engineers and U. S. Geol. Survey, 32 p.

Cope, E. D., 1893, A preliminary report on the vertebrate paleontology of the Llano Estacado: Texas Geol. Survey 4th Ann. Report, p. 1-137.

Cramer, S. L., 1973, Paleocurrent study of the Upper Triassic sandstones, Texas High Plains: MS thesis, West Texas State University, 31 p.

Cummins, W. F., 1890, The Permian of Texas and its overlying beds: Texas Geol. Survey 1st Ann. Report, p. 183-197.

_____, 1891, Report on the geology of northwestern Texas: Texas Geol. Survey 2nd Ann. Report, p. 357-552.

_____, 1891, Report on the geography, topography, and geology of the Llano Estacado or Staked Plains: Texas Geol. Survey 3rd Ann. Report, p. 129-174.

_____, 1893, Notes on the geology of northwest Texas: Texas Geol. Survey 4th Ann. Report, p. 179-238.

Darton, N. H., 1899, Preliminary report on the geology and water resources of Nebraska west of the one hundred and third meridian: U. S. Geol. Survey 19th Ann. Report, pt. 4, Hydrology, p. 719-785.

Dickson, R. E., D. P. Drake, and T. J. Reese, 1977, Measured sections and analyses of uranium host rocks of the Dockum Group, New Mexico and Texas: Bendix Field Engineering Corp. Report GJBX-9 (77), 68 p.

Drake, N. F., 1891, Stratigraphy of the Triassic Formation of northwest Texas: Texas Geol. Survey 3rd Ann. Report, p. 227-247.

Elias, M. K., 1931, The geology of Wallace County, Kansas: Bull. Univ. Kansas, v. 32, no. 7, p. 1-254.

Evans, G. L., 1949, Upper Cenozoic of the High Plains: West Texas Geol. Soc. and New Mexico Geol. Soc. Guidebook, Field Trip no. 2, Cenozoic Geology of the Llano Estacado and Rio Grande Valley, p. 1-22.

_____, and G. E. Meade, 1945, Quaternary of the Texas High Plains: Univ. Texas Bull. 4401, p. 485-507.

Fandrich, J. W., 1966, The Velloso Dome: West Texas State University Geol. Soc. Guidebook, SASGS Ann. Field Trip, Geology of Palo Duro Canyon State Park and the Panhandle of Texas, p. 25-30.

Frye, J. C., and A. B. Leonard, 1957a, Ecological interpretations of Pliocene and Pleistocene stratigraphy in the Great Plains region: Univ. Texas Bur. Econ. Geology Report of Inv. no. 29, 11 p.

_____, 1957b, Studies of Cenozoic geology along eastern margin of Texas High Plains, Armstrong to Howard counties: Univ. Texas Bur. Econ. Geology Report of Inv. no. 32, 62 p.

_____, 1959, Correlation of the Ogallala Formation (Neogene) in western Texas with type localities in Nebraska: Univ. Texas Bur. Econ. Geology Report of Inv. no. 39, 46 p.

Gidley, J. W., 1903, The fresh-water Tertiary of northwestern Texas: Bull. Am. Mus. Nat. History, v. 19, Art. 26, p. 617-635.

Gould, C. N., 1905, Geology and water resources of Oklahoma: U.S. Geol. Survey Water-Supply Paper 148, 178 p.

_____, 1906, The geology and water resources of the eastern portion of the Panhandle of Texas: U. S. Geol. Survey Water-Supply and Irrigation Paper 154, 54 p.

_____, 1907, The geology and water resources of the western portion of the Panhandle of Texas: U. S. Geol. Survey Water-Supply and Irrigation Paper 191, 57 p.

_____, 1924, A new classification of Permian red beds of southwestern Oklahoma: Am. Assoc. Petroleum Geologists Bull., v. 8, no. 3, p. 322-341.

_____, and F. E. Lewis, 1926, The Permian of western Oklahoma and the Panhandle of Texas: Oklahoma Geol. Survey Bull. 13, 29 p.

Green, F. E., 1954, The Triassic deposits of northwestern Texas: Ph.D. dissertation, Texas Tech University, 196 p.

Gregory, J. T., 1962, The genera of phytosaurs: Am. Jour. Sci., v. 260, p. 652-690.

Grubb, H. W., 1966, Importance of irrigation water to the economy of the Texas High Plains: Texas Water Development Board Report 11, 56 p.

Hills, J. M., 1942, Rhythm of Permian seas—a paleogeographic study: Am. Assoc. Petroleum Geologists Bull., v. 26, no. 2, p. 217-255.

Hirschfeld, S. E., and S. D. Webb, 1968, Plio-Pleistocene Megalonychid sloths of North America: Bull. Florida State Mus., v. 12, no. 5, p. 213-296.

Hood, H. Charles, 1976, Paleocurrent investigations in the Quartermaster Formation (Upper Permian) Palo Duro Canyon State Park: Unpub. report, West Texas State University, 16 p.

_____, 1977a, Geology of Fortress Cliff Quadrangle, Randall County, Texas: MS thesis, West Texas State University, 123 p.

_____, 1977b, Geology of Palo Duro Canyon, Randall County, Texas, *in* Underwood, James R., Jr., and Hood, H. Charles, eds., Geology of Palo Duro Canyon and vicinity, Randall County, Texas: Field Trip Guidebook, Mid-Continent Regional Meeting of Am. Assoc. Petroleum Geologists, Amarillo, Texas, September 11, 1977, p. 42-49.

Hoots, H. W., 1925, Geology of a part of western Texas and southeastern New Mexico, with special reference to salt and potash, U.S. Geol. Survey Bull. 780, p. 33-126.

Hughes, J. L., 1966, Stratigraphy and paleontology of the Palo Duro area: West Texas State University Geol. Soc. Guidebook, SASGS Ann. Field Trip, Geology of Palo Duro Canyon State Park and the Panhandle of Texas, p. 5-14.

Jacquot, L., L. C. Geiger, B. R. Chance, and W. Tripp, 1970, Soil Survey of Randall County, Texas: U. S. Soil Conservation Service, 62 p.

Johnston, C. S., 1937, Osteology of *Bysmachelys canyonensis*, a new turtle from the Pliocene of Texas: Jour. Geology, v. 45, no. 4, p. 439-447.

_____, 1938, Preliminary report on the vertebrate type locality of Cita Canyon, and the description of an ancestral coyote: Am. Jour. Sci., v. 35, no. 20, p. 383-390.

_____, 1939, Preliminary report on the late middle Pliocene, Axtel locality, and the description of a new member of the genus *Osteoborus*: Am. Jour. Sci., v. 237, no. 12, p. 895-898.

_____, and D. E. Savage, 1955, A survey of various late Cenozoic vertebrate faunas of the Panhandle of Texas, pt. I: Univ. California Publications in Geol. Sciences, v. 31, no. 2, p. 27-50.

Judson, S., 1950, Depressions of the northern portion of the southern High Plains of eastern New Mexico: Geol. Soc. America Bull., v. 61, p. 253-274.

Massingill, G. L., 1975, Geology of calcium carbonate materials used for the manufacture of portland cement, Bushland, Texas: MS thesis, West Texas State University, 40 p.

Matthews, W. H., III, 1969, The geologic story of Palo Duro Canyon; Univ. Texas Bur. Econ. Geology Guidebook 8, 51 p.

Nicholson, J. H., 1956, Stratigraphic study of Palo Duro Basis (abs.): Am. Assoc. Petroleum Geologists Bull, v. 40, no. 2, p. 426-427.

_____, 1966, Subsurface geology of the Palo Duro Basin: West Texas State University Geol. Soc. Guidebook, SASGS Ann. Field Trip, Geology of the Palo Duro Canyon State Park and the Panhandle of Texas, p. 20-24.

Patton, L. T., 1923, The geology of Potter County: Univ. Texas Bur. Econ. Geology and Technology Bull. 2330, 180 p.

Pettijohn, F. J., 1975, Sedimentary Rocks, 3rd ed., Harper and Row, New York, Evanstown, San Francisco, and London, p. 474-475.

Price, W. A., 1958, Sedimentology and Quaternary geomorphology of South Texas: Trans. Gulf Coast Assoc. Geol. Socs., v. 8, p. 41-75.

Reeves, C. C., Jr., 1966, Pluvial lake basins of West Texas: Jour. Geology, v. 74, no. 3, p. 269-291.

_____, 1970, Origin, classification, and geologic history of caliche on the Southern High Plains, Texas and eastern New Mexico: Jour. Geology, v. 78, no. 3, p. 352-362.

_____, and W. T. Parry, 1965, Geology of West Texas pluvial lake carbonates: Am. Jour. Sci., v. 263, no. 7, p. 606-615.

_____, 1969, Age and morphology of small lake basins, Southern High Plains, Texas and eastern New Mexico: Texas Jour. Sci., v. 20, no. 4, p. 349-354.

Roth, R. I., 1932, Evidence indicating the limits of Triassic in Kansas, Oklahoma, and Texas: Jour. Geology, v. 40, no. 8, p. 688-725.

_____, 1943, Origin of siliceous Dockum conglomerates: Am. Assoc. Petroleum Geologists Bull, v. 27, no. 5, p. 622-631.

_____, 1955, Paleogeology of Panhandle of Texas: Am. Assoc. Petroleum Geologists Bull, v. 39, no. 4, p. 422-443.

_____, N.D. Newell, and B. H. Burma, 1941, Permian pelecypods in the lower Quartermaster Formation, Texas: Jour. Paleontology, v. 15, no. 3, p. 312-317.

Savage, D. E., 1955, A survey of various late Cenozoic vertebrate faunas of the Panhandle of Texas, pt. II, Proboscidea: Univ. California Publications in Geol. Sciences, v. 31, no. 3, p. 51-74.

_____, 1960, A survey of various late Cenozoic vertebrate faunas of the Panhandle of Texas, pt. III, Felidae: Univ. California Publications in Geol. Sciences, v. 36, no. 6, p. 317-344.

Schultz, G. E., ed., 1977, Field conference on Late Cenozoic biostratigraphy of the Texas Panhandle and adjacent Oklahoma: Field Trip Guidebook, Killgore Research Center Dept. Geology and Anthropology, Special Pub. 1, West Texas State University, Canyon, Texas, 160 p.

Schaeffer, B., and J. T. Gregory, 1961, Coelacanth fishes from the continental Triassic of the western United States: Am. Mus. Novitates, no. 2036, 18 p.

Sellards, E. H., W. S. Adkins, and F. B. Plummer, 1932, The geology of Texas, Vol. I, Stratigraphy: Univ. Texas Bur. Econ. Geology Bull. 3232, 1007 p.

Totten, R. B., 1954, Palo Duro Basin, Texas: Am. Assoc. Petroleum Geologists Bull., v. 38, no. 9, p. 2049-2051.

_____, 1956, General geology and historical development, Texas and Oklahoma panhandles: Am. Assoc. Petroleum Geologists Bull., v. 40, no. 8, p. 1945-1967.

Trauger, F. D., C. J. Mankin, and J. P. Brand, 1972, Road log of Tucumcari, Mosquero, and San Jon country: New Mexico Geol. Soc. Guidebook, 23rd Field Conf., East-Central New Mexico, p. 12-45.

Udden, J. A., 1915, Potash in the Texas Permian: Univ. Texas Bur. Econ. Geology Bull. 17, 59 p.

Underwood, James R., Jr., and Wayne Lambert, 1974, Centroclinal cross strata, a distinctive sedimentary structure: Jour. Sed. Petrology, v. 44, no. 4, p. 1111-1113.

—————, and Gerald E. Schultz, 1975, History of geology and anthropology at West Texas State University: The Compass, v. 52, no. 3, p. 41-48.

—————, and H. Charles Hood, eds., 1977a, Geology of Palo Duro Canyon and vicinity, Randall County, Texas: Field Trip Guidebook, Mid-Continent Regional Meeting of Am. Assoc. Petroleum Geologists, Amarillo, Texas, September 11, 1977, 70 p.

—————, 1977b, Field trip road log, Palo Duro Canyon and vicinity, *in* Underwood, James R., Jr., and Hood, H. Charles, eds., Geology of Palo Duro Canyon and vicinity, Randall County, Texas: Field Trip Guidebook, Mid-Continent Regional Meeting of Am. Assoc. Petroleum Geologists, Amarillo, Texas, September 11, 1977, p. 7-41.

U. S. Geological Survey, 1956, Fortress Cliff Quadrangle (7.5 minute series), scale 1:24,000.

Webb, S. D., 1965, The osteology of *Camelops*: "Science," Bull. Los Angeles County Mus., no. 1, 54 p.

West Texas State University Geological Society, 1959, Guidebook, Palo Duro Field Trip, 25 p.

Wilcox, R. E., G. A. Izett, and H. E. Powers, 1970, The Yellowstone Park region as the source of the Pearlette-like ash beds of the Great Plains (abs.): Am. Quat. Assoc., 1st meeting, p. 151.

Wood, H. E., R. W. Chaney, J. Clark, E. H. Colbert, G. L. Jepsen, J. B. Reeside, Jr., and C. Stock, 1941, Nomenclature and correlation of the North American continental Tertiary: Geol. Soc. America Bull., v. 52, no. 1, p. 1-48.

Photo A. Typical folded gypsum, Velloso Dome. Note hammer for scale.

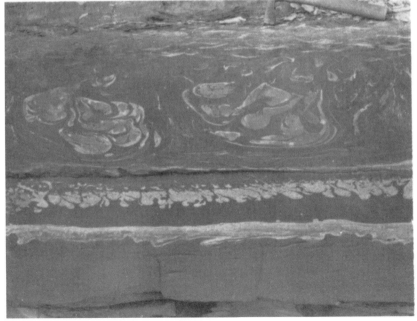

Photo B. Striking "flame structures" found in Permian siltstones.

Photo C. Triassic Peak. Quartermaster—Tecovas—Trujillo boundaries shown.

Photo D. Catarina Caves. Arrows show a few of the entrances.

Photo E. The Lighthouse, trademark of Palo Duro Canyon.

Photo F. Velloso Dome. Massive, folded gypsum in center of photo.

Photo G. Capitol Peak, composed of the Quartermaster and Tecovas formations.

Photo H. Fortress Cliff. Trujillo-Ogallala unconformity marked.

Photo I. The Rock Garden, as seen between Crossings 4 and 5.

Photo J. Devil's Slide, a colorful—and dangerous—spur of Tecovas mudstone.

ARCHEOLOGY OF PALO DURO CANYON

Jack T. Hughes
Professor of Anthropology
West Texas State University

INTRODUCTION

An archeological survey of the Texas Panhandle that was initiated by Floyd V. Studer early in this century (Studer, 1931) has been continued to the present by West Texas State University. On a cooperative basis, the Panhandle-Plains Historical Museum and the Department of Geosciences, through its Archeological Research Laboratory at Killgore Research Center, have recorded more than 1700 sites in the region.

A great many archeological sites have been recorded along the Palo Duro Canyon, partly because the canyon is close to WTSU, but mainly because it has been one of the most attractive areas for human habitation in the Panhandle throughout the 12,000 or so years that people have lived in the region. Indians living in and around the canyon had access not only to the varied geological and biological resources of the canyon but also to the resources of the bordering uplands. The canyon provided an abundance of sheltered camping places convenient to supplies of water, wood, stone, game and wild plant food. The bordering uplands, covered with grass and dotted with lakes, afforded campsites with good views in the midst of bison, antelope, and waterfowl.

Although much of the canyon has been searched for archeological sites, mostly by the museum and laboratory at WTSU but also to some extent by other agencies, such as the Texas Historical Commission (Malone, 1970; Pearson, 1974; Katz, 1976), most of the vast and rugged territory in and around the main canyon and its tributaries still remains to be explored. At most of the hundreds of sites which have been located and recorded, investigations have been confined to surface inspecting and collecting. Test excavations, seldom extensive, have been conducted at a good many sites. Only a few sites—mostly small but important ones which were threatened with destruction—have been largely or completely excavated. These investigations have produced great quantities of records and collections, all of which have been processed and stored, but few of which have been analyzed and reported.

Despite the limited number of published reports on archeological surveys and excavations in the Palo Duro Canyon area, enough information is available for a review of the types of sites which occur in the area (Fig. 1), and for an outline of the main stages of cultural development during Indian habitation of the area (Fig. 2). The only previous summaries of the archeology of the canyon are very brief accounts in newspapers, magazines, and guidebooks, like the article by Moore (1966).

TYPES OF SITES

The prehistoric Indian sites along Palo Duro Canyon are found in many different kinds of places and represent a wide variety of activities. Campsites (Fig. 3) marked by quantities of burned hearth stones and boiling pebbles, flint flakes, various artifacts, and other remains are especially common around the falls at the heads of most of the tributary canyons, but also occur on high places along the canyon rims, on bedrock benches along the slopes, and on alluvial terraces along the floors. The habitation sites range from small overnight camps to large seasonal camps, and permanent villages (Fig. 4) are present at a few places. Deep mortar holes (Fig. 5) in talus boulders and bedrock ledges occur at many of the camps. Flexed burials in small stone-filled graves (Fig. 6) are found at some of them.

Rock shelters (Fig. 7) are present at many places under the cliffs of Ogallala caliche along the canyon rims and at a few places under the cliffs and boulders of Trujillo sandstone along the canyon slopes and floors. Most of the larger overhangs were used for habitations, and some of the smaller ones for burials. Carvings and paintings (Fig. 8) are found in some of the rock shelters, and elsewhere on cliffs and boulders. Rock art sites of Palo Duro Canyon have been described by Jackson (1938), Kirkland (1942), Kirkland and Newcomb (1967), and most recently and fully by Upshaw (1972).

At many places the slopes below the caprock have concentrations of pebbles and cobbles, eroding from the basal Ogallala (Potter) gravels, which show signs of lithic workshop activity. The largest cobbles are a gray-brown silicified siltstone (Potter chert) which was especially popular for coarse tools such as choppers and hammers. At several places in the deeper parts of the canyon, outcrops of a purple bed in the Tecovas shales contain large lenses of a colorful jasper which have been extensively quarried (Fig. 9) and are surrounded by great quantities of work-shop debris. At most sites in the Palo Duro Canyon area, the Tecovas jasper was the preferred material for points, knives, scrapers, etc., and is more abundant than the better-known Alibates agate from the quarries on the Canadian River northeast of Amarillo.

At many places along the canyon floor, cutbanks along stream channels reveal masses of bison bones buried in alluvial terraces of late Pleistocene and Recent age. A few of these bone beds (Fig. 10) have been shown to be places where bison were killed by prehistoric Indians, and many others probably will prove to be bison kill sites.

Prehistoric Indian sites of various kinds are especially numerous in the upper, better-watered portions of the main canyon and its tributaries, where many of the best sites have been damaged or destroyed by dam-building and other development activities, and by relic-digging vandals.

The archeological sites in the Palo Duro Canyon area, as elsewhere in the Texas Panhandle, can be described in terms of four main stages of cultural development. Beginning with the earliest, these are the PaleoIndian stage of late Ice Age big-game hunting, the MesoIndian (or Archaic) stage of post-glacial foraging, the NeoIndian stage of developing horticulture, and finally, the Historic stage of increasing European involvement.

THE PALEOINDIAN STAGE

Radiocarbon dates at numerous sites in the Great Plains indicate that the PaleoIndian stage of cultural development began about 10,000 B.C. and ended about 5,000 B.C. The PaleoIndians were primarily hunters of Pleistocene big-game animals who roamed freely in small groups over vast areas in pursuit of their quarry. PaleoIndian cultures are characterized by several different types of lanceolate spear points. The PaleoIndian stage spanned the closing phases of the Pleistocene, when the cool wet (Anathermal) climate was becoming warmer and drier, and the herds of mammoth, horse, camel, and giant bison were dwindling toward extinction.

The points of the earlier (Clovis and Folsom) cultures are fluted; those of the later (Plano) cultures are parallel-flaked. During the early PaleoIndian stage, the Clovis people of about 10,000 B.C. hunted mammoths with large fluted points (Fig. 2,a), and the Folsom people of about 8,000 B.C. hunted giant bison with small fluted points (Fig. 2,b). During the late PaleoIndian stage, various Plano cultures hunted both extinct and modern bison with various kinds of parallel-flaked points (Fig. 2,c), generally made with consummate skill.

Surface surveys have shown that the PaleoIndian big-game hunters were thoroughly familiar with the Palo Duro Canyon area. Stray points—usually basal fragments—of Clovis, Folsom, and various Plano types have been found at many places along the rim of the main canyon and its tributaries. These finds probably represent briefly occupied lookout stations where the nomadic hunters replaced their broken spear points. The distinctive points have been found in greater numbers at several places which may have been favorite spots for temporary camps. These campsites occur at lakes near the canyon rim, on the rim around the heads of tributary canyons, and in the higher, older alluvial terraces along the canyon floor. Some of the mammoth and giant-bison remains which have been found at several places in the alluvial terraces probably represent PaleoIndian kills.

Very little excavation has been done at PaleoIndian sites in the Palo Duro Canyon area. At the Flint Ridge site (A560) in the Palisades development on the main canyon, several test pits in a high terrace have produced some unusually small parallel-flaked points and other artifacts. This site appears to be a camp of one of the Plano cultures. The tests need to be completed before the finds are analyzed and reported.

As part of archeological salvage at Mackenzie Reservoir in the upper part of Tule Canyon, the Rex Rodgers site (A957 Area II), a PaleoIndian bison kill, has been excavated and reported (Willey, Harrison, and Hughes, 1978a; Speer, 1975). At this site, the remains of six individuals of the extinct *Bison antiquus* accompanied by five PaleoIndian spear points were preserved in a high terrace. The points are broad and lanceolate with concave and thinned or fluted bases. Three have side notches near the base, like San Patrice points, and have been named Rex Rodgers points (Fig. 2,d). The other two are unnotched (Fig. 2,e) and are reminiscent of Clovis, Folsom, and Plainview points. The Rex Rodgers site has been radiocarbon-dated at 7,441 B.C.

A skull of an extinct *Bison occidentalis* excavated from a site (P180) at the base of a high terrace in the Timbercreek development on the main canyon has been radiocarbon-dated at 8,850 B.C. (Schultz and Cheatum, 1970). Although no artifacts were found at the site, it is the right age for a PaleoIndian kill.

THE MESOINDIAN STAGE

The MesoIndian (or Archaic) stage in the Southern Plains began about 5,000 B.C. and ended early in the Christian era. The MesoIndians were small groups of foragers who thoroughly exploited the seasonally-changing plant and animal resources within a particular territory. MesoIndian cultures are characterized by many different types of barbed dart points that appear to have been used with the atlatl or spear-thrower. A warm dry (Altithermal) climate during the early MesoIndian stage seems to have shifted about 2,000 B.C. toward the moderate (Medithermal) climate of modern times during the late MesoIndian stage.

In northwestern Texas, the MesoIndian cultures are poorly known, especially the earlier ones (Hughes, 1976). The earlier MesoIndian sites are marked by a few kinds of dart points (Fig. 2,f & g), and by a limited variety of artifacts such as gouges (Fig. 2,h), choppers, hammers, and boiling pebbles. Bison and other large-mammal remains are scarce, suggesting that the larger game animals may have virtually abandoned the region during the 3,000-year "Long Drouth" of the Altithermal, and that any MesoIndians who remained may have been forced to eke out an existence on the limited food resources provided by a desert-like flora and fauna. The culture manifested at the Bitter Creek site (A1319) near Lakeview in Hall County may be representative of the early MesoIndian stage (Hughes and Hood, 1975).

The later MesoIndian sites are marked by quantities of dart points, mainly corner-notched (Fig. 2,i & j), and by a large and varied artifact inventory, including an abundance of knives, scrapers, grinding implements, and hearth stones as well as boiling pebbles. Remains of large mammals, especially bison, are common, suggesting a return of big game to the region with the onset of essentially modern Medithermal climate, and a larger population of late MesoIndians supported by a more abundant and diverse food supply. The culture manifested at the Little Sunday site (A160) in Palo Duro Canyon may be typical of the late MesoIndian stage (Hughes, 1955).

The distinctive artifacts called "gouges" seem to be diagnostic of the early MesoIndian stage in northwestern Texas (Hughes, 1975). Sites with gouges are much more common in the Rolling Plains of the southeastern Panhandle (Hughes, 1972, 1973) than they are elsewhere in the Panhandle, suggesting that the Rolling Plains may have been more attractive during the Altithermal than the High Plains to the west, including the Palo Duro Canyon area. Although gouges occasionally are found along the canyon and its tributaries, occupation of the area seems to have been very limited during the early MesoIndian stage, and few sites of this period have yet been studied. During archeological salvage at Mackenzie Reservoir, gouges were found in test excavations at the Blue Clay site (A957 Area I) (Willey, Harrison, and Hughes, 1978b.)

In contrast with the early MesoIndian stage, numerous sites of the late MesoIndian stage have been recorded in the Palo Duro Canyon area, indicating a great deal of activity in the area with the beginning of modern climate. Most of the sites are camps at upland playas, along canyon rims, around tributary head-springs, on benches and terraces within the canyons, and in rock shelters. The camps are marked by clusters of hearth stones and boiling pebbles, flint flakes, bone fragments, and other remains, usually sparse and superficial, but sometimes abundant or deeply buried. Mortar holes are present at many of the camps, and slab-covered burials in small shallow graves sometimes occur. The Meso-Indian skulls tend to be long-headed. Much of the quarry-workshop activity in the canyon doubtless was carried out by the late Meso-Indians, and some of the rock art may be this early. Some of the bison remains in the canyon evidently represent late MesoIndian kills, like that at the Twilla site (A73) and others which have been reported from the Rolling Plains to the southeast (Tunnell and Hughes, 1955; D. Hughes, 1977).

Although most of the late MesoIndian sites in the Palo Duro have only been examined and recorded, excavations have been conducted at several sites, and the findings at a few of the sites have been analyzed and published. Test excavations as yet un-reported by WTSU and other agencies have encountered late MesoIndian materials in the lower levels of several open camps. WTSU has tested a campsite (A4) on the Wright place, on a ter-race between Palo Duro and Tierra Blanca creeks, above the head of the main canyon. Possible late MesoIndian burials have been recovered from this site, from another site (A26) in the same vicinity, and from two others (A329 and A426) on the main stream in the lower part of the state park. Dr. Waldo R. Wedel of the Smithsonian Institution tested a campsite (A729) near the pour-off of Thomas Draw on the northern rim of the main canyon above the park. Emerson L. Pearson of the Texas Historical Com-mission tested a campsite (A148) on a terrace near Water Cross-ing No. 2 in the park, and two sites at the head of North Cita Canyon on the Reynolds Ranch, one on the upland (A159) and the other deeply buried in a terrace (A866).

Also not yet reported are tests by WTSU at several rock shelters in the canyon where late MesoIndian materials were found in the lower levels. These include a large shelter (A334) under the caliche caprock to the north of the head of the main canyon, and a small shelter (A335) under the limestone rimrock to the south of the main canyon head, both on the Blackburn place; a small shelter (A485) under an Ogallala ledge near the pouroff of Blue Spring Draw on the northern rim of the main canyon above the park; and a large shelter (A5) under the caliche caprock near the head of South Cita Canyon on the Schaeffer Ranch. Charcoal from the late MesoIndian level in the Blue Spring shelter was dated at 295 A.D.

Work by various agencies, including WTSU, has been reported at several open camps with late MesoIndian materials in the canyon. Wedel (1975) has summarized testing by the Smithsonian at a deeply stratified site (A883) near the pouroff of Chalk Hollow on the northern rim of the main canyon above the park. Late MesoIndian materials in the lower levels were dated from 1445 to 350 B.C. Pearson (1974) has described tests for the Texas Historical Commission at a site (A704) on a bench near Capitol Peak in the park. The site has a late MesoIndian component. Susanna and Paul Katz (1976) have reported tests for the Commission at a prolific site (A1301) with a late MesoIndian component on a terrace in the lower part of Tule Canyon. Tests at the County Line site (A741), a similar site in the Mackenzie Reservoir area in the upper part of Tule Canyon, have been reported by WTSU (Willey and Hughes, 1978a).

Excavations have been reported by WTSU at two small rock shelters in the Palo Duro Canyon area, both with late MesoIndian remains in the lower levels. One of these is the Canyon Country Club cave (A251), under an Ogallala caliche cliff bordering the Palo Duro Creek valley well above the head of the main canyon, where the lower levels were dated at 880 to 150 B.C. (Hughes, in press). The other is the Deadman shelter (A959 Area II), under a Trujillo sandstone ledge on Deadman Creek in the Mackenzie Reservoir area, where the lower levels were dated at 120 to 210 A.D. (Willey and Hughes, 1978b).

Carol O. Jokerst has described (1972) the partial skeleton of a probable late MesoIndian found eroding from deep in the edge of a terrace (A138) in the upper part of Palo Duro Canyon, above the Farm Road 1541 bridge.

THE NEOINDIAN STAGE

In the Southern Plains the NeoIndian stage began early in the Christian era and ended with the arrival of Coronado in 1541 A.D. The NeoIndians were hunting and gathering people who became increasingly dependent on gardening to supplement their diet. NeoIndian cultures are characterized by the presence of arrow points and/or pottery. Early in the NeoIndian stage, around 500 A.D., the climate in the Panhandle area seems to have been somewhat moister than it is today.

With increasing reliance on corn, bean, and squash horticulture, the NeoIndians became more sedentary and their populations expanded, so that the small temporary camps of the early NeoIndians were gradually replaced by the large permanent villages of the late NeoIndians. In the Great Plains, the early NeoIndian cultures have been assigned to a Plains Woodland tradition and the late NeoIndian cultures to a Plains Village tradition (Wedel, 1961).

The early NeoIndian cultures of the Texas Panhandle are very poorly known. They are characterized by several kinds of small barbed arrow points (Fig. 2,k & l). In the northern Panhandle, the barbed arrow points may be accompanied by thick cordmarked pottery like that of Woodland cultures in the Great Plains, and sometimes by plain brown pottery from Mogollon cultures in southern New Mexico. This complex has been reported at the Lake Creek site (A48) in the Canadian River breaks (Hughes, 1962). In the Palo Duro Canyon area, the barbed arrow points are usually accompanied only by the Mogollon brownware. The upper levels at the Deadman shelter (A959 Area II) in the Mackenzie Reservoir are typical of this complex, for which the name "Palo Duro culture" has been proposed (Willey and Hughes, 1978b).

One of the late NeoIndian cultures of the Panhandle is comparatively well known. This is the Antelope Creek culture (Krieger, 1946), whose distinctive slab-house village ruins are especially numerous in the middle part of the Canadian River breaks across the Panhandle. These villages, which have been investigated much more extensively than other kinds of sites in the Panhandle, seem to have been inhabited from about 1200 to 1450 A.D. Although the use of building stone is reminiscent of the Puebloan cultures in eastern and northern New Mexico, and various Puebloan trade items are present in the ruins, the Antelope Creek culture closely resembles other cultures of the Plains

Village tradition in architectural features, stone and bone artifacts, pottery, etc. The culture is characterized not only by its slab houses but also by several kinds of small triangular arrow points (Fig. 2,m & n), a distinctive kind of cordmarked pottery, and various other traits. The Antelope Creek people seem to have left the region about a century before the arrival of Coronado, perhaps because of drouth conditions and Apache troubles. They may have been partly ancestral to the historic Pawnee of Nebraska (Hughes, 1974).

The varieties of NeoIndian sites, both early and late, in the Palo Duro Canyon area are much like those of the late MesoIndian stage. Many temporary campsites of the Antelope Creek culture have been recorded in the canyon, suggesting that it was a favorite hunting ground for these people, and a few permanent village sites are known, one (A739) as far south as Tule Canyon. Several burials of the Antelope Creek culture have been found, mostly in rock shelters. The skulls tend to be broad-headed. The Antelope Creek people did not quarry the local Tecovas jasper as much as the earlier groups, preferring to import Alibates agate from their Canadian River headquarters.

A good many sites with NeoIndian components have been investigated in the Palo Duro, mainly by WTSU, but most of the investigations have not yet been reported. NeoIndian components are present at a number of the sites with MesoIndian components already mentioned: the Canyon Country Club cave (A251), the Wright site (A4), the two Blackburn shelters (A334 and A335), the Thomas Draw site (A729), the Chalk Hollow site (A883), the Blue Spring shelter (A485), the Water Crossing No. 2 site (A148), the Capitol Peak site (A704), the two Reynolds sites (A159 and A866), the Schaeffer shelter (A5), the lower Tule site (A1301), the Blue Clay site (A957 Area I), the County Line site (A741), and the Deadman shelter (A959 Area II).

The NeoIndian components at some of these sites are of special interest. At the Canyon Country Club cave, an early NeoIndian component (the Palo Duro culture) in the middle levels was dated at 300 to 680 A.D., while a late NeoIndian component (the Antelope Creek culture) in the upper levels was dated at 1250 to 1330 A.D. At the Chalk Hollow site, the Blue Spring shelter, and the Deadman shelter, the Palo Duro culture in the upper levels was dated respectively at 370 to 870 A.D., 815 to 1110 A.D., and 465 to 710 A.D. A burial probably representing the Palo Duro culture was found in the Deadman shelter.

It seems significant that remains of the Prairie vole (*Microtus*

ochrogaster) were found in the Palo Duro culture levels at the
Canyon Country Club cave, the Blue Spring shelter, and the
Deadman shelter. Since the Prairie vole no longer lives in the
Panhandle, preferring the moister regions to the east, the climate
of the Panhandle may have been wetter around the middle of the
first millennium A.D. than it is today.

NeoIndian components have been encountered in unreported
work at a good many other sites in the Palo Duro Canyon area. A
shelter (A180) under the limestone rimrock to the south of the
main canyon head on the Blackburn place, very similar to A335,
has produced several burials and various artifacts of the Antelope Creek culture. West of the Farm Road 1541 bridge, an infant
burial accompanied by numerous beads of *Olivella* shell, turquoise, and other materials was found eroding from a crevice
(A598) in the caliche cliff bordering a small tributary canyon.
Test excavations at a site (A16) on a terrace in Camp Don Har-
rington have revealed a possibly early component of the Antelope Creek culture, with another burial.

In the Palisades development, on the talus slope below a large
collapsed overhang (A530) of the caprock, an important component of the Antelope Creek culture has been extensively tested
and dated at 1320 to 1485 A.D. In the Lake Tanglewood development, a test in a small overhang (A634) of the caprock has yielded
materials of the Antelope Creek culture, including human
skeletal remains. On a terrace in the same development, a slab
house (A254) of the Antelope Creek culture has been excavated
and dated at 1120 and 1280 A.D.

Excavations in a large rock shelter (A178) in a cliff of Trujillo
sandstone near the upper falls of the Palo Duro have produced
Antelope Creek materials, including many perishable items. On
Timber Creek Canyon, a crevice (A585) in the caprock contained a
burial of the Antelope Creek culture with a variety of grave goods.
Excavation of a large rock shelter (A174) under a resistant layer
of basal Ogallala opal at the head of a major tributary canyon
near the Wayside community yielded much evidence of Neo-
Indian occupation, including a burial.

Reported work at NeoIndian sites not previously mentioned
includes testing at the Road Cut (A953 Area I), Snail Bed (A954),
and Deadman Terrace (A959 Area I) sites in the Mackenzie Reservoir area (Hughes and Willey, 1978).

THE HISTORIC STAGE

The final stage of Indian cultural development in the Pan-handle is the Historic stage, which began with the Coronado expedition in 1541 A.D. and ended with the Mackenzie campaign in 1874. During the Historic stage, the region was dominated by the Apache until about 1700, when they were replaced by the Comanche. Coming from the north, as the Apache had done a few centuries earlier, the Comanche forced the Apache southward, and were joined much later by their allies, the Kiowa and Chey-enne.

The Apache span the transition from prehistory to history in the Panhandle. They seem to have reached the region only a century or two before Coronado, who described them as large bands of bison-hunting foot-nomads. They depended almost entirely on the buffalo herds for food and fuel, weapons, tools, and containers, clothing, bedding, and tenting, and used large dogs to help transport their few possessions from camp to camp. By the time they left the region, they seem to have changed very little, except for becoming more warlike horse-nomads, with a few metal items, glass beads, and other European trade goods. They alternately traded and raided among the eastern Pueblo villages, ultimately contributing to the abandonment of the settlements, as may have happened earlier to the Antelope Creek villages. Some Apache groups seem to have lived in permanent villages and done a little gardening, probably in imitation of their more sedentary neighbors.

Many campsites in the Palo Duro Canyon area and elsewhere in the Panhandle have fragments of a thin black micaceous pot-tery like the cooking pots of the eastern and northern Pueblos, and pieces of a handsome glaze-polychrome ware from the same sources, as well as obsidian, turquoise, and other trade items from New Mexico. Most of the sites possess tiny triangular arrow points (Fig. 2,o) and small end scrapers. The sites occur on both rims and terraces of the canyon, and are often extensive. Al-though some of these sites may represent Puebloan hunters or traders, most of them probably are Apache sites. One large site of this kind (A264) on Tierra Blanca Creek near Hereford has many stone house foundations (Holden, 1931).

Very little work has been done at the many sites with probable Apache components that have been recorded in the Palo Duro Canyon area. At the Canyon Country Club cave (A251), possible Apache materials were found in the top level, dated at 1550 and

1650 A.D., and a burial may have been made from this level. Apache materials may be present at one of the Reynolds sites (A159) and in the top levels at some of the other sites previously mentioned.

Tests have been made at a large campsite (A152) of probable Apache affiliation on the canyon rim overlooking the Palo Duro Club. On the slope of a tributary canyon near the club, portions of a large olla were found eroding from underneath a caliche ledge (A1373). Since the glaze-polychrome vessel is in the style of Middle Glazes C and D, which were made at Pecos Pueblo between 1425 and 1500 A.D., it may have been cached by the Apache. A smaller, unbroken vessel was found in a similar situation a little further down the main canyon. A possible Apache dwelling below the collapsed rock shelter (A530) in the Palisades development has been tested. Probable Apache materials were found in tests at an extensive campsite (A288) on a terrace near the junction of Cita Canyon with the main Palo Duro.

Tests have been reported (Katz, 1976) at another extensive camp (A1299) with probable Apache materials on a terrace near the junction of Tule Canyon with the main Palo Duro. A date of 1590 A.D. was obtained at this site.

Stone circles or tipi rings are present at a few campsites around the Palo Duro and elsewhere in the Panhandle. Most of these features probably represent Apache or later Comanche occupation.

In the Panhandle after 1700 A.D., the Comanche, with the aid of horses and a variety of European trade goods, became much more effective buffalo-hunters than any of their predecessors in the region, or most of their contemporaries elsewhere in the Great Plains. Like the Mongols of Asia, they became superb horsemen, with a highly mobile culture based on hunting and herding, trading and raiding. They dominated the region for more than a century and a half, until diminishing buffalo herds weakened them sufficiently that the U. S. Army, equipped with modern weapons, was finally able to conquer them in the massive campaign of 1874 (Taylor, 1962). After a series of engagements, culminating with the Battle of Palo Duro, the surviving remnants of the Comanche and their allies were confined to reservations in Indian Territory.

Comanche sites in the Palo Duro and elsewhere have received very little archeological attention. Cartridge cases and other relics of the Palo Duro battle have been found at the mouth of Cita

Canyon, but efforts to find traces of the burned Indian encampment have not yet been successful. Early-day cowboys found tipi poles at Comanche campsites in the canyon, and a few probable Comanche burials in the cliffs. Two historic Indian burials with mirrors were found in a caliche overhang (A651) on the Brown place on Tierra Blanca Creek above the head of the main canyon. Comanche and other historic Indian burials have been described from several places in the Staked Plains (Word and Fox, 1975).

Excavations at the Sand Pit site (A953 Area II), a probable Comanche camp of the late 1700's in the Mackenzie Reservoir area, have provided a fascinating glimpse of a group in transition from the Stone Ages to the Metal Ages (Willey, Harrison, and Hughes, 1978c). Arrow points, end scrapers, and gun flints of Alibates agate were mixed with knives and fleshers of iron, and with gun flints and glass beads of European origin. Another probable Comanche camp in the same area, the Sandstone Ledger site (A958), produced iron arrow points (Fig. 2,p) and possessed some interesting petroglyphs (Willey and Hughes, 1978c). The fireplaces at both of these sites were very small ash lenses about the size of a dinner plate.

CONCLUSIONS

With the Battle of Palo Duro in 1874, nearly 12,000 years of Indian history in the canyon came to an end, and Anglo history began—barely 100 years ago. The evidence of the long habitation of the canyon by Indians is abundant but inconspicuous; they left the gorge and its life essentially as they had found it. In recent decades, much of the canyon has been altered far more radically and irreversibly, by dams, roads, and buildings, than during all of the earlier millenia combined. These construction activities, coupled with mindless, self-serving relic digging, have destroyed forever a great deal of our priceless and irreplaceable heritage from the prehistoric past, which should constitute a public trust to be preserved for the benefit of future generations.

Many years of archeological research in the canyon, conducted chiefly by WTSU and mainly on an emergency salvage basis, have barely scratched the surface, but an outline of the sequence of prehistoric events is beginning to take shape. For some 5,000 years, PaleoIndian big-game hunters roamed the canyon—Clovis mammoth hunters succeeded by Folsom giant-bison hunters and finally by Plano hunters of both giant and modern bison—while the cool wet climate of the terminal Pleistocene gradually became warmer and drier.

During the "Long Drouth" of the next 3,000 years, the canyon seems to have been virtually devoid of both game and people, although there was some occupation by early MesoIndian gatherers like the Bitter Creek culture. The beginning of essentially modern climate seems to have initiated a nearly 2,000-year span of hunting and gathering by late MesoIndian groups like the Little Sunday culture.

For the next 1,000 or so years, when the climate may have been somewhat moister than it is today, the canyon seems to have been occupied by incipient horticulturalists of the early NeoIndian stage, mainly the Palo Duro culture, with influences from the Southwestern Mogollon tradition, and possibly the Lake Creek culture, with influences from the Plains Woodland tradition. This was followed by 300 or 400 years of occupation by developed horticulturalists of the late NeoIndian stage, mainly the Antelope Creek culture of the Plains Village tradition, with Puebloan influences.

Not long before the dawn of history, these villagers were replaced by bison-hunting Apache foot-nomads, who became horse-nomads after Spanish contact, but were in turn replaced after a stay of 300 or 400 years by the more effective Comanche horse-nomads. After fewer than 200 years, the Comanche in their turn were replaced by Anglo cattlemen.

During the last century, the cattlemen were soon joined by dry-land subsistence farmers, who have recently turned into industrialized irrigation farmers and cattle-feeders. For thousands of years, nature raised the grass to feed the buffalo which fed the Indians; now the farmers raise the grain to feed the cattle which feed much of the world.

When one surveys the entire span of human existence in the Palo Duro area, the most impressive fact is the accelerating rate of radical change, both environmental and cultural. It seems unlikely that we face a long and placid future.

Some patterns persist, however—both major and minor. An example of a major enduring pattern is the tendency, one way or another, from the earliest times onward, for meat procurement to remain central to human life on the Staked Plains. An example of a minor enduring pattern is the tendency of modern tourists from the Panhandle to return from visits to the Pueblos in New Mexico with the same things that the Antelope Creek people brought back to their villages—pretty painted pots and turquoise jewelry.

REFERENCES

Holden, William C.
    1931.   Texas Tech Archaeological Expedition, Summer, 1930. Texas Archaeological and Paleontological Society Bulletin, Vol. 3, pp. 43-52.

Hughes, David T.
    1977.   Analysis of Certain Prehistoric Bison Kills in the Texas Panhandle and Adjacent Areas. M.A. thesis, The University of Arkansas, Fayetteville.

Hughes, Jack T.
    1955.   Little Sunday: An Archaic Site in the Texas Panhandle. Texas Archeological Society Bulletin, Vol. 26, pp. 55-74.

    1962.   Lake Creek: A Woodland Site in the Texas Panhandle. Texas Archeological Society Bulletin, Vol. 32, pp. 65-84.

    1972.   Archeology. In Ark-Red Chloride Control Part I, Areas VII, VIII, and X, Texas. Report submitted to the U. S. Army Corps of Engineers by West Texas State University.

    1973.   Archeology. In Environmental Inventory and Assessment of Areas VI, IX, XIII, XIV, and XV, Red River Chloride Control Project, Oklahoma and Texas. Report submitted to the U. S. Army Corps of Engineers by West Texas State University.

    1974.   Prehistory of the Caddoan-speaking Tribes. Garland Publishing Inc., New York and London.

    1975.   Some Early and Northerly Occurrences of the Clear Fork Gouge. Paper presented at Reunion Sobre Aspectos de Arqueologia e Historia del Noreste, Monterrey, Nuevo Leon, Mexico.

    1976.   The Panhandle Archaic. In The Texas Archaic: A Symposium, edited by Thomas R. Hester, Center for Archaeological Research, The University of Texas at San Antonio, Special Report No. 2, pp. 28-38.

    in press   The Canyon Country Club Cave, Randall County, Texas. Texas Historical Commission, Austin.

Hughes, Jack T., and H. Charles Hood
    1975.   An Archeological Survey in the Lakeview Watershed. Report submitted to the Soil Conservation Service by West Texas State University.

Hughes, Jack T., and Patrick S. Willey, assemblers
    1978.   Archeology at Mackenzie Reservoir. Texas Historical Commission, Office of the State Archeologist, Archeological Survey Report No. 24, Austin.

Jackson, A. T.
   1938.   Picture-writing of Texas Indians. The University of Texas Pub. No.
           3809, Austin.

Jokerst, Carol O.
   1972.   A Floodplain Burial in Randall County, Texas. Lower Plains Arche-
           ological Society Bulletin No. 2 (for 1971), pp. 1-4.

Katz, Susanna R. and Paul R.
   1976.   Archeological Investigations in Lower Tule Canyon, Briscoe County,
           Texas. Texas Historical Commission, Office of the State Archeologist,
           Archeological Survey Report No. 16, Austin.

Kirkland, Forrest
   1942.   Indian Pictographs and Petroglyphs in the Panhandle Region of
           Texas. Texas Archaeological and Paleontological Society Bulletin,
           Vol. 14, pp. 9-26.

Kirkland, Forrest, and W. W. Newcomb, Jr.
   1967.   The Rock Art of Texas Indians. The University of Texas Press, Austin.

Krieger, Alex D.
   1946.   Culture Complexes and Chronology in Northern Texas. The Univer-
           sity of Texas Pub. No. 4640, Austin.

Malone, James M.
   1970.   Archeological Reconnaissance in the Mackenzie Reservoir Area of
           Tule Canyon. Texas State Historical Survey Committee and Texas
           Water Development Board, Archeological Survey Report No. 8, Austin.

Moore, Ray
   1966.   Archeology of Palo Duro Canyon. West Texas State University Geolog-
           ical Society Guidebook for 1966 Southwestern Association of Student
           Geological Societies Annual Field Trip, pp. 53-57.

Pearson, Emerson L.
   1974.   Soil Characteristics of an Archeological Deposit: Randall County,
           Texas. Texas Archeological Society Bulletin, Vol. 45, pp. 151-189.

Schultz, Gerald E., and Elmer P. Cheatum
   1970.   *Bison occidentalis* and Associated Invertebrates from the Late Wis-
           consin of Randall County, Texas. Journal of Paleontology, Vol. 44,
           No. 5, pp. 836-850.

Speer, Roberta D.
   1975.   Fossil Bison Remains from the Rex Rodgers Site, Briscoe County,
           Texas. M.S. thesis, West Texas State University.

Studer, Floyd V.
   1931.   Archeological Survey of the North Panhandle of Texas. Texas Archae-
           ological and Paleontological Society Bulletin, Vol. 3, pp. 70-75.

Taylor, Joe F.
  1962.   The Indian Campaign on the Staked Plains, 1874-1875. Panhandle-Plains Historical Society, Canyon, Texas.

Tunnell, Curtis D., and Jack T. Hughes
  1955.   An Archaic Bison Kill in the Texas Panhandle. Panhandle-Plains Historical Review, Vol. 28, pp. 63-70.

Upshaw, Emily
  1972.   Palo Duro Rock Art: Indian Petroglyphs and Pictographs. M.A. thesis, West Texas State University.

Wedel, Waldo R.
  1961.   Prehistoric Man on the Great Plains. The University of Oklahoma Press, Norman.

  1975.   Chalk Hollow: Culture Sequence and Chronology in the Texas Panhandle. Actas del XLI Congreso Internacional de Americanistas, Vol. 1, pp. 271-278, Mexico, D.F.

Willey, Patrick S., Billy R. Harrison, and Jack T. Hughes
  1978a.   The Rex Rodgers Site. In Archeology at Mackenzie Reservoir, assembled by Jack T. Hughes and Patrick S. Willey.

  1978b.   The Blue Clay Site. In Archeology at Mackenzie Reservoir, assembled by Jack T. Hughes and Patrick S. Willey.

  1978c.   The Sand Pit Site. In Archeology at Mackenzie Reservoir, assembled by Jack T. Hughes and Patrick S. Willey.

Willey, Patrick S., and Jack T. Hughes
  1978a.   The County Line Site. In Archeology at Mackenzie Reservoir, assembled by Jack T. Hughes and Patrick S. Willey.

  1978b.   The Deadman's Shelter Site. In Archeology at Mackenzie Reservoir, assembled by Jack T. Hughes and Patrick S. Willey.

  1978c.   The Sandstone Ledger Site. In Archeology at Mackenzie Reservoir, assembled by Jack T. Hughes and Patrick S. Willey.

Word, James H., and Anne Fox
  1975.   The Cogdell Burial in Floyd County, Texas. Texas Archeological Society Bulletin, Vol. 46, pp. 1-63.

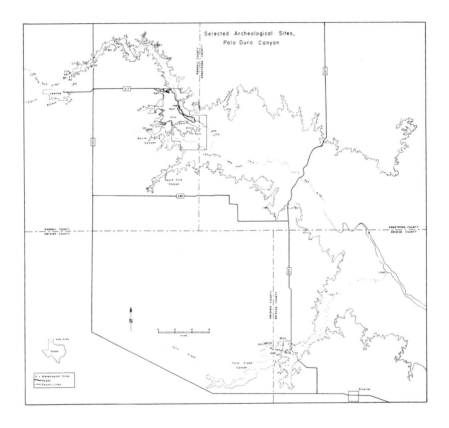

Selected Archeological Sites,
Palo Duro Canyon

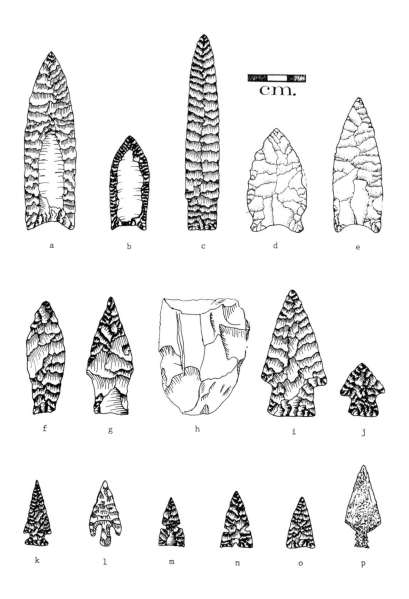

Figure 2. Some artifacts typical of the archeological stages in the Palo Duro Canyon area. PaleoIndian stage: a, Clovis point; b, Folsom point; c, Eden point; d, notched Rex Rodgers point; e, unnotched Rex Rodgers point. MesoIndian stage: f, Pandale point; g, Trinity point; h, gouge; i, Lange point; j, Ellis point. Neo-Indian stage: k, Scallorn point; l, Deadman point; m, Washita point; n, Harrell point. Historic stage: o, Fresno point; p, metal point.

Figure 3. Test excavations at Site A4, an open camp on a terrace between Palo Duro and Tierra Blanca creeks north of Canyon.

Figure 4. A slab-house village ruin (Site A739) is located at the base of this butte in Tule Canyon.

Figure 5. Mortar holes in a sandstone boulder at an open camp (Site A868) near a spring in Dry Creek Canyon.

Figure 6. A burial partially exposed in a rock shelter (Site A180) under the caprock on Tierra Blanca Creek northeast of Canyon.

Figure 7. View of Site A174, a large rock shelter under the caprock at the head of a tributary canyon near Wayside.

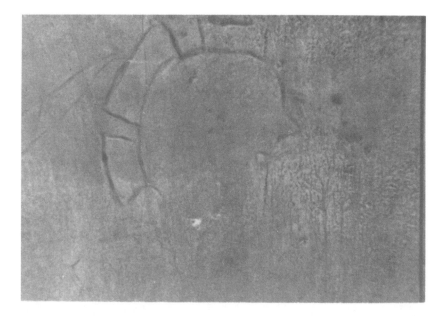

Figure 8. Profile carved in sandstone at a rock shelter (Site A370) in Thomas Draw.

Figure 9. A Tecovas jasper quarry (Site M82) is located at this road cut on the Claude-Wayside highway across Palo Duro Canyon.

Figure 10. Excavating the Rex Rodgers Site (A957 Area II), a PaleoIndian bison kill now covered by Lake Mackenzie.

THE PALEONTOLOGY OF PALO DURO CANYON

Gerald E. Schultz
Department of Geosciences
West Texas State University

During the past century, the Texas Panhandle has acquired an excellent reputation as a source of museum-worthy vertebrate fossils and today holds a key position in the field of paleontology or the science of prehistoric life. To the average visitor, the region must appear to be another monotonously flat and uninteresting portion of the High Plains. Actually, however, the Staked Plains of Texas or Llano Estacado, as the region south of the Canadian River is called, stands as a high plateau bounded on two sides by steep escarpments which separate it topographically from the Low Rolling Plains to the east and the Pecos Valley of New Mexico to the west. Several large canyons have cut for great distances into the escarpment on the east and mark the headwater tributaries of the Red, Pease, Brazos, and Colorado rivers of Texas. These canyons and the adjacent "Breaks of the Plains" have exposed, over extensive areas, strata of several geologic ages in which many fine vertebrate fossils have been found. These fossils are now in the collections of Harvard and Yale universities, the American Museum of Natural History, the Smithsonian Institute, the University of California, the University of Michigan, and, of course, the Panhandle-Plains Historical Museum and West Texas State University.

Palo Duro Canyon is one of the most rugged, scenic, and geologically significant areas of the Texas Panhandle. It begins in northeastern Randall County about 12 miles east of the town of Canyon and 15 miles southeast of Amarillo where Palo Duro Creek has cut a "miniature Grand Canyon" 600 to 800 feet deep into brightly colored sedimentary rocks of Permian, Triassic, and late Tertiary age. Joined here by several tributary canyons it then continues southeastward for about 40 miles as the Prairie Dog Town Fork of the Red River through Armstrong County and into Briscoe County where it widens out and merges into the Low Rolling Plains. The most scenic part of the canyon near its head in Randall County is now a state park.

Formation of the upper canyon and its tributaries, Timbercreek Canyon, Big and Little Sunday canyons, North and South Cita canyons, and Tule Canyon, began less than a million years ago. A variety of geological processes were involved. Lengthening and deepening of the canyon was accomplished primarily by stream erosion. Widening of the canyon and its tributaries was effected by slope wash and by mass movement, i.e. gravitational processes such as slump, debris flow, creep, and rock slide followed by removal of this material downstream.

Fossil remains of prehistoric animals have been known from the Palo Duro for nearly 100 years. In 1892, while assisting geologist W. F. Cummins with explorations for the State Geological Survey of Texas, Professor E. D. Cope, an eminent paleontologist and a devout Quaker from Pennsylvania, discovered bones and teeth of a crocodile-like reptile known as a phytosaur. Since that time, many fossils of 3-toed horses, camels, rhinoceroses, mastodons, ground sloths, deer, peccaries, dogs, and cats as well as lower forms such as land turtles, phytosaurs, and amphibians have been discovered in the eroded "breaks" along the eastern escarpment of the Plains and along the Canadian River drainage.

In Palo Duro Canyon, the oldest sedimentary rocks exposed are those of the Permian Period which closed the Paleozoic Era about 230 million years ago. These rocks consist of the massive, bedded gypsum of the Cloud Chief Formation and the overlying reddish-orange siltstones and shales of the Quartermaster Formation which form the canyon floor and the lower part of the brightly colored Spanish Skirts at the base of the canyon walls and which may also be seen along the Canadian River and Lake Meredith.

During late Permian time, a shallow land-locked embayment of the sea covered much of west Texas. Sediments deposited in and near the edge of this sea contained iron which oxidized to form the bright red colors seen in the siltstones of the Quartermaster Formation. Cross-bedded sediments containing asymmetrical ripple marks indicative of continental stream deposits occur interbedded with shallow marine deposits containing symmetric wave ripple marks. This alternating sequence of continental and marine sediments was deposited during a series of marine transgressions and regressions, or times of alternating rise and fall of sea level (Matthews, 1969). As the Permian Period drew to a close, the sea gradually retreated to the southwest.

Permian rocks in the Palo Duro area are unfossiliferous. Farther east, some poorly preserved marine clams and snails have been found in a dolomite lens at the base of the Quartermaster (Roth, Newell, and Burma, 1941). Deltaic deposits of early and middle Permian age have produced amphibian and reptile remains in north central Texas and central Oklahoma but no vertebrates are known from the late Permian of west Texas.

By the latter part of the Triassic Period, which immediately followed the Permian Period and which opened the Mesozoic Era or Age of Reptiles, the environment in the Texas Panhandle had changed considerably. At this time, about 190 to 200 million years ago, low energy streams flowed northwest across the region depositing sand and fine gravel in channels and muds or clays on floodplains. These sediments formed the bright lavender, yellow, and orange shales and siltstones and white sandstones of the Tecovas Formation and the massive greenish-gray sandstone and conglomerate ledges and the maroon mudstones of the overlying Trujillo Formation. These layers form most of the canyon walls and are well exposed in prominent features such as the Spanish Skirts and the Devil's Slide (Tecovas Fm.) and Sad Monkey Point (Trujillo Fm.). Together, these formations comprise the Dockum Group. During Tecovas time the climate was humid. Small lakes, swamps, and abundant vegetation covered the floodplains of meandering streams. The region encompassing northwest Texas, New Mexico, and Arizona at this time probably resembled the present Amazon River drainage basin of South America. By Trujillo time, the climate was somewhat drier and the streams were more braided as in the Canadian and Red rivers today.

The most abundant Triassic fossils in the canyon are the teeth and bony plates of phytosaurs, large reptiles which resembled the alligators and crocodiles in appearance (Fig. 1). Their occurrence was first reported by Cope (1893) and later by Green (1954) and Gregory (1962). Although they did not give rise to crocodilians, phytosaurs are thought to have lived in similar river and swamp environments and to have had similar habits. Some had broad, heavy skulls and are believed to have fed on amphibians and smaller reptiles while others had long, narrow snouts and probably fed on fish and other small creatures. These carnivores were surely misnamed since the term "phytosaur" means literally "plant reptile." Their teeth were sharp, pointed, and frequently serrated along the edges and were covered with hard, shiny enamel which made them very durable. Except for size differences and a tendency to become laterally compressed, they showed little variation from front to back in the jaw. A peculiar feature of the skull consisted of the backward position of the nostrils immediately in front of the eyes rather than at the anterior end of the snout as in modern crocodilians. A primitive phytosaur skull

minus the snout was collected from the Tecovas Formation
near the north boundary of the park and is now on exhibit in the
Panhandle-Plains Museum. Parts of one skeleton were found in
Big Sunday Canyon.

Fig. 1   Phytosaurs, large amphibious alligator-like reptiles from the late Triassic
         Period, 190 million years ago. Note position of the nostrils on top of the
         head near the eyes.

Another common creature in the Texas Panhandle during
Triassic time was *Metoposaurus* or *Buettneria*, an amphibian
somewhat resembling a modern salamander but reaching a
length of six or seven feet (Fig. 2). Its skull was flattened and
exceptionally large compared with its body. The eyes were placed
on top of the head and included a pineal or so-called "third eye"
which was located in the middle of the skull and which was probably light sensitive. The long, slender jaws with their wide gape
suggest that this creature may have submerged itself in the water
in order to snap at fish when the opportunity occurred. The sprawly
weak limbs and the bulky body made it unlikely that *Metoposaurus* was able to support itself on dry land for any length of
time. Although fragmentary remains of this creature have been
found in the Tecovas Formation in Palo Duro Canyon, the best
material comes from a site on Sierrita de la Cruz Creek northwest

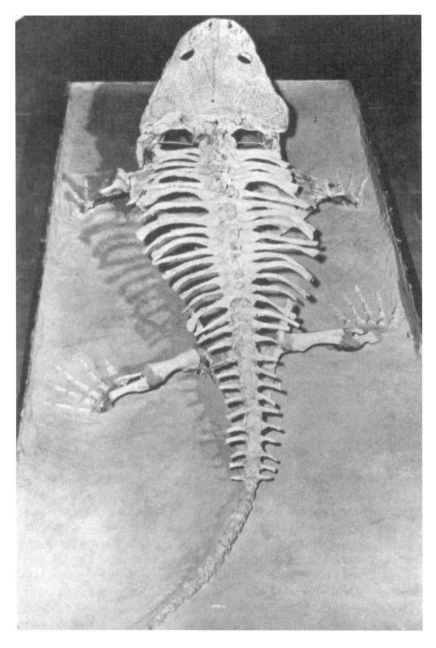

Fig. 2 Skeleton of *Metoposaurus ("Buettneria")*, a large flat-headed amphibian collected from the Upper Triassic Tecovas Formation northwest of Amarillo, Texas. (Photo courtesy of Panhandle-Plains Hist. Soc.)

of Amarillo where the WPA in 1940 excavated an impressive number of skulls and skeletons for the Panhandle-Plains Historical Museum—one of the largest collections of this species in North America.

Desmatosuchus was a strange-looking reptile not unlike a crocodile in general appearance but characterized by flat bony plates down the back and several pairs of long, pointed spines extending laterally from the neck. Small peg-like teeth indicate that this creature was a plant-eater. Although much less common than remains of phytosaurs, fossil spines and other bones of this animal have been found in the lower part of the Tecovas Formation in Big Sunday Canyon. Remains of fish which lived in Triassic streams and lakes of the region occasionally turn up in the Tecovas Formation. *Ceratodus*, a lungfish similar to that of Australia today, is represented by flattened wing-shaped tooth plates about one inch long. These plates bore a number of radiating ridges and were mounted on the roof of the mouth where they were used to crush mollusks and shellfish. In 1960, a skull of *Chinlea*, a coelacanth or fleshy-lobed fish, was found in Big Sunday Canyon (Schaeffer and Gregory, 1961; Schaeffer, 1967). Coelacanths lived in freshwater streams during their early history and, until recently, were thought to have become extinct at the end of the Age of Dinosaurs about 65 million years ago. In 1938, a coelacanth was dredged up from the deep Mozambique Channel between Madagascar and the mainland of Africa. Since that time additional specimens of this "living fossil" have come to light.

Among the small fossils found in the Tecovas shales are small, oblong stony objects called coprolites. These pellets represent the fossilized excrement of phytosaurs and metoposaurs and are usually red or lavender in color and about one inch in length. Analysis of coprolites may reveal chips of bone and teeth and, hence, information about the diet of these animals.

The Tecovas shales are generally more fossiliferous than the Trujillo Formation, particularly with respect to the vertebrates, although some phytosaur teeth have been found in the latter. On the other hand, plant remains are equally represented in both formations. Carbonized impressions of stems and bark of conifers, ferns, and horsetails occur on bedding planes in the gray sandstones of the Trujillo. A most unusual specimen in the Panhandle-Plains Museum consists of the impression of what some experts think may be a palm leaf (Ash, 1976). If such is the case, it would be one of the oldest "flowering plants" or angiosperms on record. The specimen, assigned to the genus *Sanmiguelia*, was collected in 1934 from the Trujillo sandstone in South Cita Canyon (Fig. 3). Petrified logs and lignitic woody fragments, mostly of a drab gray color, occur in the Tecovas shales. Invertebrates are represented in the Trujillo by numerous small freshwater clams similar to the modern genus *Unio*. Shells and shell casts of these clams occur at a site in North Cita Canyon.

At the top of the Trujillo Formation, an unconformity or erosional surface marks a long hiatus or missing time interval between the end of the Triassic Period and the late Tertiary when the overlying Ogallala Formation was deposited about five million years ago. During the Jurassic and Cretaceous periods which succeeded the Triassic, dinosaurs flourished on the earth only to become extinct at the end of the Cretaceous Period of the Mesozoic Era. No dinosaurs have been found in Palo Duro Canyon although a small bipedal form called *Coelophysis*, about six feet long, occurs in Triassic shales elsewhere in the Texas Panhandle and in northern New Mexico. Large dinosaur bones were collected in the 1930's from the Jurassic age Morrison Formation near Kenton and Boise City, Oklahoma. Rocks of Cretaceous age containing numerous fossil oysters of the genus *Gryphaea* occur near Tucumcari, New Mexico. It is not known whether Jurassic and Cretaceous rocks were ever deposited in the Palo Duro area but stream-worn *Gryphaea* shells, probably derived from Cretaceous rocks to the west, occur in the lower part of the late Tertiary age Ogallala Formation near the park road and at a few places in South Cita Canyon.

The Tertiary Period comprises most of the Cenozoic Era or Age of Mammals which began about 65 million years ago. During this time many large mammals evolved in the Great Plains and intermountain basins of the West. Rocks and fossils of early and middle Tertiary age are missing in the Texas Panhandle. If they were ever present, erosion had removed all traces of them by late Tertiary time when the Ogallala Formation was deposited. The Ogallala represents a vast complex of sands, silts, gravels, and caliche extending southward from western Nebraska to the Edwards Plateau of Texas. These fluvial deposits were laid down by streams flowing eastward from the Rocky Mountains during the late Miocene and early Pliocene epochs of the Tertiary Period between ten and four million years ago. The caliche "caprock" at the top of the Ogallala forms the High Plains surface for hundreds of miles. In some parts of the Panhandle, the channel sands and floodplain clays have produced a diverse fauna of 3-toed

Fig. 3 *Sanmiguelia lewisi* Brown, a palm-like leaf from the Upper Triassic Trujillo Formation of South Cita Canyon. This specimen, PPHM no. 1101,
contains two leaf impressions. (Photo courtesy of Panhandle-Plains Hist.
Soc.)

horses, camels, rhinoceroses, deer, antelope, mastodons, bone-eating dogs, saber-tooth cats, and large tortoises or land turtles, e.g. in the vicinities of Clarendon, Claude, Miami, Canadian, and Higgins. Many prominent universities and museums have sent collecting parties into the region during the last 80 years. The Panhandle-Plains Museum also possesses impressive fossil collections from these localities.

In the Palo Duro Canyon area, the Ogallala Formation is quite thin, about 20 to 40 feet compared with about 400 to 500 feet along the Canadian River near Canadian, and it forms the canyon rim in some parts of the canyon as in Fortress Cliff. A few localities have produced fossils four or five million years old from the late Hemphillian Mammal Age; most of these are not in the park proper but in the more inaccessible tributaries such as Dry Canyon on the Christian Ranch near Claude (Johnston and Savage, 1955; Savage, 1955) and North Cita Canyon on the Harrell (formerly Axtel) Ranch (Johnston, 1939; Johnston and Savage, 1955). These sites have produced hundreds of fossil horse teeth. The Axtel faunal locality is noted for the upper and lower jaws of a new species of large bone-crushing dog named *Osteoborus hilli* (Johnston, 1939) in honor of Dr. Joseph A. Hill, former president of West Texas State College (University) (Fig. 4). A few horse teeth and part of a large tortoise shell were found in 1964 in a sand layer by the park road where it begins its descent to the canyon floor. Fossil prairie grass seeds occur in small pockets in the brown sand behind the Coronado Visitor Center (West Texas State University Geological Society, 1976).

One of the most spectacular fossil localities in the Palo Duro and the Panhandle as well was discovered by the late Floyd V. Studer of Amarillo in the 1930's. The site is in North Cita Canyon near the park boundary (see map, page 8). Fossils occur here in a sequence of light-colored sands and silts deposited about two to three million years ago during the Pliocene Epoch of the Tertiary Period in a basin eroded into the Ogallala Formation. This basin was approximately four miles in diameter and extended from the south edge of Big Sunday Canyon across the head of Little Sunday Canyon to the north side of North Cita Canyon and was intermittently occupied by a playa lake. Fossil evidence suggests that this basin was surrounded by broad, grassy plains. Animals living near the basin apparently came there to drink and perhaps to die. Their remains were washed into low areas, buried and fossilized only to be exposed later by headward erosion of the tributary canyons.

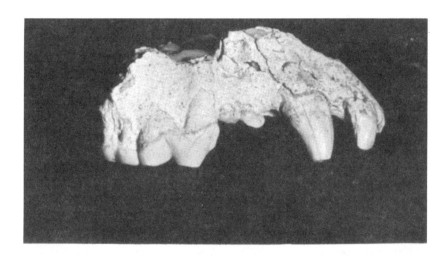

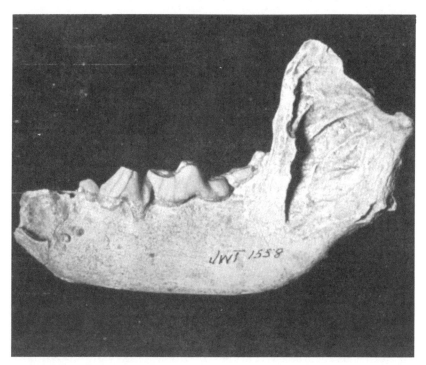

Fig. 4   Upper and lower jaws of *Osteoborus hilli* Johnston, a bone-crushing dog
from the Axtel local fauna of early Pliocene (late Hemphillian) age, Ogallala Formation, North Cita Canyon. (Photo courtesy Panhandle-Plains
Hist. Soc.)

At the time of discovery of the Cita Canyon fossil site, C. Stuart Johnston was Curator of Paleontology and Archeology at the Panhandle-Plains Museum (Fig. 5). Johnston had assumed this position in 1934 along with that of Assistant Professor of Geology at West Texas State College. He had completed most of his course requirements for the doctorate in the field of vertebrate paleontology at the University of Oklahoma and had developed a strong interest in the Tertiary mammalian paleontology and the archeology of the region. He was particularly attracted by the Panhandle's rich Miocene and Pliocene fossil beds which offered great research opportunities. During the five years preceding his untimely death in 1939, Johnston worked untiringly to build up the collections of fossils and artifacts in the museum and to develop a Department of Geology and Archeology on the campus. In these efforts, he was aided by his young and attractive wife, Margaret (Fig. 5). When WPA funds became available, Johnston applied for and received a series of grants totaling close to $100,000 by means of which large numbers of men were employed excavating fossils from approximately 15 sites in the Panhandle. Within a period of about five years, many thousands of specimens were collected for the museum, a task which would have taken a handful of dedicated students several lifetimes to complete under normal circumstances. As many as 75 men were employed at one time on these projects. Margaret supervised much of the field work while Johnston, himself, supervised the extensive preparation and cataloging of fossils in the small basement laboratory of the museum, developed exhibits, taught classes, and continued the work toward his doctorate. The discovery of a rich Pliocene fossil bed in Cita Canyon provided him with a close, convenient and significant dissertation subject. With the help of WPA, a large crew of men worked year-round at the site from 1936 until about 1940 (Fig. 6). These efforts produced numerous remains of horses, camels, mastodons, deer, antelope, peccaries, ground sloths, glyptodons, carnivores, tortoises, and water birds. Several species were new to science and included two cats, a coyote, a hyena, two birds, and two tortoises.

Horses are the most abundant mammals in the Cita Canyon fossil assemblage being represented by hundreds of teeth, jaws, and leg bones. They include a large zebra-like form named *Dolichohippus* (Fig. 7) and a small less abundant type called *Nannippus* which retained three toes on each foot.

Camels include several varieties ranging from dromedary-size to llama-size. Pronghorn antelope (Fig. 8) are represented by two

Fig. 5 C. Stuart and Margaret Johnston at the "Horse Quarry" on the McDaniel Ranch near Silverton, Texas during WPA excavations in 1937. Johnston was Curator of Paleontology at the Panhandle-Plains Historical Museum while his wife, Margaret, supervised field excavations. (Photo courtesy Panhandle-Plains Hist. Soc.)

Fig. 6 WPA crew excavating fossils in North Cita Canyon in 1936. This Pliocene or Blancan age quarry was worked for about five years in the 1930's and yielded hundreds of fossils including horse, camel, deer, antelope, peccary, mastodon, sloth, glyptodon, saber-tooth cat, bone-crushing dog, and hyena. (Photo courtesy of Panhandle-Plains Hist. Soc.)

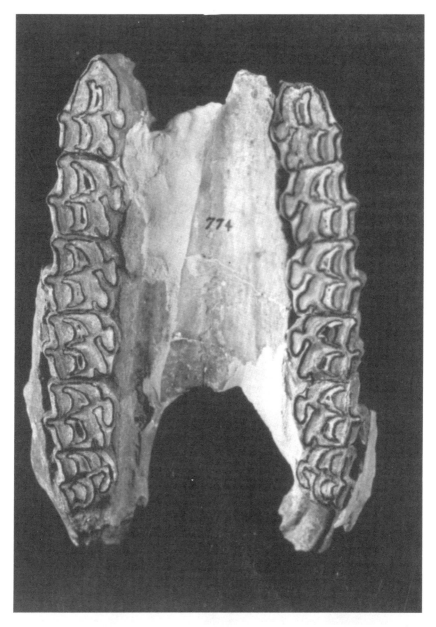

Fig. 7   Upper teeth and palate of *Equus (Dolichohippus)*, a horse similar to the
modern Grevy zebra of East Africa. This horse was common in the Cita
Canyon local fauna of mid-to-late Pliocene (Blancan) age, North Cita Canyon, Randall County, Texas. (Photo courtesy of Panhandle-Plains Hist.
Soc.)

Fig. 8 Extinct pronghorn antelope from the Pliocene (Blancan age) Cita Canyon local fauna. Two species are represented by two distinctly different horn cores. (From a painting by Gustav Sundstrom in the Panhandle-Plains Historical Museum.)

different species distinguished by the shape of the bony core supporting the horny sheath but otherwise very similar to the modern variety. *Platygonus* (Fig. 9) was a peccary similar to the modern javelina of south Texas and Mexico. Deer were also present.

Fig. 9   *Platygonus*, a late Tertiary and Pleistocene (Ice Age) peccary or javelina which occurs in the Cita Canyon local fauna.

Stegomastodon (Savage, 1955) was a cousin to the elephant but, unlike the latter, it was a browser of soft leafy vegetation and had low-crowned teeth with rounded nipple-like cusps. Long cylindrical tusks emerged from the skull but the lower jaw was short and tuskless.

Ground sloths were large, shaggy-furred beasts reaching a length of about 10 feet and possessing sharp claws and a long tubular skull with simple peg-like teeth lacking enamel. Two varieties, *Megalonyx* (Hirschfeld and Webb, 1968) and *Glossotherium* (Fig. 10) were present at Cita Canyon. These animals migrated northward from South America during late Tertiary time. Although extinct, they are survived by their cousins, the tree sloths of Central and South America.

Fig. 10   *Glossotherium*, a late Tertiary and Pleistocene ground sloth found in the
Cita Canyon local fauna. These animals were immigrants from South
America and became extinct at the end of the Pleistocene or Ice Age. They
are related to the modern tree sloths of Central and South America.

Related to the ground sloths were the glyptodonts (Fig. 11)
which resembled armadillos but which were much larger and had
a rigid shell or carapace made of numerous polygonal plates
joined tightly together at their margins rather than the more
flexible, overlapping style of covering seen in the modern armadillos. *Glyptotherium*, as the Cita Canyon variety was called,
may have reached a length of five feet and may have stood up to
three feet high. Bony plates covered the head and rings of bony
plates encircled the tail. Some varieties had spikes or knobs on the
end of the tail which functioned as a club or mace. Glyptodonts
were not native to North America but migrated northward from
South America during the Pliocene Epoch.

   Carnivores comprise a small but significant part of the fauna
from Cita Canyon. With the abundance and diversity of prey
animals available, it is not surprising that a variety of carnivores, some of them rare, have been found at the site. Cats include
a large saber-toothed form called *Ischyrosmilus johnstoni* (Mawby, 1965) (Fig. 12) which used its long canines to stab its prey so
that it would bleed to death. This species is represented in the

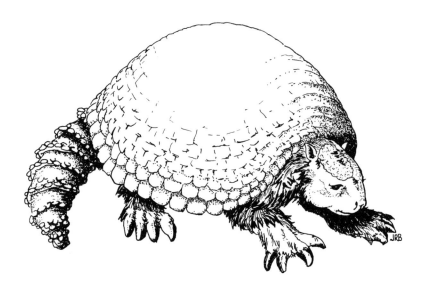

Fig. 11   *Glyptotherium*, a late Tertiary glyptodont which occurs in the Cita Canyon local fauna. These animals were immigrants from South America and resembled armadillos but were much larger and had a rigid armor of fused bony plates covering the body and rings of bony plates covering the tail.

museum's collections by a partial skull, several jaws and teeth, and assorted limb bones. *Felis studeri* (Savage, 1960) was either a puma or a cheetah and is represented by a skull, jaws, and assorted limb bones and vertebrae. It was named in honor of the late Floyd Studer, amateur archeologist and benefactor of the museum, by Don Savage, a former student and distinguished graduate of West Texas State College. Don, who learned paleontology under Johnston, is now Head of the Paleontology Department at the University of California at Berkeley. Studer is credited with having first reported the Cita Canyon site to Johnston in 1935.

An ancestor to the modern coyote was described by Johnston (1938) on the basis of three excellent skulls and given the name *Canis lepophagus* (Fig. 13). The role of scavenger was played primarily by a large, massive but short-jawed, bone-crushing dog called *Borophagus* and by an extremely rare hyena called *Chasmaporthetes johnstoni* (Stirton and Christian, 1940, 1941) known only from a right lower jaw possessing certain cat-like characters in the teeth (Fig. 14). A short-faced bear is represented by

Fig. 12   *Ischyrosmilus johnstoni* Mawby, a late Tertiary (Pliocene) saber-tooth cat from the Cita Canyon local fauna. These cats had long, sharp, stabbing canines and powerful front legs but were probably not graceful runners like some modern cats. (From a painting by Gustav Sundstrom in the Panhandle-Plains Historical Museum.)

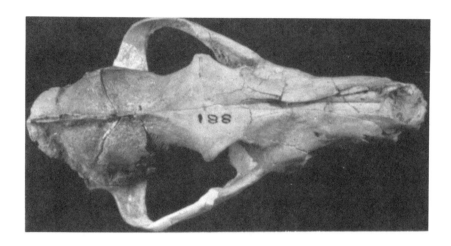

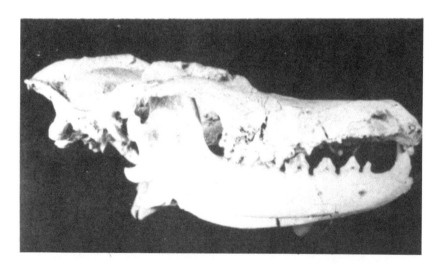

Fig. 13   *Canis lepophagus* Johnston, a new species of ancestral coyote from the
          Cita Canyon local fauna, Blancan age. Upper figure is top view of the
          "type" skull, PPHM, no. 881. Lower figure is side view of skull and jaws,
          no. 722. (Photo courtesy Panhandle-Plains Hist. Soc.)

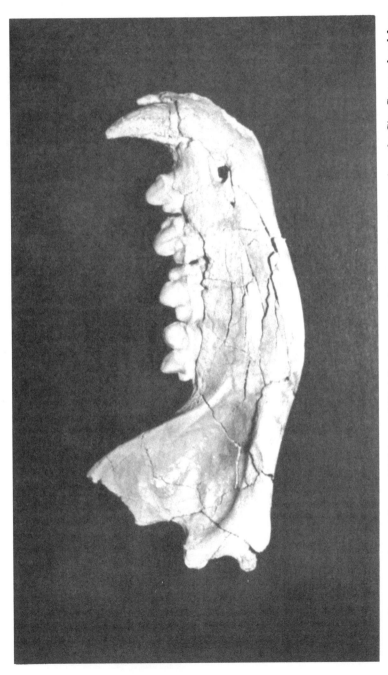

Fig. 14 *Chasmaporthetes johnstoni* (Stirton and Christian), a new and rare species of hyena from the Cita Canyon local fauna, Blancan age. This is the type specimen, a right lower jaw, PPHM no. 2343. (Photo courtesy Panhandle-Plains Hist. Soc.)

two molar teeth and a leg bone while the smaller and rarer carnivores include gray fox, badger, skunk, and raccoon.

Large land turtles or tortoises similar to those now living in the
Galapagos Islands roamed the Cita Canyon area at this time also
(Fig. 15). Several large shells, a skeleton, and an egg were collected here (Johnston, 1937; Auffenberg, 1962) (Fig. 16). These
animals have been found in other parts of the Great Plains in
deposits of the late Tertiary and the Pleistocene or Ice Age. Since
these animals require a frost-free climate, it is thought that winters in much of the Plains were milder than those of the present.
Large tortoises could not survive the extreme temperatures of the
Great Plains today.

Recently, the author has collected a variety of interesting rodents, rabbits, and shrews to supplement the larger animals in
the Cita Canyon fauna. About 15 tons of sand were collected in
burlap sacks and wet-screened to remove the sediment and obtain a concentrate of small jaws, teeth, and bone scrap. The
rodents include gophers, ground squirrels, and mice. Lower forms
are present also and include frogs, toads, snakes, and several

Fig. 15   *Geochelone*, a large land tortoise from the late Tertiary and Pleistocene.
These animals require frost-free climates and could not survive in the
Texas Panhandle today although their modern counterparts live in the
Galapagos Islands.

Fig. 16   Excavation of fossil land tortoise in Cita Canyon. Photograph shows bottom part of shell (plastron) and internal skeletal bones. Top of shell (carapace) has been removed. Shell was about 3 feet long and 2 feet wide. (Photo courtesy of Panhandle-Plains Hist. Soc.)

water birds as well as a wild turkey (Miller and Bowman, 1956).
Microvertebrates, as these small forms are called, are more sensitive to climatic and other ecologic factors than larger animals
and, therefore, aid in reconstructing environmental conditions in
the immediate area at the time they lived there. The Cita Canyon
fauna lived during the Pliocene Epoch which closed the Tertiary
Period and immediately preceded the Pleistocene Epoch or Ice
Age. A fauna similar to that from Cita Canyon has been found
100 miles farther south in Blanco Canyon near Crosbyton. This
fauna, known for nearly 100 years, is the basis for what paleon-
tologists call the Blancan Mammal Age. Both faunas are summarized in a paper by Johnston and Savage (1955).

During the Pleistocene or Ice Age, which began about one and
one half million years ago, glaciers advanced and retreated several times over the northern part of the continent. The Southern
High Plains including the Texas Panhandle were never glaci-
ated, however, but climates in this region during periods of glacial advance farther north were marked by cooler summers and
milder winters with more rainfall than at present. Interglacial

Fig. 17   *Mammuthus*, the mammoth. This Pleistocene immigrant from Asia
roamed over much of North America. Southern forms were probably
smooth-skinned like the Indian elephant while northern forms developed
woolly coverings for colder climates. Note long curved tusks.

times were warm and subtropical.

In the Palo Duro region, Pleistocene fossils have been found in sediments overlying those of the Cita Canyon basin and in terrace gravels and alluvium which occur as fill in some of the tributary valleys. Most notable of the larger animals were the mammoth and the bison. Both were veritable latecomers to North America having entered it by way of the Bering Land Bridge from Asia. The former (Fig. 17) was represented by the Imperial mammoth and the somewhat later Columbian mammoth. Since climates in the region were mild, it is unlikely that these animals were woolly as were the northern varieties but rather they probably resembled the closely related modern Indian elephant except for their somewhat larger size and their long curved upper tusks. Their cheek teeth were large with flat grinding surfaces and were composed of many flat enamel plates arranged vertically in rows. Remains of tusks and tooth enamel plates are not uncommon finds in the Palo Duro area.

Bison (Fig. 18) arrived in North America during late Pleistocene time. Early varieties are rare as fossils and were charac-

Fig. 18   *Bison.* The bison is a late Pleistocene immigrant from Asia. Early forms had long heavy horns. Later forms developed shorter horns as in the modern Plains bison.

terized by much longer horn cores than the modern species. Later bison more nearly resembled the living variety and their teeth and skulls frequently weather out of the dark, reddish-brown alluvium in the small valleys and draws which feed the Palo Duro. The teeth closely resemble those of cattle to which the bison is related.

Screenwashing of sediment from several Pleistocene sites in Cita Canyon has yielded an abundance of small snails, rodents, and shrews which live today farther north in the Great Plains and give evidence of cooler climates in Texas. Some of these fossils occur in a clay beneath a layer of fine volcanic ash (Pearlette Type O) which erupted from Yellowstone Park 600,000 years ago and was carried to its present site by prevailing winds (Wilcox, Izett, and Powers, 1970).

Today, tourists may visit the newly developed Coronado Interpretative Center and Museum in Palo Duro Canyon State Park and see examples of fossils and rocks found in the park. Dioramas tell the story of the formation of the canyon and show restorations of prehistoric animals and reconstructions of early geologic landscapes. The Panhandle-Plains Historical Museum in Canyon contains a superb collection of fossils from the Palo Duro and surrounding region. Many of these fossils have been donated by ranchers and other Panhandle residents while others were obtained through the aid of WPA and West Texas State University. A few of the more spectacular fossils are on public display in the museum basement but the greater part of this rich and extensive collection remains in storage where it is available for research studies. With the eventual construction of a new connecting wing between the museum annex and the main building, space will be available for a Hall of Geology and Paleontology, now in the planning stage, in which visitors will be able to see new and better displays of Panhandle fossils than have been possible previously. Meanwhile, the many visitors to Palo Duro Canyon State Park can see a great outdoor geologic museum with new displays appearing everyday.

* * * * * * * *

Acknowledgments. The author is grateful to the Panhandle-Plains Historical Society for the loan of photographs used in this article. Pen-and-ink line drawings of the animals were made by John R. Brown through an Organized Research Grant at the Killgore Research Center, West Texas State University.

LITERATURE CITED

Ash, S. R., 1976, Occurrence of the controversial plant fossil *Sanmiguelia* in the Upper Triassic of Texas: Jour. Paleontology, v. 50, no. 5, p. 799-804.

Auffenberg, Walter, 1962, A new species of *Geochelone* from the Pleistocene of Texas: Copeia, no. 3, p. 627-636.

Cope, E. D., 1893, A preliminary report on the vertebrate paleontology of the Llano Estacado: Geol. Survey Texas, 4th Ann. Rept., 1892, p. 1-137.

Green, F. E., 1954, The Triassic deposits of northwestern Texas: Unpublished Ph.D. dissertation, Texas Tech University, 196 p.

Gregory, J. T., 1962, The genera of phytosaurs: Amer. Jour. Sci., v. 260, p. 652-690.

Hirschfeld, S. E., and S. D. Webb, 1968, Plio-Pleistocene megalonychid sloths of North America: Bull. Florida State Mus., v. 12, no. 5, p. 213-296.

Johnston, C. S., 1937, Osteology of *Bysmachelys canyonensis*, a new turtle from the Pliocene of Texas: Jour. Geology, v. 45, p. 439-447.

_____, 1938, Preliminary report on the vertebrate type locality of Cita Canyon and the description of an ancestral coyote: Amer. Jour. Sci., 5th series, v. 35, p. 383-390.

_____, 1939, Preliminary report on the late Middle Pliocene, Axtel locality and the description of a new member of the genus *Osteoborus*: Amer. Jour. Sci., v. 237, p. 895-898.

Johnston, C. S. and D. E. Savage, 1955, A survey of various late Cenozoic vertebrate faunas of the Panhandle of Texas; Part I: introduction, description of localities, preliminary faunal lists: Univ. California Publ. Geol. Sci., v. 31, no. 2, p. 27-50.

Matthews, W. H., III, 1969, The geologic story of Palo Duro Canyon: Guidebook 8, Texas Bureau Econ. Geol., Univ. Texas, Austin, Texas, p. 1-51.

Mawby, J. E., 1965, Machairodonts from the late Cenozoic of the Panhandle of Texas: Jour. Mammalogy, v. 46, no. 4, p. 573-587.

Miller, A. H., and R. I. Bowman, 1956, Fossil birds of the late Pliocene of Cita Canyon, Texas: Wilson Bull., v. 68, no. 1, p. 38-46.

Roth, R. I., N. D. Newell, and B. H. Burma, 1941, Permian pelecypods in the lower Quartermaster Formation, Texas: Jour. Paleontology, v. 15, no. 3, p. 312-317.

Savage, D. E., 1955, A survey of various late Cenozoic vertebrate faunas of the Panhandle of Texas; Part II: Proboscidea: Univ. California Publ. Geol. Sci., v. 31, no. 3, p. 51-74.

_____, 1960, A survey of various late Cenozoic vertebrate faunas of the Panhandle of Texas; Part III: Felidae: Univ. California Publ. Geol. Sci., v. 36, no. 6, p. 317-344.

Schaeffer, Bobb, 1967, Late Triassic fishes from the western United States: Bull. Amer. Mus. Nat. History, v. 135, art. 6, p. 287-342.

Schaeffer, Bobb, and J. T. Gregory, 1961, Coelacanth fishes from the continental Triassic of the western United States: Amer. Mus. Novitates, no. 2036, p. 1-18.

Stirton, R. A., and W. G. Christian, 1940, A member of the Hyaenidae from the Upper Pliocene of Texas: Jour. Mammalogy, v. 21, no. 4, p. 445-448.

_____, 1941, *Ailuraena* Stirton and Christian referred to *Chasmaporthetes* Hay: Jour. Mammalogy, v. 22, no. 2, p. 198.

West Texas State University Geological Society, 1976, Guidebook of Palo Duro Canyon, p. 1-21.

Wilcox, R. E., G. A. Izett, and H. E. Powers, 1970, The Yellowstone Park region as the source of the Pearlette-like ash beds of the Great Plains (abs.): Am. Quat. Assoc., 1st meeting, p. 151.

THE VEGETATION OF PALO DURO CANYON

Robert A. Wright
Department of Biology
West Texas State University

INTRODUCTION

The vegetation of an area is the sum total of the plants growing in that area. Individual plants are organized into populations of species by interbreeding. Interbreeding acts as a cohesive force within a population giving its individuals certain characteristics in common that distinguish them from members of other populations. Thus oaks differ in a number of obvious ways from junipers. One species of juniper differs in a number of more subtle ways from another species of juniper. In turn, all the populations of an area are organized into groups called plant communities. Each particular type of community has its own characteristic appearance and structure, which distinguishes it from other communities. There are striking differences between a grassland community and a woodland community. They do not look alike, and the woodland community has a more complex structure, consisting perhaps of a tree stratum, a stratum of shrubs, and a floor stratum of grasses and forbs. Coming around full circle, the plant communities of an area make up the entire vegetation. The point of this discussion is to show that the vegetation of an area is not just a random assortment of plants, but rather is the end of a spectrum of hierarchially organized systems of increasing complexity.

Consider the vegetation of Palo Duro Canyon. Here is a rich pattern of communities, such as juniper woodland, mesquite flats, and riverine woodland. What are the physical forces responsible for the particular hierarchy we can observe here? The most influential are two sets of environmental factors: climate and soil. An appreciation of the vegetation of Palo Duro Canyon requires some knowledge of these factors and how they operate to shape the living landscape of the canyon. Thus, what would otherwise seem to be a digression into irrelevant matters of climatology and pedology by this rationale assumes pertinence.

If we were, however, to restrict our attention to these aspects, we would have a narrow and incomplete picture of what we wish to view. Bohm (1969), in his characterization of hierarchies, gives us a program for enlarging our perspective. He has described a metaphysics of process. In this view of the universe, things are only relatively constant and thus cannot be fundamental. What is fundamental is a complex hierarchy of larger and smaller flow patterns in which things are abstractions of what is relatively constant within a process of movement and transformation. Thus the shape of a cloud, to use Platt's (1970) example, has only a relative constancy within a process of masses of moist air, continually condensing and evaporating, moving through them. Things do not last forever. Things come into existence, remain relatively stable for some time, and then pass out of existence.

Viewed through Bohm's metaphysical lenses, the present vegetation of Palo Duro Canyon is seen to be as fleeting as a summer cloud. At one magnification, we see an ephemeral mosaic landscape, ever changing through long eons by the mass movement of floras across its surface in response to changes in the configuration of the earth and continental climate. At another magnification, we see more recent changes occurring over hundreds of years as the relative positions of populations within the vegetation are changed in response to the local environment. Therefore, the vegetational pattern of Palo Duro Canyon should be considered in the larger context of the historical development of the vegetation, from the ancient floras that occupied our continent millions of years ago to the modifications in the vegetation brought about in more recent time.

We can further enrich our appreciation by applying another aspect of Bohm's flow-picture. This is that each thing is the center of vast processes, extending ultimately over the entire universe. This means that things can only be understood if considered in their holistic relationship to other things. Palo Duro Canyon is part of a vast escarpment system that occurs throughout the Central Plains from Montana and North Dakota south through the Llano Estacado to the Edwards Plateau. It is biologically related to this system and to other breaks in the topography by a common scarp woodland. The particular series of escarpments that extend from about the area of Palo Duro Canyon south to the Edwards Plateau is genetically related to the Llano Estacado from which it was formed by geologic processes. The Llano Estacado, likewise, is genetically related to the Rocky Mountains by geologic events. And on it goes. Of course, we cannot extend our coverage to the entire universe, but we should consider, for example, the vegetation of Palo Duro Canyon as it relates to the vegetation of the total escarpment system and to the physical environment of the Llano Estacado.

THE PHYSICAL ENVIRONMENT

CLIMATE

We can discuss the climate of the Llano Estacado as an entire unit because of the essential uniformity of its climate, owing in part to its essential uniformity of topography. Wendorf (1975) has summarized the climatic data. The average annual precipitation increases from about 14 inches in the south to about 22 inches in the north. The precipitation is unevenly distributed throughout the year: low precipitation in the winter, high in the spring, low in the mid-summer, and high in the late summer and fall. Days are hot during the summer; the daily maximum usually from 90° to 95° F, but occasionally higher than 100° F. During the coldest months of winter, December and January, the temperature usually reaches a maximum in the low 50's and drops to a minimum in the mid 20's. Almost constantly blowing wind is characteristic of the Llano Estacado. The greatest wind velocities come in the early spring and the lowest in the late summer. The average mean wind speed ranges from about 9 m.p.h. in the south to about 14 m.p.h. in the north. The high winds and low relative humidity result in high evaporation rates. Class A pan evaporation is 110 inches per year at Midland and 100 inches at Amarillo.

The combination of high evaporation, high temperature, and high constant wind drastically reduces the effectiveness of the precipitation. Lotspeich and Coover (1962) present evidence indicating that soils are seldom wetted by a single rain below 6 inches. In most years, they report, the soil is not wetted below 2 to 3 inches, and the deeper soil layers are wetted only during abnormally wet years.

A grassland climate is usually characterized by low effective moisture and a marked dry season. The climate of the Llano Estacado, as we see from the above description, satisfies the criterian and can be considered as a grassland climate. This view implies that grasslands in general, and the Llano Estacado in particular, are climatically determined. It is instructive in this regard to consider how climatic conditions are correlated with vegetation types. Gleason and Cronquist (1964) tell us how:

Modern encyclopedias give statistics about the climate for

many cities and countries, and most good atlases have maps
showing the climate of the world. Botanists have charted the
distribution of the principal types of vegetation over the
world, and that is also shown on maps in many atlases. So all
we have to do is compare the known climate with the known
vegetation and try to find some correlation between them.

As Sauer (1944) points out, the rainfall and temperature values
associated with a particular vegetation type, like grassland, may
be found to apply to areas covered with some other type of vegetation. Such exceptions place the causal relation in doubt. Thus,
although the majority of ecologists consider grasslands to be
climatically determined, we must consider a minority opinion. We
will do this later.

TOPOGRAPHY AND SOIL

Even those who approve of the climate-vegetation correlation
method concede that local topographic and soil conditions may
so drastically modify climatic effects as to determine the type of
vegetation to be found in an area. This is especially important in
considering the vegetation of escarpments.

The surface of the Llano Estacado is flat. As a generality this is
certainly true. The occasional minor topographic breaks in relief
only accentuate the essential flatness. Topographic irregularities are provided by a few east-flowing modern and ancient stream
beds and by the thousands of small, shallow playa lakes that dot
the surface.

The soils of the Llano Estacado and Palo Duro Canyon have
been discussed by Lotspeich and Coover (1962), Lotspeich and
Everhart (1962), and Jacquot et al. (1970). The soils spread over
the Llano are mainly eolian. During Pleistocene time, winds blew
soil material out of what is now the Pecos Valley of New Mexico.
The prevailing wind direction was then and is now from the
southwest to the northeast. As the winds carried this material
across the plains, the coarser material was dropped first, the finer
material was carried longer distances. This differential settling
of mineral material gave rise to a soil gradient across the Llano,
with sandy soils in the southwestern corner grading into silty
clay loam and clay loam soils in the northeastern corner.

Relatively coarse textured soils are associated with stream
channels and with the east and southeast rims of playas. The
soils of the playas themselves are finer in texture than the sur-

rounding soils, with pure clay often occurring in the center of the larger playas.

The sharpest topographic relief is provided, of course, by the eastern escarpment and the reentrant canyons cut into the surface of the Llano Estacado by stream erosion. These areas are characterized by a great diversity of soils. This brings us to the soils of Palo Duro Canyon. Near the borders of the canyon, the clay loam soil of the Llano Estacado grades into a calcareous, grayish-brown soil with a granelly loam or loam surface. Within the canyon itself, the caliche escarpments, sandstone bluffs and ledges, talus slopes, and dissected red bed plains are grouped together by soil scientists into the well-named Rough Broken Land. Soils of colluvial footslopes grade from grayish-brown sandy loam into brown loam. The nearly level floodplains and adjacent gently sloping footslopes support deep, calcareous alluvium. Common on the canyon floor are red or reddish-brown very fine sandy loam soils that are derived from reddish sandstone and siltstone.

THE PRESENT VEGETATION

Those vast areas of nearly level or gently rolling terrain of the Llano Estacado where the soils are deep and fine-textured are presently dominated by blue grama[1] and buffalo grass. Dominance by these grasses of low stature explains the origin of the name "short grass plains." The dense sod of these short grasses occurring over thousands of acres gives the vegetation an essentially homogenous appearance. Here and there the monotony is relieved by taller grasses extending above the short grass sod. These are the mid grasses such as silver bluestem, sand dropseed, and purple three-awn. A touch of occasional color is added by forbs like scarlet globe-mallow, purple coneflower, Indian blanket, Mexican hat, and blazing star.

Scattered over the Llano Estacado are topographic irregularities and peculiar soil types that provide habitats for minor communities. Modern and ancient streambeds with relatively coarse soils provide suitable moisture conditions for the development of a sagebrush-mixed prairie community. There sand sagebrush shares the landscape with tall and mid grasses, such as little bluestem, sand bluestem, and Canada wild rye. Playa lakes often

[1] Scientific names are given in the appendix.

have a distinctive flora. Within the larger playas the perennial grasses of the plains are displaced by annual grasses and forbs.

Associated with the change in soil from the plains to the land bordering the escarpment is a change in vegetation. Now we focus our attention on the area of Palo Duro Canyon. As we approach the canyon we can see the short grasses decreasing in relative abundance and mid grasses, such as little bluestem and sideoats grama, increasing. Especially conspicuous are the increasing numbers of shrubs, particularly the evergreen, scale-leaved junipers. Just along the rim of the canyon the shrubby mountain mahogany becomes a conspicuous addition to the vegetation.

Rough Broken Land comprises the rugged terrain of the sides of the canyon, extending from the Ogallala Formation down through the Trujillo and Tecovas to the upper part of the Quartermaster. On the steeper canyon slopes above and the Spanish skirts below, plants are unable to gain a foothold as geologic erosion removes soil material about as fast as it is formed. On other less steep areas, the well-drained escarpment soils are ideal for the development of scarp woodland. The deep and woody roots of trees and shrubs are especially well adapted for exploiting these soils for the deeply infiltrating moisture. Species common to this woodland are one-seeded juniper, red-berry juniper, forestiera, small-leaved sumac, and lemon sumac. On drier slopes mesquite, feather plume, and four-winged saltbush are especially conspicuous. In the heads of small canyons the environment is mesic enough to support Rock Mountain cedar and eastern red cedar.

Below the canyon slopes, extending to the creek, there is a great diversity of plant life. At first glance the vegetation seems to be almost chaotic, without discernible pattern, but closer inspection reveals that topography and soils have sorted the vegetation into communities. A particular rank and grouping of species is characteristic of the fertile terraces, another of the red beds, and still another of the riverine habitat.

The greatest diversity of species occurs on the terraces. The loamy soils are high in fertility and can hold much moisture. Not only are most of the species of the plains and scarp woodland found there but new species also make their appearance. There are trees and shrubs such as one-seeded juniper, red-berry juniper, small-leaved sumac, lemon sumac, mesquite, hackberry, forestiera, soapberry, wafer ash, and lotebush; mid grasses such as little bluestem, sideoats grama, sand dropseed, alkali sacaton, and vine-mesquite; and short grasses such as blue grama, hairy grama, and buffalo grass. Also scattered over the terraces are desert Christmas cactus, prickly pear cactus, and yucca. Within this general vegetational matrix are smaller assemblages of plants, where a single species or group of species dominates to such an extent as to be more important than the other components of the vegetation. Extensive stands of mesquite and small but locally heavy stands of yucca, of prickly pear cactus, and of annual forbs (weeds) reflect a past history of disturbance. In some areas Lilliputian topographic features are important in determining especially the species of grass present. Slight depressions which receive additional water may be dominated by vine-mesquite and/or alkali sacaton. Not far away are microridges on which little bluestem and sideoats grama assume dominance. On the intervening more nearly level area blue grama is usually the most abundant species of grass.

Compared to the terraces, the vegetation on the relatively sandy soils of the Permian red beds is depauperate. However, the particular nature of the community depends, primarily, on the depth of the soil. The shallower, droughty soils support a sparse cover of blue grama, hairy grama, and sand dropseed with a few scattered, stunted individuals of red-berry juniper and mesquite. The deeper soils support a denser growth of mid grasses, like sideoats grama and bluestems, and shrubs like red-berry juniper and small-leaved sumac.

A riverine woodland community has developed in the alluvial soils along the margins and narrow floodplains of the Prairie Dog Town Fork of the Red River. Especially conspicuous are the large, broad-leaved cottonwood trees. Willow, saltcedar, and buttonbush are other woody plants that are restricted to this habitat. Other trees and shrubs, such as hackberry and wafer-ash, which are adapted to somewhat wider ranges of environmental conditions, extend into this community from surrounding areas. Although tall grasses are not confined to the floodplains, it is there that switchgrass, Indian grass, and big bluestem reach their best development.

HISTORY OF THE VEGETATION

Let us now attempt to reconstruct the development of the vegetation of our area (Palo Duro Canyon and the related escarpment system and the Llano Estacado) through geologic and recent times. With threads of evidence from fossil floras, fossil pollen, and historical documents we can weave together the story. Unfortunately there is not a complete record available for our area, but records from nearby areas are adequate to arrive at a reasonable reconstruction of the processes and events.

Geologic History

The ancient geologic history has been preserved in fossil and stratigraphic records. The interpretations of these records by Chaney (1947), MacGinitie (1953), Elias (1942), and especially Axelrod (1948, 1950, 1952, 1958) allow us to descend into the past; to view macroscopically the continental events occurring through the Cenozoic to the Pleistocene that are important in understanding the derivation of the present vegetation.

The account begins with a description of the vegetation of North America during Palocene-Eocene times. It is only in these relatively recent times, geologically speaking, that knowledge of fossil plants is great enough to allow an adequate analysis of vegetation as controlled by the environment. During these times, the North American continent was covered by two vast forests: The Arcto- and Tropical-Tertiary forests. North of about 45° latitude to the Arctic Ocean, sweeping from the Pacific Ocean to the Atlantic, was the Arcto-Tertiary Forest. This magnificent forest consisted of a mixture of temperate conifers and deciduous hardwoods, including cedar, fir, hemlock, pine, and spruce; alder, ash, dogwood, maple, and oak. Later in geologic history climatically induced events would separate the conifers and hardwoods, and eventually segregate them into two distinctive forests. South of about 45° latitude, extending to Patagonia was the Tropical-Tertiary Forest, dominated by artocarpus, avocado, fig, and magnolia. A broad area of overlap existed between these two giant forests.

From Eocene time, through the Oligocene, and into the Miocene, a gradual cooling of the climate forced a migration to the south of these Tertiary forests. The Arcto-Tertiary Forest advanced toward our area, but events that had been taking place in the southwestern part of the continent would prevent it from becoming fully established here. These events resulted in the development of the Madro-Tertiary Flora, which would eventually come to dominate much of southwestern North America.

During the middle Eocene, a distinctive group of plants began to evolve in relatively arid habitats, possibly in the localized rain shadows of minor mountains. These plants evolved from subtropical and warm temperate components of the Tropical-Tertiary Forest. They would eventually evolve into small-leaved, drought-resistant sclerophylls and microphylls, similar to those now occurring in the semiarid and arid parts of southwestern North America. During the period of expansion of this early Madro-Tertiary Flora, through the Oligocene, it had a generalized composition. Events occurring during the later Cenozoic resulted in a segregation of this generalized flora into a number of derivative communities. It was during this interval that the major mountain systems (Sierra Nevada, Coast, Transverse, Cascade, Sierra Madre, and Rocky Mountains) reached their present heights. These geologic events caused a differentiation of climates, especially the development of extensive rain shadows on the lee sides of the mountain masses. Secular climatic changes, such as lowering of winter temperatures, were also occurring. The derivative elements of the Madro-Tertiary Flora owe their existence to the environmental diversity created by these changes. Today we find representatives of all these elements in our area.

The Sierra Madrean woodland element was pushed to the south by low winter temperatures, until it came to occupy its present position in the Cape Region of Baja, California, northern Sierra Madres, and the mountains of southwestern United States. The conifer woodland element consisted of species adapted to lower winter temperatures. This element evolved into the modern pinyon pine and digger pine communities of western North America. The warmer, essentially frost-free areas of northeastern Mexico and adjacent Texas became the home of an arid subtropical scrub element. A plains grassland element evolved on the Great Plains.

The story of the development of the plains grassland element is part of the larger story of the development of the central grasslands of North America. This story begins with the evolution of woodland and forest grasses of Cretaceaus time. In response to lower rainfall conditions, these grasses eventually evolved into plains grasses. Communities in which these grasses were important began to develop and expand during the Eocene, through the Oligocene and Miocene, and with accelerated speed into the Pliocene. There are differing views on the evolution of grasslands in the Great Plains region. Because of the increased number of contradictions in the interpretation of the fossil record as more recent times are approached, it becomes increasingly difficult to reconstruct a generally acceptable model of what happened. The traditional view has been that extensive grasslands have been in existence since the mid-Miocene (Clements, 1920; Cain, 1944). This idea is not based on direct evidence, but has been inferred from other evidence, especially the prominent role grazing animals had in this region during those times. A minority view, that we will consider in detail later, holds that treeless grassland has a much more recent origin. According to this view, the Great Plains was occupied by an admixture of trees and grasses—a savanna. Despite these differing views, it is evident that grasses were becoming of increasing importance during the Tertiary.

The expansion of grassland or savanna in the center of the continent figured into the splitting of the Arcto-Tertiary Forest into eastern and western components. The western component came to be dominated by conifers and the eastern by deciduous trees. The eastern component interests us in one respect. Many of the grass species native to the tall grass prairie that occur in our area on special sites had their origin in the wooded regions of the middle west and southeast (Wells, 1970).

The Pleistocene scene was dominated by repeated advances and retreats of glaciers. The continental ice sheets did not reach into the Llano Estacado; thus no moraines, no scouring of bedrock, no deposition of glacial drift occurred in this area. Nevertheless there were changes in climate and in the living landscape. The majority view, mentioned above, is that grasses became more luxuriant during periods of increased moisture but were never replaced by trees or shrubs (Antevs, 1954). Reconstruction of Pleistocene environments based primarily on fossil pollen indicate more dramatic changes (Wendorf, 1961, 1970 and Wendorf and Hester, 1975). The advancement of glaciers decreased temperatures and increased precipitation far to the south of the ice sheets. In response to these climatic changes, the aspect of the landscape was altered. Playa lakes filled with water, and woody plants became increasingly conspicuous components of the vegetation. Then when glaciers retreated, temperatures climbed and precipitation dropped. Larger lakes gradually decreased in size, smaller lakes dried up, and woody plants became restricted to escarpments or slopes of draws. During the Pleistocene a number of these advances and retreats occurred. From about 30,000 to 17,000 B.C., the dominant vegetation type was a sagebrush savanna. Favored areas supported pine, oak, juniper, and a scattering of spruce. The Tahoka pluvial period followed and lasted to sometime from 11,500 to 9,500 B.C. During this period, conditions were favorable to the growth of conifers. A boreal forest dominated by pine and spruce covered the Llano Estacado. Following the Tahoka, there may have been some relatively minor pluvial periods, but the general tendency was one of slowly increasing aridity.

One idea of what occurred during post-glacial times is that with advancing aridity, the climate eventually became unsuitable for the growth of woody plants on the plains. These plants retreated from the plains and became confined to the stream channels and escarpments that afforded compensation for the environmental adversity. Grasses assumed sole dominance over the plains. Thus this idea is in agreement with the majority opinion mentioned earlier of the ancient history of a treeless grassland. Grasslands are viewed as climatically determined. The plains are simply too dry for the existence of trees.

On the other hand, Wells (1965, 1970a, 1970b) believes that most of the grassland province of North America is climatically capable of supporting certain xerophytic species of trees. In favor of this idea he cites several lines of evidence, such as the recent invasion of woody species from scarp woodlands onto grasslands and the success of experimental tree plantations on the plains. As to the possible environmental factors responsible for the presence of grassland, Wells (1970a) believes that "wind driven grass fires, whether ignited by lightning or by man, must be accorded a key position in the hierarchy." Fires are not as harmful to grasses as they are to woody plants. The regenerating buds of grasses are at or just below the soil surface, where they escape the severest heat. On the other hand, the buds of shrubs and seedling trees are at the ends of twigs above ground, where they are easily damaged by fire. Thus recurrent fires would prevent reproduction of woody plants. Wells contends that vast conflagrations sweeping over the smooth prairie topography for great distances were in this way important in the development of treeless prairie. These fires would advance across the prairie until quenched by rain or checked by abrupt breaks in the topography. As abrupt breaks in topography, escarpments acted as natural firebreaks and provided a refuge for shrubs and trees.

Recent History

By several thousand years ago the general pattern of vegetation of our area was established: grasses covered the plains, trees and shrubs were largely confined to the escarpments. Now we direct our attention to questions concerning changes that have occurred in more recent times within this vegetational matrix.

Specifically the questions concern changes in the distribution of mesquite and in the nature of the grass covering of the plains. These subjects considered in their broad contexts have provided fuel for heated controversy among ecologists for many years. We will focus our attention on the controversies as they apply to our own area. Since we are dealing with the recent past, the fossil record is of no use; we must turn to historical documents.

Mesquite. "Oldtimers state with absolute finality that when the Canyon (Palo Duro Canyon) was first used by cattle these flats were perfectly open and free from mesquite" (Jones, 1951). In fact, it is a common belief among Texas old-timers that mesquite was brought into Texas from Mexico by cattle. This idea was given some scientific respectability by Shelford's (1944) statement that mesquite spread from south central Texas northward into west central Oklahoma in fairly recent times. Shelford (1963) gives a map showing the changes in geographical distribution of mesquite in Mexico and southwestern United States. In about 1600 A.D. mesquite was confined to the southwestern corner of Texas. By 1923 it had greatly increased in geographical distribution, especially to the north and east. This idea that mesquite has increased in geographical distribution within historical times has been disputed by Malin (1953). From a study of historical documents, Malin came to the belief that mesquite has not increased its geographical range since about 1800. He does believe that there has been an increase in the density of the plants in areas where they have long been present in relatively small numbers.

The word of old-timers and of Shelford indicates that mesquite has been a fairly recent introduction into our area. Malin gives us some reason to doubt this. To answer the question, we will use Malin's approach and search historical documents for evidence. Where a possibility exists of violating the meaning of the authors, it is necessary to quote verbatim from the original sources.

Starting in 1786 there was a series of Spanish expeditions for the purpose of establishing direct routes from Santa Fe to San Antonio, to Natchitoches, and to St. Louis. Among those who recorded these expeditions were Jose Mares, Santiago Fernandez, and Francisco Amangual. Loomis and Nasatir (1967) have reprinted the diaries of these individuals. All quotations of their diaries are from Loomis and Nasatir.

In 1787 Jose Mares and two companions left Santa Fe to find a short route to San Antonio. They traveled across the Llano Estacado to what seems to be Tule Canyon. The second day after descending the eastern escarpment Mares wrote: "Set out the east, skirting the same arroyo, through mesquite land." Five days later he wrote: "Travelled across a plain. Arroyo on left. Stopped in same arroyo. Much permanent water and many groves of different trees, cottonwoods, and some mesquite."

In 1788 Santiago Fernandez left the Taovaya villages on the Red River to return to Santa Fe. On August 1 he descended to the Prairie Dog Town Fork of the Red River. On the next day he wrote in his diary: "On the 2nd, at 4 in the morning [we set out] in the same direction [and] travelled continuously across a plain until [we arrived at] some springs of water, where we took our siesta until 3 o'clock; then we proceeded to a thicket of mesquite, in which we stopped."

Captain Francisco Amangual traveled from San Antonio to Santa Fe in 1808. On May 12 the caprock of the Llano Estacado was sighted. The following entries were made as the expedition traveled parallel to the escarpment:

May 12
We travelled over high and level ground, covered with flat hills, and a few *canadas* covered with mesquite trees.... Then we continued until we ascended an elevation from which we sighted an extensive plain and a strip of mesquite trees a long distance away. The guide said that there was nothing [but plains] ahead, and that it was impossible for us to go across during the day without exposing our men and animals to die of thirst. It was decided to travel in a different direction, along some *canada* with water, ... [which were] covered with grass and a few mesquite.

May 13
We continued to travel over a high and level country, covered with red sand and some clumps of mesquite trees that were high and thickly wooded.... After traveling a short distance, we crossed an extensive plain, with many small lakes and pools of rain water. There were some clumps of mesquite trees and small cottonwoods; the place is a delightful valley, about 1 league in extent in every direction; its length was cut short by an elevation, very large and level, which we climbed. We again descended to another level . . . that had similar *canadas* and much water and grass, and a few mesquite trees toward the edges.

The first expedition sponsored by the United States govern-

ment to explore our area was led by Major Stephen Long. Dr.
Edwin James, botanist and surgeon for the expedition, reported
the first botanical description of mesquite, from plants that he
observed along the upper Canadian River in August of 1820
(James, 1905).

Twenty-five years after the Long Expedition, a party under the
direction of Lieutenant James Abert traveled through the Texas
Panhandle. On September 5 the expedition entered the Panhandle. The entry in Abert's journal (Carroll, 1941) for that date
reads:

> We saw today an abundance of musquit [mesquite], a species
> of "leguminoseae", which has been thought of by some
> persons to be the same as the "acacia arabica". It is a thorny
> shrub, scarcely ever attaining the height of 5 feet. The
> legumes are long, sabre-form, cylindrical, and nearly white,
> filled with a solid substance of sweetish taste and from which
> the Comanches and Kioways manufacture a kind of flour.

On September 10 the party was moving down the Canadian
River valley in the central Panhandle.

> At an early hour in the morning we were on our way, and
> soon leaving the bottom, entered a more desolate country
> than we had hitherto seen. The high and dry table lands were
> covered with but a few scattered plants, and were altogether
> desert-like.
> The cacti and musquit were most abundant. In one place we
> noticed a quantity of the long pods of the last mentioned
> plant, which had evidently been thrown there by human
> hands.

The first of the expeditions led by Captain Randolph Marcy
crossed the Panhandle in 1849. His journal (Marcy, 1850) contains several mentions of mesquite. The expedition has been
traveling for a number of days over "high rolling prairie" and
"elevated plateau" when on June 12 they came onto the Llano
Estacado. "We have seen a few mezquite [mesquite] bushes
during the past three days." The next day they marched parallel
to the bluffs bordering the Llano Estacado over a "very smooth
Prairie." The entry for that day reads: "We passed a great deal of
the small mezquite and numberless plants of the jointed cactus
today."

In 1852 Marcy was charged with leading a party to explore the headwaters of the Red River. On June 28 they were at the base of the Llano Estacado, probably in what is now Briscoe County. Marcy (1854) wrote "As Capt. McClellan and myself were passing to-day along under the bluffs, we saw in advance of us a herd of antelopes quietly feeding among some mezquite trees. . . ."

After exploring the Prairie Dog Town Fork of the Red River to its headwater in Palo Duro Canyon, Marcy's party started their return trip down the Red River. Writing of the South Fork of the Red River:

> We find much more mezquite timber upon this branch of the river than upon the other. Indeed, I have never seen much of this wood above the thirty-sixth degree of north latitude; but south of this it appears to increase in quantity and size as far as the twenty-eight degree. Upon the Canadian River I have observed a few small bushes; but the climate in that latitude appears too cold for it to flourish well.

In 1854 Marcy led another expedition; this one to explore the headwaters of the Brazos and Big Wichita rivers. Since their travels were mainly in the country to the southeast of the Llano Estacado, most of the report does not concern us. However, one part is pertinent. Marcy was sufficiently impressed by the numerous mesquite he had encountered in his three expeditions that he summarized his observations (Marcy, 1856). He noted that "It [mesquite] covered a great portion of the country over which we travelled. . . ." He also mentioned that mesquite often occurred "upon the most elevated arid prairies, far from watercourses."

Bigelow prepared a botanical profile of forest trees along the route followed by the Whipple expedition of 1853-1854. Mesquite was found in sufficient abundance at the northern edge of the Llano Estacado along the Canadian River to deserve being noted on the profile. Torrey's report of his examination of Bigelow's plant collection gives the collection site as "Plains, on the Canadian" (Whipple, 1856).

This survey of historical documents should leave no doubt that mesquite has been present in our area for a long time. Certainly its occurrence predates the introduction of cattle. Furthermore, the evidence shows that mesquite was not entirely limited to drainage courses but was at least present on some areas of the plains.

Short grass plains. The Llano Estacado is part of the short grass plains. A number of ecologists have claimed that before disturbance by domestic livestock what is now short grass plains was then a mixed grass prairie, with such mid grasses as needle-and-thread grass and western wheat grass coexisting with the shorter blue grama and buffalo grasses. One of America's pioneer ecologists, Frederic Clements, first came to this realization in the summer of 1915; a summer of very high rainfall. Mid grasses suddenly appeared over the plains and in some places grew so densely as to completely obscure the shorter grasses. It seems that the high rainfall offset grazing pressure. Clements (1920, 1934) found other evidence in favor of this idea: mid grasses returned to areas that had been protected for long periods of time, and photographs taken on the Hayden Expedition in 1870 showed areas of the Great Plains covered with mid grasses.

Clements and Chaney (1937) claimed that a century before they wrote the mixed grass prairie still possessed the cover that had characterized it since postglacial times: mid grasses with an open understory of short grasses clothing the plains from Saskatchewan to Texas. If their description is true, then it should be reflected in historical documents.

There are a number of reasons why the descriptions of the plains in historical documents are not entirely satisfactory. For one thing, most of the expeditions that crossed the Texas Panhandle kept close to the Canadian River; consequently, the upland plains were not adequately described. Also, the recorders of these expeditions were from the forested East, and grasses did not seem to capture their imaginations. Although some of the early travelers were botanists, or had some training and interest in botany, they were plant collectors and not plant ecologists. Plant ecology had yet to be developed. Even the taxonomic identification of the grasses was not at all satisfactory. For example, Roe (1951) documents that the name "buffalo grass" was applied to a number of different species of grass.

Despite these drawbacks, we can still use the historical record to some advantage. A description of the nature of the grass covering of the plains is still derivable from historical records. Although most of these records concern the Canadian River valley, they are not entirely devoid of descriptions of the uplands. Also, the early observers need not have been trained ecologists to distinguish between taller and shorter grasses.

The first written report of the nature of the grassland of the Llano Estacado was made by Castenada, chronicler of Coronado's expedition of 1540. He wrote (Winship, 1896): "The grass grows tall near these lakes; away from them it is very short, a span or less." He also noted that as the large expedition traveled over the plains: "The grass never failed to become erect after it had been trodden down and although it was short, it was as fresh and straight as before." Obviously, if taller grasses were present in any appreciable amounts on the plains, the grass would have remained trodden down for a considerable time after being trampled by the large numbers of livestock of Coronado's party.

On June 14, 1849 Marcy climbed out of the Canadian River valley onto the plains in the present Oldham County. He wrote of his impression of the country (Marcy, 1850):

> When we were upon the high tableland, a view presented itself as boundless as the ocean. Not a tree, shrub, or any other object, either animate or inanimate, relieved the dreary monotony of the prospect; it was a vast, illimitable expanse of desert prairie—the dreaded "Llano Estacado" of New Mexico; or, in other words, the great Zahara of North America. It is a region almost as vast and trackless as the ocean—a land where no man, either savage or civilized permanently abides; it spreads forth into a treeless, desolate waste of uninhabited solitude, which always has been, and must continue, uninhabited forever; even the savages dare not venture to cross it except at two or three places, where they know water can be found. The only herbage upon these barren plains is a very short buffalo grass, and, on account of the scarcity of water, all animals appear to shun it.

Lieutenant J. H. Simpson prepared a number of maps of the country over which Marcy's expedition of 1849 passed. An inscription on one of the maps indicated that between 100° and 100° 30' "Buffalo grass begins to appear." On another map for 100° 30' to 104°: "The grass, an alternation and sometimes a commixture of Buffalo and Prairie, with an occasional patch of Mesquite; begins to become rather scarce after reaching Shady Creek." On the map for 104° to 107°, Simpson noted: "Pasturage on alternation of buffalo and mesquite grass beyond Tucumcari creek rather scanty; a search for better generally rewarded" (Simpson, 1850).

During his second expedition Marcy (1854) wrote: "The grass upon the Staked Plains is generally a very short variety of mesquite, called buffalo grass, from one to two inches in length, and gives the plains the appearance of an interminable meadow that has been recently mown very close to the earth."

Marcy's expedition to the headwaters of the Brazos approached the Llano Estacado from the southeast. W. B. Parker, a civilian member of the group, gave an account of that corner of the Staked Plains (Parker, 1856):

> The view was the most extensive and glowing in the sunset, the most striking that we had enjoyed during the whole trip, combining the grandeur of immense space—the plain extending to the horizon on every side from our point of view—with the beauty of the contrast between the golden carpet of buffalo grass and the pale green of the mesquite tree dotting its surface.

Records pertaining to the original condition of the present day short grass plains in areas other than the Llano Estacado have been examined by Larson (1940) and Malin (1947). Descriptions by many explorers and travelers—Lewis and Clark, Abert, Fremont, Emory, Wislizenus, Cross, Elliot, Hayden, Dodge—convinced them that even in pristine times short grasses dominated these areas.

Thus we are presented with a seeming incongruity. On the one hand are the observations showing that taller grasses have increased in abundance on areas protected from grazing or in times when grazing pressure has been somehow offset. On the other hand is the evidence indicating that much of the Great Plains, including the Llano Estacado, was dominated by short grasses long before the introduction of domestic livestock.

It takes no great imagination to see where we should look for a resolution to the apparent contradiction. If grazing by domestic livestock has been held responsible for the replacement of mid grasses by short grasses, but if the short grass plains predates grazing by domestic livestock, then, obviously, we should consider the role of other types of grazing animals—the native grazers. The most important of the native grazing mammals of the Great Plains, in terms of impact on the vegetation, were the buffalo, blacktail prairie dog, and pronghorn antelope (Costello, 1969).

Estimates of the numbers of buffalo in primitive times vary from 30 million to 200 million (Haines, 1970). Even if we take the lowest estimate, we are led to some awesome values. Assuming an average weight of 1,000 pounds, the total biomass of these 30 million buffalo would be 30 billion pounds. The total biomass of humans in the United States today is only about 27 billion pounds (using a population estimate of 225 million and an average weight of 120 pounds). No small part of this biomass on the hoof trampled the plains of the Texas Panhandle. From the first description by Castenada in 1540 until Charles Goodnight and his cowboys drove 10,000 buffalo out of Palo Duro Canyon in 1876, the literature provides evidence of great numbers (see Roe, 1951 for references).

Concerning the impact of the buffalo on the vegetation, Stewart (1936) wrote: "In every instance seasonal migrations of the herds permitted recovery of the vegetation between grazing periods." Likewise, Clements (1936) believed that extensive overgrazing was prevented by migrations. Such seasonal migrations would have been especially important to the vegetation of the Llano Estacado, since they would have taken these animals northward out of our area during the summer growing season. But such does not seem to have been the case. Roe (1951), in his magistral book, disposes of the myth of annual migrations. There is no way to do justice to his argument here; all that can be said is that his evidence is overwhelming.

At the other extreme from the positions of Stewart and Clements is that of Larson (1940), who holds that the entire short grass plains owes its existence to overgrazing by buffalo. Costello (1969) seems to take a less extreme position, proposing that the buffalo "maintained the prairies in a short grass condition," but "they practiced a form of deferred and rotation grazing in which overgrazed areas might be untouched for several years allowing the vegetation to recover to its former productivity." Costello's contention, ignoring the anthropomorphic wording, is a reasonable one. The movements of buffalo to "greener pastures" can be viewed as an evolutionary mechanism that would prevent them from so overexploiting their entire habitat as to drastically reduce its productivity and subject the species to the danger of extinction by mass starvation.

The blacktail prairie dog also had a drastic effect on the vegetation. Their numbers must have been astronomical. Merriam (1902) estimated a population of 400 million prairie dogs in a town 25,000 square miles in an area located between San Angelo and Clarendon, Texas. Even if we agree with Koford's (1958) criticism that Merriam's density estimate was at least twice as high as warranted, that still leaves a lot of prairie dogs. This impression is intensified by the historical record. The most detailed accounts were those written by Marcy about prairie dog towns he came across in his expeditions of 1849, 1852, and 1854. Most of the towns were encountered during the Red River expedition. He noted that their abundance was likely the reason the Comanches named one fork of the Red River Ke-che-a-qui-ho-no or Prairie Dog Town River.

Schaffner (1926) was the first author to consider the ecological effects of blacktail prairie dogs on grassland. He thought that they were responsible for extending and perpetuating short grass communities. Their grazing caused drying of the soil and reduced reproduction of taller grasses. Koford's (1958) observations led him to the same conclusion: "In mixed prairie, prairie dogs alone can both produce and maintain the short-grass association."

Nelson (1925) was told by George Bird Grinnell that in all the conversations he had had with men familiar with the western plains in the middle of the nineteenth century it had been agreed that pronghorn antelope were far more abundant than buffalo. Nelson considered a conservative estimate of pronghorn numbers to have been 30 to 40 million. The numbers indicate that the pronghorns were among the most important of the grazing mammals, but they played a role in the economy of the plains different from those of the buffalo and blacktail prairie dog. Pronghorns show a much greater preference for forbs and browse than do the other two grazers.

Their different food preferences may have resulted in a mutually favorable situation for the buffalo and pronghorns. According to this argument, close grazing by buffalo reduced the grass cover, providing forbs and small shrubs an opportunity for increase. Such areas became less desirable for buffalo but more desirable for the pronghorns. Continued grazing by pronghorns eventually reduced the abundance of forbs and browse, giving the grasses a competitive edge. Thus pronghorns accelerated the recovery of these sites to a condition again favorable for buffalo. There is some evidence for such a relationship. Buechner (1950) found a similar type of mutually favorable interaction between cattle and pronghorns in the Trans-Pecos area of Texas.

The above discussion indicates that the pristine grassland of the Great Plains was neither a continuous short grass plains nor a continuous mixed prairie, even on uniform topography and soils. Rather at any one time there must have been a mosaic of communities: some dominated by forbs because of close grazing by buffalo and prairie dogs; others less closely grazed by buffalo and prairie dogs, dominated by short grasses; some dominated by forbs but recovering, under antelope grazing, from the effects of the transient buffalo; yet others in which a mixture of short grasses and forbs was maintained by the sedentary prairie dogs; some with a small contingent of mid grasses among the short grasses as they recovered from grazing; and still others so long ungrazed as to be mixed prairie.

A Scenario

This section on the history of the vegetation can be concluded with the presentation of a scenario. Because of the sketchy and ambiguous nature of much of the evidence and the consequent speculative nature of its interpretation, a number of plausible scenarios could be created. They would differ primarily in the particular order of the scenes and in the timing of the entrance and exit of the actors. The justification for the particular one given here is simply that it is constructed from the evidence I find most convincing.

We begin, arbitrarily, with a scene as things might have been about 10,000 years ago as the Laurentide and Cordilleran ice sheets retreated, freeing North America of glacial ice. As the glaciers faded in the north, the pluvial lands to the south were subjected to a secular, if erratic, trend of decreasing precipitation. The boreal forest of spruce and pine that covered the Llano Estacado[2] was gradually replaced by a more open forest of pine, juniper, and oak. As the drying trend continued, the trees became even more widely spaced, allowing the development of an under-story of grasses. Gradually the density of the trees became so low as to allow grasses to begin to become dominant, and there evolved that combination of grassland and forest called a savanna.

Even as these events were beginning, Early Man had already put in a conspicuous appearance. A population explosion occurred about 11,000 to 12,000 years ago, perhaps the result of a late Wisconsin migration out of Alaska with the opening of a passage through Canada by glacial retreat (Haynes, 1970). Activities of these early inhabitants set into action a chain of events

---

[2] Since "Llano Estacado" means "Staked Plains," it is clearly improper to speak of a forest covering the Llano Estacado. Simply to avoid cumbersome wording, "Llano Estacado" in this section will be used to refer to the area that eventually would become the Llano Estacado.

that profoundly effected the ecology of the Great Plains area, including the Llano Estacado.

Sometime around 7,000 B.C., the Early Hunters discovered an efficient way to kill large numbers of their prey (Hester, 1967). Perhaps the first inkling in this direction came as they passively observed the effects of fires which escaped from their abandoned campfires (Stewart, 1956). They soon learned to actively manipulate fire to their advantage: with fire drives large numbers of animals could be stampeded into arroyos and canyons and there easily slaughtered (Saur, 1944).

During the early post-pluvial years on the wooded Llano Estacado, fires were fairly rare, set by lightning and accidentally by man, with small and localized effects. As precipitation became more seasonal, dry seasons became more pronounced and the vegetation became more flammable. The dry, strong winds associated with the dry season were available for spreading fires over larger and larger areas. Following the destruction of forest trees by fire, grasslands expanded by a series of jumps from preexisting enclaves within the forest. Thus fires and an unfavorable climate conspired to drive trees from the uplands. The trees found refuge especially along escarpments.

The expansion of grassland provided an occasion for grazing mammals to increase in numbers. With the increase in size of the buffalo herds, taller grasses were grazed down in many areas, providing a favorable habitat for prairie dogs. Continued grazing of some of these areas by buffalo and prairie dogs caused an increase in forbs that were attractive to pronghorn antelope. These ecological relationships resulted in the development of the mosaic of communities mentioned earlier. Such was the appearance of the Great Plains several thousand years ago. In the southern High Plains short grass and severely disturbed communities were probably more common than in the north. Not only was there an abundance of grazing animals but drought likely was more common and severe. Drought will damage taller grasses more than shorter ones, and if prolonged will greatly reduce the cover of even a short grass stand.

Ever since the end of the Ice Age and of pluvial conditions, many species have found in Palo Duro Canyon a sanctuary from hostile environments. Species from a variety of ancestral areas entered the canyon, not all at once, but staggered, with groups of ecologically related species arriving during climatic periods favorable to them. Also, within the canyon the dominance relations among these groups of species changed with the changing climate. Thus even as the spruce and pine were being eliminated from the uplands, they dominated the vegetation of much of the canyon. Tall grasses such as big bluestem, Indian grass, and switch grass were the most abundant of the herbaceous plants. Then as the years passed and the climate became progressively less cool and moist, spruce and pine relinquished dominance and eventually passed out of existence. Their place in the dominance hierarchy was taken by more xerophytic trees and shrubs: juniper, oak, mountain mahogany. At the same time short grasses like blue grama and buffalo grass became prominent on some of the more droughty sites.

By several thousand years ago, the character of the vegetation of Palo Duro Canyon was already determined, to a large extent by species of Madro-Tertiary derivation. By that time in geologic history, the Madro-Tertiary Flora had long since segregated into its component elements. Representatives of each of the elements occupied particular aspects of the canyon according to their ecological predispositions. The Sierra Madrean woodland element made the greatest contribution to the canyon's flora. Species derived from this element—forestiera, hackberry, lotebush, lemon sumac, small-leaved sumac, mountain mahogany, oak, soapberry—became established in all habitats, although they were not particularly abundant on the more xeric or more mesic sites. Associated with this assemblage were grasses derived from the plains grassland element: blue grama, buffalo grass, sand dropseed. The arid subtropical scrub element contributed species, such as mesquite and feather plume, that were preadapted to the more xeric sites. The significant contributions of the conifer woodland element were Rocky Mountain cedar and one-seeded juniper. These two species occurred together in nearly all the habitats available to junipers, but the Rocky Mountain cedar was more abundant in the more mesic situations while the one-seeded juniper was more abundant in the more xeric situations. They shared many of their sites, especially the drier ones, with the redberry juniper, whose ancestry can be traced to the conifer woodland element. The other species of juniper, Eastern red cedar, migrated into the canyon from the east, ultimately from the area occupied by derivatives of the Arcto-Tertiary Flora. In accordance with its evolutionary history in eastern North America, this species was preadapted to the more mesic juniper habitats. Also coming from the east and likewise favoring the mesic hab-

itats were many of the taller grasses: little bluestem, big bluestem, Indian grass, and switch grass.

By the time Coronado led his expedition across the Llano Estacado and into Palo Duro Canyon, the general pattern of vegetation of plains and canyon had long been established and would
stay essentially the same for several hundred years into the
future. Even the virtual elimination of buffalo in the mid-1870's,
and the reduction in the population sizes of other grazing mammals, did not relieve grazing pressure long enough to allow mid
grasses to make a comeback. The niche left vacant by the
elimination of the buffalo was soon filled by domestic cattle, as
they were brought onto the plains in large numbers in the late
1870's and into the 1880's. The subsequent grazing by livestock
and cessation of recurrent and extensive grassland fires did effect
some changes in the vegetation. No longer subject to purging
by fire, small junipers began to appear on the grasslands bordering the scarp woodlands. Mesquite was further spread by cattle
throughout Palo Duro Canyon and onto the plains. The mesquite
seeds passed through their digestive tracts not only unharmed
but with successful germination practically insured: their hard
seedcoats were scarified by gastic juices and they emerged from
the digestive tract already fertilized and watered.

APPENDIX

Common and scientific names of organisms mentioned in text:

Animals

Antelope
Antilocarpa americana

Blacktail prairie dog
Cynomys ludovicianus

Buffalo
Bison bison

Plants

Alder
Alnus spp.

Alkali sacaton
Sporobolus airoides

Artocarpus
Artocarpus spp.

Ash
Fraxinus spp.

Avocado
Persea spp.

Big bluestem
Andropogon Gerardi

Blazing star
Liatris spp.

Blue grama
Bouteloua gracilis

Buffalo grass
Buchlöe dactyloides

Buttonbush
Cephalanthus occidentalis

Maple
Acer spp.

Mesquite
Prosopis glandulosa

Mountain mahogany
Cercocarpus montanus

Needle-and-thread grass
Stipa comata

Oak
Quercus spp.

One-seeded juniper
Juniperus monosperma

Pine
Pinus spp.

Pinyon pine
Pinus edulis

Prickly pear cactus
Opuntia phaeacantha

Purple coneflower
Echinacea angustifolia

Canada wildrye
Elymus canadensis

Cedar
Thuja spp.

Cottonwood
Populus Sargentii

Digger pine
Pinus sabiniana

Desert Christmas cactus
Opuntia leptocaulis

Dogwood
Cornus spp.

Eastern red cedar
Juniperus virginiana

Feather plume
Dalea formosa

Fig
Ficus spp.

Fir
Abies spp.

Forestiera
Forestiera pubescens

Four-wing saltbush
Atriplex canescens

Hackberry
Celtis occidentalis

Hairy grama
Bouteloua hirsuta

Hemlock
Tsuga spp.

Indian blanket
Gaillardia pinnatifida

Purple three-awn
Aristida purpurea

Red-berry juniper
Juniperus Pinchotii

Rocky Mountain cedar
Juniperus scopulorum

Salt cedar
Tamarix aphylla

Sand bluestem
Andropogon Hallii

Sand dropseed
Sporobolus cryptandrus

Sand sagebrush
Artemisia filifolia

Scarlet globe-mallow
Sphaeralcea coccinea

Sideoats grama
Bouteloua curtipendula

Silver bluestem
Bothriochloa saccharoides

Small-leaved sumac
Rhus microphylla

Soapberry
Sapindus Drummondii

Spiderwort
Tradescantia occidentalis

Spruce
Picea spp.

Switch grass
Panicum virgatum

Vine-mesquite
Panicum obtusum

Indian grass
Sorghastrum nutans

Juniper
Juniperus spp.

Lemon sumac
Rhus trilobata

Little bluestem
Andropogon scoparius

Lotebush
Ziziphus obtusifolia

Magnolia
Magnolia spp.

Wafer-ash
Ptelea trifoliata

Wavy-leaf thistle
Cirsium undulatum

Western wheatgrass
Agropyron Smithii

Willow
Salix exigua

Yucca
Yucca angustifolia

LITERATURE CITED

Antevs, Ernst. 1954. Climate of New Mexico during the last glaciopluvial. J. Geol. 62:182-191.

Axelrod, D. I. 1948. Climate and evolution in western North America during Middle Pliocene time. Evolution 2:127-144.

_____. 1950. Evolution of desert vegetation in western North America. Carnegie Inst. Wash. Publ. 590:215-306.

_____. 1952. A theory of angiosperm evolution. Evolution 6:29-60.

_____. 1958. Evolution of the Madro-Tertiary Geoflora. Bot. Rev. 24:433-509.

Bohm, David. 1969. Further remarks on order, p. 41-60. *In* C. H. Weddington [ed.], Towards a theoretical biology. Aldine Publ. Co., Chicago.

Buechner, H. K. 1950. Life history, ecology, and range use of the pronghorn antelope in Trans-Pecos Texas. Am. Midland Naturalist 43:257-354.

Cain, S. A. 1944. Foundations of plant geography. Harper Brothers, N. Y.

Carroll, H. B. 1941. Gúadal Pá: the journal of Lieutenant J. W. Abert from Bent's Fort to St. Louis in 1845. Panhandle-Plains Historical Rev. 14.

Chaney, R. W. Tertiary centers and migration routes. Ecol. Monographs 17:139-148.

Clements, F. E. 1920. Plant indicators. Carnegie Inst. Wash. Publ. 290:1-388.

_____. 1934. The relict method in dynamic ecology. J. Ecol. 22:39-68.

_____. 1936. Nature and structure of the climax. J. Ecol. 24:252-284.

_____ and R. W. Chaney. 1937. Environment and life in the Great Plains. Carnegie Inst. Wash. Suppl. Publ. 24 (revised ed.): 1-54.

Costello, D. F. 1969. The prairie world. Thomas Y. Crowell Co., N. Y.

Elias, M. K. 1942. Tertiary prairie grasses and other herbs from the High Plains. Geol. Soc. Am. Sp. Paper 41:1-176.

Gleason, H. A. and A. Cronquist. 1964. The natural geography of plants. Columbia Univ. Press, N. Y.

Haines. Francis. 1970. The buffalo. Thomas Y. Crowell Co., N. Y.

Haynes, C. V. 1970. Geochronology of man-mammoth sites and their bearing on the origin of the Llano complex, p. 77-92. *In* Dort, W., Jr., and J. K. Jones, Jr. [eds.], Pleistocene and recent environments of the central Great Plains. Univ. Press of Kansas, Lawrence.

Hester, J. J. 1967. The agency of man in animal extinctions, p. 169-192. *In* Martin, P. S. and H. E. Wright, Jr. [eds.], Pleistocene extinctions, the search for a cause. Proc. VII Congr. Intern. Assoc. Quaternary Research, Nat. Acad. Sci. - Nat. Research Council. Yale Univ. Press, New Haven.

Jacquot, L., L. C. Geiger, B. R. Chance, and W. Tripp. 1970. Soil survey of Randall County, Texas, U.S.D.A., Soil Conservation Service, in cooperation with Texas Agr. Exp. Sta.

James, Edwin. 1905. An account of an expedition from Pittsburg to the Rocky Mountains, performed in the years 1819, 1820; under the command of Major Stephen Long, 1823. *In* Thwaites, R. G. [ed.], Early western travels, 1748-1846. Vol. 14-17. Arthur H. Clark Co., Cleveland.

Jones, P. V., Jr. 1951. The Palo Duro, great canyon of the plains. Texas Game and Fish v. 29 (June).

Koford, C. B. 1958. Prairie dogs, white faces, and blue grama. Wildl. Monographs, No. 3, p. 1-78.

Larson, Floyd. 1940. The role of the bison in maintaining the short grass plains. Ecology 21:113-121.

Loomis, N. M. and A. P. Nasatir. 1967. Pedro Vial and the roads to Santa Fe. Univ. Oklahoma Press, Norman.

Lotspeich, F. B. and J. R. Coover. 1962. Soil forming factors on the Llano Estacado: parent material, time, and topography, Texas J. Sci. 14:7-17.

_____ and M. E. Everhart. 1962. Climate and vegetation as soil forming factors on the Llano Estacado. J. Range Management 15:134-141.

MacGinitie, E. D. 1953. Fossil plants of the Florissant beds, Colorado. Carnegie Inst. Wash. Publ. 599.

Malin, J. C. 1947. The grassland of North America: prolegomena to its history. James C. Malin, Lawrence, Kansas.

_____. 1953. Soil, animal, and plant relations of the grassland, historically reconsidered. Sci. Monthly 76:207-220.

_____. 1956. The grassland of North America: its occupance and the challenge of continuous reappraisals, p. 350-366. *In* W. L. Thomas [ed.], Man's role in changing the face of the earth. Univ. Chicago Press.

Marcy, R. B. 1850. Report of exploration and survey of route from Fort Smith, Arkansas, to Santa Fe, New Mexico, made in 1849. House Ex. Doc. 45, 31st Congress, 1st Session, Public Doc. 577. Washington, D. C.

_____. 1854. Explorations of the Red River of Louisiana in the year 1852. . . . Sen. Ex. Doc. 54, 32nd Congress, 2nd Session, Public Doc. 666, Washington, D. C.

_____. 1856. Message of the President of the United States, communicating a copy of the report and map of Captain Marcy of his exploration of the Big Wichita and the headwaters of the Brazos Rivers, 1854. Sen. Doc. 60, 34th Congress, 1st Session, Public Doc. 621, Washington, D. C.

Merriam, C. H. 1902. The prairie dog of the Great Plains, p. 257-270. *In* Yearbook U. S. Department of Agriculture 1901.

Nelson, E. W. 1925. Status of the pronghorned antelope. U. S. Department of Agriculture, Dept. Bull. 1346.

Parker, W. B. 1856. Notes taken during the expedition through unexplored Texas, in the summer and fall of 1854. Hayes and Zell Publ., Philadelphia.

Platt, John. 1970. Hierarchial growth. Bull. Atomic Scientists 26:2-4, 46-48.

Roe, F. G. 1951. The North American buffalo. Univ. Toronto Press.

Saur, C. O. 1944. A geographic sketch of early man in America. Geographical Rev. 34:529-573.

Schaffner, J. H. 1926. Observations on the grasslands of the central United States. Ohio State Univ. Studies, Contrib. Botany 178.

Shelford, V. E. 1944. Deciduous forest, man, and the grassland fauna. Science 100: 135-140, 160-162.

_____. 1963. The ecology of North America. Univ. Illinois Press, Urbana.

Simpson, J. H. 1850. Report and map of the route from Fort Smith, Arkansas, to Santa Fe, New Mexico. Sen. Ex. Doc. 12, 31st Congress, 1st Session, Publ. Doc. 554.

Stewart, G. 1936. History of range use, p. 119-133. *In* The western range. Sen. Doc. 199. Washington, D. C.

Stewart, O. C. 1956. Fire as the first great force employed by man, p. 115-133. *In* W. L. Thomas [ed.], Man's role in changing the face of the earth. Univ. Chicago Press.

Wells, P. V. 1965. Scarp woodlands, transported grassland soils and concept of grassland climate in the Great Plains region. Science 148:246-249.

_____. 1970a. Vegetational history of the Great Plains: a post-glacial record of coniferous woodland in southeastern Wyoming, p. 186-202. *In* Dort, W., Jr. and J. K. Jones, Jr. [eds.], Pleistocene and recent environments of the central Great Plains. Univ. Press of Kansas, Lawrence.

_____. 1970b. Historical factors controlling vegetation patterns and floristic distributions in the central plains region of North America, p. 211-221. *In* Dort, W., Jr. and J. K. Jones, Jr. [eds.], Pleistocene and recent environments of the central Great Plains. Univ. Press of Kansas, Lawrence.

Wendorf, Fred. 1961. A general introduction to the ecology of the Llano Estacado, p. 12-31. *In* Wendorf, F. [ed.], Paleoecology of the Llano Estacado. Fort Burgwin Research Center Publ. No. 1, Ranchos de Taos, N. M.

_____. 1975. The modern environment, p. 1-12. *In* F. Wendorf and J. J. Hester [eds.], Late pleistocene environments of the southern High Plains. Fort Burgwin Research Center Publ. No. 9, Ranchos de Taos, N. M.

_____ and J. J. Hester. 1975. Preface, p. vii-ix. *In* F. Wendorf and J. J. Hester [eds.], Late pleistocene environments of the southern High Plains Fort Burgwin Research Center Publ. No. 9, Ranchos de Taos, N. M.

Whipple, A. W. 1856. Reports of the explorations and surveys to ascertain the most practicable and economical route for a railroad from the Mississippi River to the Pacific Ocean, 1853-4. House Ex. Doc. 91, 33rd Congress, 2nd Session.

Winship, G. P. 1896. The Coronado expedition (1540-42), Fourteenth Annual Report of the Bureau of American Ethnology, Part I, p. 329-367. Government Printing Office.

MAN AND THE PALO DURO CANYON: FROM CORONADO TO GOODNIGHT

William C. Griggs
Director
Panhandle-Plains Historical Museum

The wealth of the New World, discovered by adventurers such as Hernan Cortés in Mexico and Francisco Pizarro in Peru, led many early sixteenth-century Spaniards to believe that vast quantities of additional riches were theirs for the finding. When Mexico's Viceroy Antonio de Mendoza dispatched Fray Marcos de Niza[1] and Estevancio[2] to search for the fabled El Dorado,[3] this enthusiasm for gold rose to a new height. Upon his return, de Niza's reports led many to believe that the legendary seven cities of gold actually existed. Adventurous would-be *conquistadores* vied for places on the new expedition which was sure to come.

Francisco Vásquez de Coronado, the governor of the state of Nueva Galicia, was named as the commander of the army which left Mexico City in 1540 to find glory, fame, and wealth in the northern reaches of the Spanish provinces. With approximately one thousand men, the Coronado expedition marched up Mexico's western shore past Culiacán into present New Mexico. They conquered Háwikuh, one of the southernmost Zuni pueblos, then Tusayán, an adobe city of the Hopis. From this point they continued to Tiguex, a village on the Rio Grande near present Ysleta, before continuing to the Pecos pueblo of Cícuye. All of northern New Mexico was under their control.

The victory of Coronado's *conquistadores* was a hollow one.

---

[1] Fray Marcos de Niza was a Franciscan Friar who came to America in 1531. He served in Peru, then in Nicaragua, before arriving in Mexico in 1539. See George Parker Winship, *Fourteenth Annual Report of the United States Bureau of Ethnology*, Part I (Washington: Government Printing Office, 1896), p. 28.

[2] Estevancio, or Estevan, was a Negro who, as a member of the Pánfilo de Narváez expedition, was shipwrecked on the Texas coast along with Cabeza de Vaca, Andrés Dorantes de Carranza, and Alonso de Castillo Maldonado. The four wandered through Texas for eight years with Indians before returning to Mexico City. See *Ibid.*, p. 14. Also, see Walter Prescot Webb, ed., *The Handbook of Texas* (2 vols.; Austin: Texas State Historical Association, 1952), Vol. I, p. 574.

[3] *El Dorado* was a mythical place in Spanish South America that was supposed to be fabulously rich. This myth carried over to the Spanish exploration of North America. See *Ibid.*, p. 347.

None of their dreams of gold, silver, or precious jewels had been realized. All that the followers of Francisco Vásquez de Coronado found by the end of 1540 were mud buildings, a hostile people, and a small quantity of turquoise. The huge expedition mounted by Viceroy Mendoza to the upper edge of New Spain seemed to be a failure in every respect. Small wonder, then, that imaginations were rekindled when a Plains Indian slave of the Puebloans nicknamed by the Spaniards *"El Turco"*—the Turk—told of another magical land named Quivira where the dreams of those who would follow in the footsteps of Cortés and Pizarro might be realized. The expedition of Coronado and his followers to find this city of gold resulted in the first written account of the huge, flat "buffalo plains" of the present Texas Panhandle. Too, their written reports were the first descriptions by Europeans of what is now called the Palo Duro Canyon.[4] According to Pedro de Casteñeda, a chronicler of the journey, it was a "large ravine" that was "a league wide from one side to the other, with a little bit of a river at the bottom, and there were many groves of mulberry trees near it, and rosebushes with the same sort of fruit they have in France."[5] Here, Coronado's army rested several days before a decision was made to divide the command. Coronado, with thirty men, was to proceed to the north in search of the fabled city. The remainder of the army was to return to the settlements on the northern Rio Grande. Coronado located Quivira in present Kansas, but found no riches. Only straw huts and copper trinkets offered a substitute for the searched-for wealth.

In addition to being the first Europeans to see the Palo Duro Canyon, the men in Coronado's expedition were the first to see the native inhabitants of the region now known as the Panhandle-Plains. Two different tribes, the Querechos and the Teyas, were found. Although they were allied both linguistically and culturally, the two groups were enemies. It is probable that both were

---

[4] *Palo Duro* is a Spanish name which means "hard wood" after the abundance of juniper that is still found on the canyon floor. The Palo Duro Canyon is located approximately twelve miles east of the City of Canyon, Texas. The best original narrative of the Coronado expedition is found in the narrative of Pedro de Casteñeda of Najera, Spain. See Winship, *Annual Report*, pp. 186-308.

[5] *Ibid.*, p. 237

bands of the tribe which later became known as the Apaches.[6]
One account describes the two groups of Indians in this way:

> They are very well built, and painted, and are enemies of one
> another. They have no other settlement of location than
> comes from traveling around with the cows [bison]. They kill
> all of these they wish, and tan the hides, with which they
> clothe themselves and make their tents, and they eat the
> flesh, sometimes even raw, and they also even drink the blood
> when thirsty. The tents they make are like field tents, and
> they set them up over some poles they have made for this pur-
> pose, which come together and are tied at the top, and when
> they go from one place to another they carry them on some
> dogs they have, of which they have many, and they load them
> with the tents and poles and other things. . . . The sun is what
> they worship most.[7]

The Indians who lived in the vicinity of Palo Duro Canyon
changed very little from the time of Coronado's expedition until
the latter half of the seventeenth century. At that point, however,
a drastic change occurred that was to alter the history of the
Southwest. For the first time, Indians acquired horses from
Spanish herds. By 1650, it is likely that Apaches of the present
Panhandle of Texas had horses.[8] Forty years later, large numbers
of horses had completely changed the Apache life-style. With the
dog as the beast of burden, movement was slow, travel was comparatively light and camps were not moved unless a change was
necessitated by a shortage of food or water. The horse allowed the
Apache to be as mobile as the bison, his food supply. Certainly,
the horse made easier the movement of camps in and out of such
rugged areas as the Palo Duro Canyon.

By the beginning of the eighteenth century, the days of the
Apaches in the area of the upper Red River (Palo Duro Canyon)
were numbered. The Comanche Indians, whose traditional home-

[6] Frederick W. Hodge, *Handbook of Indians North of Mexico*, (2 vols.; Washington: Government Printing Office, 1907, 1912), Vol. II, p. 338. Also, see Winship,
Annual Report, p. 274. Another excellent source may be found in Charles L. Kenner, *A History of New Mexican-Plains Indian Relations* (Norman: University
of Oklahoma Press, 1969), pp. 7-8.

[7] Winship, *Annual Report*, p. 360.

[8] Ernest Wallace and E. Adamson Hoebel, *The Comanches, Lords of the South
Plains* (Norman: University of Oklahoma Press, 1952), p. 38. Also, see Francis
Haines, "Where Did the Indians Get Their Horses," *American Anthropologist*,
Vol. XL (1938), pp. 112-117. Also, see Kenner, *Relations*, p. 16.

land was in the northern and central Great Plains and west to the
Rocky Mountains, began to migrate toward the south.[9] There
were several reasons for this movement. Perhaps most important
was the territorial expansion of the powerful Sioux who, in 1700,
had begun a push to the west and south. The Sioux, as well as
other tribes who desired Comanche territory, were already armed
with muskets traded to them by Europeans in the Great Lakes
region. They were more than a match for the more primitive weapons of their Shoshonean neighbors.[10] By 1700, too, the Comanches
were already a nation of horse owners. It was only logical that
they would move closer to their source of supply near Spanish
settlements.

Regardless of the reason for the southwestern migration of the
Comanche, they came to stay. The northern intruders occupied
the former range of the Apache with comparative ease, then
moved to the south and east, claiming lands that belonged to
older, settled Texas tribes. After a century in this new land, the
Comanche had little, if any, contest for "all the country from the
Arkansas River on the north to the Mexican settlements on the
south, and from the Grand Cordillera on the west to the Cross
Timbers on the east."[11]

The Palo Duro Canyon was undoubtedly a main camping
ground for the Comanches as it had been for the Apaches before
them. The canyon provided water, protection from cold winter
winds, wood for fires and lodge poles, and stockaded buffalo hunting ground. Long broad prairies dotted the floor of the canyon,
providing excellent campsites. The Comanches ruled the Southern Plains of Texas and the deep canyons that delineate its
eastern rim with little interference for the remainder of the
eighteenth century.

The Comanches did have some contact with Europeans during
that time period, however.[12] Several diaries tell of visits to the
upper Red River and Palo Duro Canyon. In 1786, a Frenchman in

[9] Hodge, *Handbook*, Vol. I, pp. 327-329.

[10] Some Scholars believe that the Comanches were not pushed into the Southern Plains but came because the area was exceptionally well-suited to their life-
style. See Rupert N. Richardson, *The Comanche Barrier to South Plains Settlement* (Glendale: The Arthur H. Clark Company, 1933), p. 19. Also, see Hodge,
Handbook, Vol. I, p. 327.

[11] Wallace, *Comanches*, p. 12

[12] One of the best chronicles of Comanche trade with European settlements
within this time period is found in Kenner, *Relations*, pp. 23-52.

the service of Spain, Pedro (Pierre) Vial, crossed the plains of Texas en route from San Antonio de Bexar, Texas, to Santa Fe, New Mexico.[13] He was probably the first European to ever complete this journey. Although Vial did not see the Palo Duro Canyon on his first trip across the *Llano Estacado*, it was not long until another man, José Mares, did so.[14] Given a commission by Governor Fernando de la Concha of New Mexico to find a shorter route than that traveled by Vial, Mares entered the Palo Duro in August 1787. About one year later, Vial traveled the Santa Fe-San Antonio road the second time. He crossed the Palo Duro Canyon in August of 1788 accompanied by Francisco Xavier Fragoza and an escort of cavalry.[15]

Although various other European expeditions made their way through the Texas Panhandle in the late eighteenth century and early nineteenth century, few were more impressive than the group led by Captain Francisco Amagual.[16] Because of repeated intrusions of both the French and the Americans into border areas claimed by Spain, Governor Manuel Cordéro Antonio y Bustamante of Texas suggested to the Commandant-General of New Spain that a reconnaissance be made of the boundaries of Texas and New Mexico. Amagual, with two hundred men and

[13] Noel M. Loomis and Abraham P. Nasatir, *Pedro Vial and the Roads to Santa Fe* (Norman: University of Oklahoma Press, 1967), pp. 262-286. The original man'script by Pedro Vial is entitled "Diario que ... comienso á hacer desde ... San Antonio de Béjar hasta ... Santa Fé por Comision de mi Governador Don Domingo Cavello, Governador de la Provincia de los Texas ... desde el dia de Octubre de 1787 [1786]," Santa Fe, July 5, 1787. Manuscript copy in Archivo General de Mexico, Vol. LXII. See Charles Wilson Hackett, *Pichardo's Treatise on the Limits of Louisiana and Texas* ..., (4 vols.; Austin: University of Texas Press, 1931), Vol. I, p. 325. Also see Herbert Eugene Bolton, *Texas in the Middle Eighteenth Century: Studies in Spanish Colonial History and Administration* (Berkeley: University of California Press, 1915), pp. 128-129.

[14] The origin of the name *Llano Estacado* is lost in antiquity. Some accounts say that early Spanish explorers drove stakes in the ground as they crossed the plains to mark their way. Others ascribe the name to the tall spires of the yucca plant that dot the flat tableland. One account says that upright white rocks marking springs and seeps are the origin of the name. Another popular explanation interprets *estacado* as stockaded—thus "stockaded plains," an aspect the sometimes vertical rim of the caprock escarpment gives the viewer from a distance. The flat tablelands are probably the remnant of an alluvial plain formed millions of years ago as the result of erosion of the Rocky Mountains.

[15] Loomis, *Pedro Vial*, pp. 327-357.

[16] *Ibid.*, p. 461.

several wheeled vehicles, traveled from San Antonio to Santa Fe. The Palo Duro Canyon was traversed on May 23, 1808.[17]

It was not until the nineteenth century that the first exploration of the upper Red River and Palo Duro Canyon was made by Anglo-American explorers.[18] On March 5, 1852, Captain Randolph B. Marcy received orders from Major General Winfield Scott to "proceed, without unnecessary delay, to make an examination of the Red River, and the country bordering upon it. . . ."[19] Marcy's party left Fort Belknap, Texas, on May 1, en route to Cache Creek, the point at which the orders called for exploration to begin. By June 27, they reached the headwaters of the Red River. Marcy recorded that they "came in sight of the valley of the Ke-che-a-qui-ho-no, or principal branch of the Red River. Directly in front of us we could see the high table lands of the *Llano Estacado* towering up some eight hundred feet above the surrounding country, and bordered by precipitous escarpements, caped with a stratum of snow-white gypsum, which glistened in the sun's rays like burnished silver."[20] Marcy continued his exploration of the canyons that comprise the headwaters of the Red River, searching for the head of the main branch. By July 1, 1852, the Marcy expedition was in Palo Duro Canyon. Then, as now, the visitors were overwhelmed by the magnitude and beauty of the spot.

> We all, with one accord, stopped and gazed with wonder and admiration upon a panorama which was now for the first time exhibited to the eyes of civilized man. Occasionally might be seen a good representation of the towering walls of a castle of the feudal ages, with its giddy battlements pierced with loopholes, and its projecting watch-towers standing out

[17] *Ibid.*, p. 494.

[18] There were several unsuccessful attempts to reach the headwaters of the Red River in the early 1800's. In May 1806, a party led by a Captain Sparks was thwarted by a Spanish force. Zebulon M. Pike, in 1806, was ordered to search for the head of the Red River, but instead found the Rio Grande. Colonel Stephen H. Long searched for the source in 1819-1820, but was unsuccessful. See Randolph B. Marcy, *Thirty Years of Army Life on the Border* (New York: Harper and Brothers, Publishers, 1866), pp. 115-120.

[19] *Ibid.*, p. 114.

[20] *Ibid.*, pp. 144-145. Marcy states that the Comanche name of the river, *Ke-che-a-qui-ho-no*, means Prairie Dog Town River. It was so-called because of the numerous "villages" of the small rodents along the river's banks.

in bold relief upon the azure ground of the pure and trans-
parent sky above. It was as if it had been designed and exe-
cuted by the almighty artist as the presiding genius of these
dismal solitudes.[21]

But the Marcy expedition to the head of the Red River did not
effect the remoteness of the Palo Duro Canyon. It was nearly
twenty-five years before United States troops were within the
canyon's walls once again.

Although for decades before the Civil War the Comanche Indians were usually friends of both New Mexicans and Americans,
they considered themselves to be at war with Texans. They felt
free to raid frontier settlements at will, stealing horses and cattle
and capturing settlers, especially women and children. Only the
presence of the United States Army, supplemented by the roving
frontier companies of Texas Rangers, kept the Indians in check.[22]

With the advent of the Confederacy and the removal of United
States military personnel from Texas, the situation on the
western frontier deteriorated rapidly. Although some Ranger
detachments remained, they were completely unequipped to
properly patrol the far western Texas settlements. By the war's
end, hundreds of farms and homes had been abandoned as a result of Indian raids. Many houses had been burned and cattle and
horses were gone. "Widespread desolation had supplanted order-
ly settlement."[23] One writer observed that not all of the population
had been able to flee to more peaceful areas:

> Since June, 1862, not less than 800 persons have been
> murdered [up to 1868],—the Indians escaping from the troops
> by traveling at night when their trail could not be followed,
> thus giving enough time and distance to render pursuit, in
> most cases, fruitless.[24]

The Indian penchant for killing and robbing Texans on the

[21]*Ibid.*, p. 151.

[22] The best account of the activities of the pre-Civil War Rangers is found in
Walter Prescott Webb, *The Texas Rangers: A Century of Frontier Defense* (Austin:
University of Texas Press, 1965), pp. 307-344.

[23] Carl Coke Rister, *Fort Griffin on the Texas Frontier* (Norman: University of
Oklahoma Press, 1956), p. 60.

[24] P. H. Sheridan (comp.) *Records of Engagements with Hostile Indians within
the Military Division of the Missouri, 1862-1882* (Washington: Government Printing Office, 1882), p. 16, as quoted in *Ibid.*, p. 61.

frontier was not caused solely by hatred, however. Some New Mexicans were anxious to profit by trading with the Comanches, Kiowas, and Southern Cheyennes and incited the Indians to continue their pillage. Called *Comancheros*, these traders sometimes made enormous profits in their barter. One report states that the Indians gave the *Comancheros* their pick of the mules for a keg of whiskey, a pack horse for ten pounds of coffee, or a mule for five pounds of tobacco.[25] Although the Palo Duro Canyon was not one of the most important trading grounds, it was certainly used for this purpose on many occasions. One of the principal *Comanchero* roads skirted the canyon along its northwest rim.[26]

With treacherous conditions prevailing in western Texas, the Palo Duro Canyon became more remote than ever. By 1870 the *Llano Estacado* and all of its canyons and streams remained in the sole possession of the Comanches, Kiowas, and their allies. But, little known to the Indians, conditions were rapidly developing that were to lead to a sweeping change. In Kansas, W. C. Lobenstine, a fur dealer, received an order from England for five hundred buffalo hides. J. Wright Mooar, a buffalo hunter who was living at Fort Hays, filled the order. In addition he shipped an additional fifty-seven hides to a buyer in New York. The tanneries were pleased with the hides and placed huge repeat orders with both Lobenstine and Mooar.[27] Other tanneries followed suit and soon hundreds of hunters were in the field.

By 1874, the Kansas buffalo herds were decimated. Hunters began to look for new hunting grounds and quickly decided that the Texas Panhandle would be the most fruitful spot. A treaty with the Southern Plains Indian tribes at Medicine Lodge, Kansas, in 1867 caused most hunters to conclude that the Panhandle was closed to them. The Indians believed this even more adamantly. Yet when permission to enter the area was asked of Major Richard I. Dodge, the commanding officer at Fort Dodge, Kansas, his reply was "If I were a buffalo hunter, I would hunt buffalo where the buffalo are."[28] This tacit approval opened the Texas Panhandle, and ultimately Palo Duro Canyon, to Anglo-American settlement. But this was not to be an easy task.

[25] Kenner, *New Mexican-Plains Indian Relations*, p. 164.

[26] *Ibid.*, p. 181.

[27] Interview of Frank P. Hill, J. B. Slaughter, Jr., and Jim Weatherford with J. Wright Mooar, Snyder, Texas, May 15, 1936. Typescript in the archives of the Panhandle-Plains Historical Museum, Canyon, Texas.

[28] *Ibid.*

Within weeks after the first hunters ventured south of the Arkansas River into the Panhandle of Texas, Kansas supply and hide-buying firms had set up commercial establishments at a settlement called Adobe Walls on the Canadian River. Indian reaction was immediate and the Comanches, under war-chief Quanah Parker and medicine man Isatai, assembled a party of approximately three hundred warriors which quickly advanced on the buffalo hunter village and its twenty-nine inhabitants. Because of superior firepower supplied by the long-range buffalo guns of the hunters, the Indians were stymied in their efforts.[29]

The Battle of Adobe Walls, as it was called, was more damaging to the Indians than they might have presumed. The publicity regarding the fight spurred impatient demands from Texans that their lands be freed from domination by Indians. Raids in southern Colorado by Comanches and Cheyennes, combined with a Comanche and Kiowa ambush of Major John B. Jones' Texas Rangers near present Seymour, Texas, precipitated an end to President Grant's long-standing "Quaker Peace Policy" that had been advocated and instituted at the insistence of several United States religious leaders.[30]

On July 20, 1874, Secretary of War W. W. Belknap ordered "the punishment of guilty Indians wherever found . . .; the Reservation lines should be no barrier."[31] Almost immediately, orders were given to five separate commands to converge on the Texas Panhandle. General Nelson Miles' 6th Cavalry traveled south from Fort Dodge, Kansas.[32] Lieutenant John W. Davidson moved west from Fort Sill with six companies of cavalry and three companies of infantry. Major William R. Price's men were ordered to march eastward from Fort Union, New Mexico. Lieutenant-Colonel George P. Buell's command moved northwest from Fort Griffin, and Colonel Ranald S. Mackenzie's column trailed north from Fort Concho, Texas.[33]

[29] The best record to date of the Adobe Walls battle is by G. Derek West, *The Battle of Adobe Walls and Lyman's Wagon Train, 1874* (Canyon, Texas: Panhandle-Plains Historical Society, 1974).

[30] Ernest Wallace, *Ranald S. Mackenzie on the Texas Frontier* (Lubbock, Texas: West Texas Museum Association, 1965), p. 122. Also, see Thomas C. Battey, *Life and Adventures of a Quaker Among the Indians* (Boston: Lee and Shepard, 1875).

[31] *Ibid.*, p. 123.

[32] Nelson A. Miles, *Personal Recollections of General Nelson A. Miles* (Chicago: The Werner Company, 1896), p. 163.

[33] Wallace, *Mackenzie*, pp. 124-126.

Mackenzie's command, assembled from scattered units at Fort Clark and Fort Duncan, went into camp at Fort Concho on August 21, 1874. It consisted of eight companies of the 4th Cavalry plus five infantry companies.[34] "No other military expedition of equal experience, toughness, and preparation," wrote Mackenzie's biographer, "had ever gone forth to battle the Southern Plains Indians. . . ."[35]

Among the scouts that Mackenzie attached to his expedition in 1874 was a Tonkawa Indian *ex-Comanchero* named Johnson who had intimate knowledge of the country where Mackenzie's column was headed. Johnson was very well acquainted with the terrain and knew (or suspected very strongly) that the searched-for Indians would be camped in the Palo Duro Canyon.[36]

After leaving Fort Concho, Mackenzie's command headed north, establishing a supply camp on the Freshwater Fork of the Brazos River in Blanco Canyon.[37] After receiving reports from Seminole Negro Indian scouts of three Indian trails in the vicinity of the Pease River, Mackenzie decided to march in that direction. On September 25, 1874, the command camped at Tule Canyon.[38] Although trailers searched the area all around the

[34] *Ibid.*

[35] *Ibid.*, p. 126. For other accounts of the 1874 Mackenzie campaign and the "Red River War" see Miles, *Recollections*, pp. 163-175; Robert G. Carter, *On The Border With Mackenzie or Winning West Texas From the Comanches* (New York: Antiquarian Press, 1961), pp. 473-542; Robert G. Carter, *The Old Sergeant's Story: Winning the West From the Indians and Bad Men in 1870 to 1876* (New York: Frederick H. Hitchcock, 1926). The serious student of the Red River War should also consult Ernest Wallace, *Ranald S. Mackenzie's Official Correspondence Relating to Texas, 1873-1879* (Lubbock: West Texas Museum Association, 1968), and Joe F. Taylor, comp. and ed., *The Indian Campaign on the Staked Plains, 1874-1875* (Canyon, Texas: Panhandle-Plains Historical Society, 1962).

[36] Ernest Wallace, Mackenzie's biographer, states that Johnson was a half-breed Lipan Indian. See Wallace, *Mackenzie*, p. 125. Several persons claimed the honor of having been Mackenzie's chief scout and having known the location of the Indians in the Palo Duro. See Henry W. Strong, *My Frontier Days and Indian Fights on the Plains of Texas* ([Wichita Falls, Texas]: n.p.; n.d.), pp. 59-61. Also, see Jim (Cook) Lane and T. M. Pearce, *Lane of the Llano* (Boston: Little, Brown and Company, 1936), pp. 56-62. Sergeant John B. Charlton also took credit for the discovery. See Carter, *The Old Sergeant's Story*, p. 106.

[37] Colonel R. S. Mackenzie to General C. C. Auger, Commanding, Department of Texas, as printed in Carter, *On the Border*, pp. 475-476. Also, see Wallace, *Mackenzie*, p. 129. Blanco Canyon is located near present Crosbyton, Texas.

[38] Carter, *On the Border*, p. 484. Wallace, *Mackenzie*, p. 134. Tule Canyon is east of present Tulia, Texas.

campsite, no large body of Indians could be located. Signs indicated that they were near, however, and Mackenzie ordered special preparations to safeguard the cavalry horse herd in case of attack.

Mackenzie's suspicions were correct and at about ten o'clock in the evening the camp was charged by an estimated 250 Comanches. Efforts of the Indians to stampede the herd were futile and sniping was ineffectual, resulting only in the death of three horses. Nevertheless, Mackenzie ordered his troops to disperse attackers. This movement caused the Indians to lose heart and seemingly disappear into the prairie.[39]

On Sunday, September 27, Mackenzie's troops saddled their horses and headed north, not stopping to make camp until two o'clock the next morning. Shortly after the command went to sleep, it was awakened by the arrival of Sergeant John B. Charlton and the two Tonkawa Indian scouts, Johnson and Job, who announced that they had located a fresh trail. Although it was not yet four o'clock a.m., the Mackenzie command mounted immediately and as "the faint streaks of daylight came from the east" they came to "a wide and yawning chasm or cañon, which proved to be Palo Duro Cañon."[40] Below, on the edges of the stream, they saw a large Indian village. Scores of teepees dotted the plain and a huge horse herd grazed nearby.

The command to descend the narrow, winding trail was given by Mackenzie to Lieutenant William A. Thompson, who was in charge of the thirty-two Indian scouts. He was followed by Captain Eugene B. Beaumont's Company A. Mackenzie followed with the balance of the command, excepting Captain N. B. McLaughlin's First Battalion, which was ordered to stand guard at the head of the trail. Leading their horses single file, the soldiers slowly traveled the circuitous path to the canyon floor.[41]

Before the troops reached the bottom, they were spotted by a sentry located on a bluff along the canyon wall. A bullet ended his life, but not before he had yelled and waved a red blanket in warning. K'ya-been (Older man), whose teepee was near the trail's end, also saw the troops and fired his rifle twice before rushing to don war paint.[42] As Companies A and E reached the floor of the

[39] *Ibid.*, p. 135. Carter, *On the Border*, p. 487.

[40] *Ibid.*, p. 488. Also, see Carter, *The Old Sergeant's Story*, p. 106.

[41] Wallace, *Mackenzie*, p. 140. Carter, *On the Border*, p. 489.

[42] Wallace, *Mackenzie*, p. 141.

ravine, they quickly formed and started at a gallop up the canyon after the fleeing Indians. They were followed within minutes by Companies H and L, led by Mackenzie himself.[43]

The Indian village was soon in total disarray. The ground was covered with camp gear and equipment, discarded hastily in an attempt to escape capture or death at the hands of the soldiers. Many Indians took only their weapons and headed for the mouth of the canyon, hoping to save the huge horse herd that had grazed near the camp. Others, particularly women and children, scaled the walls of the Palo Duro, found cover, and poured an intense rifle and pistol fire down on the charging cavalrymen.

Pursued by Thompson's scouts, the fleeing Indians ran up the ravine almost four miles before they finally abandoned their horse herd and ran for freedom through a pass in the western end of the canyon.[44] Beaumont's Company A corralled the frightened horses, controlling them only after shooting the two leaders of the herd. As the cavalrymen turned to go back, they were met with an ever increasing fire from the Indians on the canyon walls. Captain R. G. Carter described the scene:

> The Indians who had succeeded in safely placing themselves behind the immense breastwork of rock, some 800 to 1000 feet above us, opened fire upon us and in a very few minutes made it so hot and galling that we were forced to fall back—the Indians being so thoroughly protected in their positions that we could do nothing with so many captured horses on our hands.[45]

The retreat was short-lived, however, and within minutes the troopers were once again heading in the direction of the main command. As they hurried down the canyon to get away from the Indian volleys, the trumpeter of Company L, Henry L. Hard, was shot with what seemed to be a fatal wound. The skillful medical attention given to him by Acting Assistant Surgeon Rufus Choate allowed him to "sound his trumpet-calls for many years after."[46]

[43]*Ibid.*, p. 140. The Indians consisted of a group of Kiowas led by Mamanti. The Comanches were led by O-ha-ma-ti, and the Cheyennes by Iron Shirt. See *Ibid.*, p. 139.

[44] *Ibid.*, p. 142. R. G. Carter relates that the troops went two miles up the canyon. See Carter, *On the Border*, p. 489.

[45] Carter, *On the Border*, p. 490.

[46] *Ibid.*

Captain Sebastian Gunther, commanding Company H, in an attempt to stop the withering rifle and pistol fire from the Indians on the cliffs, ordered his men to attack. When Mackenzie discovered the maneuver he called to a nearby sergeant, "Where are you going with those men?"

"To clear the bluff, sir!"

"By whose orders?"

"Captain Gunther's!"

"Take those men back to their company. Not one of them would live to reach the top."[47]

One soldier, a Private McGowan, fell to the ground as his horse was shot from beneath him. He was tugging desperately at his saddlebags when Mackenzie appeared shouting "McGowan, get away from there or you will be hit." McGowan agreed and acted as if he were about to leave the spot, then returned to the horse and resumed his efforts. Two more times Mackenzie ordered McGowan to leave. After the third order, McGowan replied, "Damned if I am until I get my tobacco and ammunition." Mackenzie gave up on his effort to persuade the private.[48]

The heavy enfilade continued from the Indians and some suspected that the column might be surrounded. One trooper, sensing that the situation was becoming desperate, said "How will he ever get out of here?" Mackenzie, within earshot of the soldier, replied "I brought you in, I will take you out." "Most of the men," said Captain R. G. Carter, "did not question when he led, we knew we depended on his care and guidance."[49]

It was near noon when Mackenzie determined to destroy the camp and supplies of the Indians and leave the canyon. Seeing Indians on top of a bluff close to the trail, Mackenzie correctly guessed that an attempt would be made to block their exit. Consequently, he ordered Captain Gunther's company to go to the top and hold the high ground till the rest of the command could get out; they reached the summit without opposition. The rest of the command piled and burned huge quantities of equipment, teepees, rifles, blankets and other supplies, then filed up the winding trail, arriving at its head one-half to three-quarters of an hour later. Not an Indian was in sight.[50]

[47] *Ibid.*

[48] *Ibid.*

[49] *Ibid.*

[50] *Ibid.*, p. 492.

Altogether, Mackenzie's command suffered one man wounded, none killed. Three horses were killed and ten were wounded. The Indians left three warriors dead on the field but it is likely that a considerable number of Indian casualties were carried away by their comrades.[51]

All in all, 1,448 horses were captured in the engagement.[52] The cavalrymen formed a corral of horsemen shaped like a parallelogram to prevent the recapture of the ponies and moved them nearly twenty miles away to the headwaters of Tule Canyon. The Tonkawa guides were allowed to select some of the best of the lot for themselves and the balance, totaling 1,048 horses, were shot.[53] It was the only way to insure that the Indians would return to the reservation and stay there.[54] Although this battle foretold the end of the Indian supremacy in the Panhandle-Plains of Texas, it was not the last battle in the Red River War.[55]

The Palo Duro Canyon was quiet by the winter of 1875. For the first time in hundreds of years, no Indian teepees dotted the canyon's floor. Where a single *Comanchero* once reported viewing twelve thousand Indian ponies, only buffalo were to be seen.[56] To the north and west, scattered *pastores*—New Mexican sheep men—grazed their flocks along the breaks of the Canadian River and near the scattered water holes on the *Llano Estacado*.

As a Texas Ranger during the Civil War, Charles Goodnight from time to time came close to the rugged edge of caprock escarpment along the edge of the plains. Even then, observing the deep canyons with live water, protection from winter winds, and high walls that took the place of fence, he must have hoped for a cattle ranch in that remote area. But the Palo Duro and other canyons were an obstacle rather than an advantage as they provided a

[51] Wallace, *Official Correspondence, 1873-1879*, pp. 123-124.

[52] *Ibid.*

[53] *Ibid.*

[54] For the view of a journalist of the Palo Duro Battle, see "Mackenzie's Expedition Through the Battle of Palo Duro Canyon" as described by a Special Correspondent of the *New York Herald*. Originally printed in the *Herald* on October 16, 1874, and reproduced in Wallace, *Official Correspondence, 1873-1879*, pp. 112-118.

[55] Mackenzie's troops had another fight on the Tule Canyon on September 26 and 27. General Miles reported engagements in the Texas Panhandle as late as December 1874. See Miles' report in Taylor, *Indian Campaign*, pp. 197-216.

[56] J. Evetts Haley, *Charles Goodnight: Cowman and Plainsman* (Norman: University of Oklahoma Press, 1949), p. 283.

refuge for the Indian and a barrier to Anglo-American settlement. Goodnight, with his partner, Oliver Loving, were forced to skirt the southern edge of the plains when they opened a well-known cattle route, the Goodnight-Loving Trail, to New Mexico and Colorado.

Goodnight, who first ranched in Palo Pinto County, worked with Loving, then John Chisum, from 1866 to 1871 in bringing thousands of Texas cattle over the long trail to New Mexico markets. In 1871, he purchased a part of the Nolan Land Grant southwest of Pueblo, Colorado, where he began ranching.[57] By 1873 his livestock assets were valued at $27,950 and he was the head of the Stock Grower's Bank of Pueblo.[58] The "panic" of 1873 was disastrous to hundreds of banks and businessmen across the country. Goodnight, whose major cash assets were invested or pledged at the bank, lost nearly all that he had except 1600 head of cattle.[59]

Within a year, Goodnight could see that the days of the Indians who lived in the Texas Panhandle were numbered. After the close of the hostilities, he made plans almost immediately to move south with his herd. By late in that year, Goodnight cows were watering on the Canadian River in two camps in eastern New Mexico, "one on Rano Creek and another ten miles west."[60] Only the *pastores* shared the range, and Goodnight was usually able to work out agreements with them for equitable division of grass and water. By early 1876 Goodnight's cows and cowboys had moved into Texas, setting up camp on the *Alamocitos*, a branch of the Canadian. There, however, Goodnight found the sheep men uncomfortably close and made plans to move further east.[61]

Although Goodnight was probably familiar with the Palo Duro Canyon, at least by reputation, it is not certain that he had ever

---

[57] Joseph G. McCoy, *Historic Sketches of the Cattle Trade of the West and Southwest* (Kansas City, Kansas: Ramsey, Millett and Hudson, 1874), p. 385.

[58] *Ibid.*

[59] Harley True Burton, *A History of the JA Ranch* (Austin: Von Boeckmann-Jones Co., 1928), p. 25. Interestingly, Goodnight was probably still relatively wealthy. He listed 1,848 cattle on his books a year earlier at a value of $27,950. The herd included "400 Texan Cows, 400 Graded Cows, 150 three-year old steers, 300 two-year old steers, 500 yearlings, and 48 bulls." He also managed to retain his Colorado ranch which he mortgaged three years later for $30,000. See McCoy, *Sketches*, p. 385, and Haley, *Goodnight*, p. 295.

[60] Haley, *Goodnight*, p. 278.

[61] *Ibid.*

actually been to the huge *arroyo.* Goodnight's biographer relates
a story about a Mexican mustanger who told of a "wild gorge that
cut the Llano in two, a wonderfully sheltered place for a ranch
that he had once seen."[62] The mustanger set out with Goodnight
and Frank Mitchell, one of Goodnight's cowboys, to find the canyon. Considerable wandering soon confused the Mexican and the
trio was about to give up before they finally reached the canyon
rim. "The guide clapped his hands in joy, and shouted '*Al fin! Al
fin!* At last! At last!' "[63]

By November 1876, Goodnight and his men were ready to make
their first descent into the Palo Duro with supplies and cattle.
Goodnight described the event in these words:

> We then made our entrance by way of the old Comanche trail
> between the junction of the Cañon Cito Blanco[64] and the main
> Palo Duro Canyon. It took us about a day and a half to work
> the cattle down this narrow and ragged trail. We then took the
> wagon to pieces and carried it down piece by piece on the
> mules. We had about six months rations and much corn. This
> was also carried down on the mules. The canyon being nar-
> row at this place prevented any buffalos from being in there.
> Hence, grass and water were found there in abundance and
> the cattle ran at their own sweet will. The portage [getting
> supplies and cattle down in the canyon] was over after two
> days.[65]

But getting men, supplies, and cattle to the bottom of the Palo
Duro was not the only major problem encountered. On the main
canyon floor were an estimated ten thousand buffalo which had
to be moved before any semblance of a ranching operation could
begin. Goodnight related in later years that he and two of his
cowhands, Leigh Dyer and "an Englishman named Hughes,"
moved the herd down the canyon fifteen miles. "Such a sight," he

[62] *Ibid.*, p. 280.

[63] Haley, *Goodnight,* p. 280. Harley True Burton, *History of the JA Ranch,*
p. 24, said that Goodnight "had passed the head of the Palo Duro during the Civil
War" and observed that it was "an ideal place to establish a cattle ranch."

[64] Cañon Cito Blanco is a small branch of the Palo Duro that is similar in many
respects to Blanco Canyon (White Canyon) near Crosbyton, Texas. Although it
has been referred to in many ways, most often as Ceta Canyon, the name in
reality, was originally *Cañoncito Blanco,* or Little White Canyon.

[65] Burton, *History of the JA Ranch,* p. 26.

said, "was probably never seen before and certainly will never be seen again. The red dust arising in clouds, while the tramp of the buffalo made a great noise. The tremendous echo of the canyon, the uprooting and crashing of the scrub cedars made one of the grandest and most interesting sights that I have ever seen."[66] This removal of the buffalo did not end the problem, however, as cowboys continued to turn back eight to fifteen hundred of the animals every day.[67]

His cattle herd settled, Goodnight went back up the *cañon* to a point where a cold rivulet of water meandered from a spring on the escarpment hundreds of feet above. There, he carefully picked out a location for a house that was later to be widely known as the "Old Home Ranch."[68]

Although Goodnight cattle occupied the floor of the *cañon*, there was no assurance that they would be able to stay there long unless he secured title to the land. Jot Gunter and William Munson, attorneys, along with John Summerfield, a surveyor, had earlier acquired title to much of the Palo Duro through redemption of State of Texas land certificates. As these astute men would have to be dealt with in any negotiations, it was obvious that Goodnight needed extensive financial backing.[69] He estimated that he would need at least 12,000 acres and that he would have to pay from seventy-five cents to a dollar and a quarter per acre.

As soon as was possible, Goodnight returned to Colorado to make plans for his wife to join him in Texas and to secure a loan to purchase the land he needed. In Denver he contacted George Clayton, an agent for the brokerage firm owned by John G. Adair. Using his Colorado ranch as collateral, Goodnight borrowed $30,000 at eighteen percent interest in March 1876.[70]

Clayton was familiar with Goodnight's success in ranching and knew of his need for capital in addition to that secured by the loan. He was also aware that his associate, John Adair, had recognized the profitability of open range ranching and had decided to look for a partner and to invest in a cattle ranch.

Adair, an Irishman, was not a cattleman. Trained for the Brit-

---

[66] *Ibid.*

[67] *Ibid.*

[68] Haley, *Goodnight*, p. 293.

[69] See Burton, *History of the JA Ranch*, p. 34, for Goodnight's explanation of the way Gunter, Munson, and Summerfield gained the certificates and land titles.

[70] Haley, *Goodnight*, p. 295. Also, see Burton, *History of the JA Ranch*, p. 26.

ish diplomatic service, Adair found that occupation unappealing and turned instead to the brokerage business. After his first trip to New York in 1866, Adair decided that he could prosper by moving to the United States. He consequently made substantial profits by borrowing money at low rates in England and loaning it at high rates in New York.[71] After meeting Cornelia Ritchie, an American, at a ball in honor of a friend of her family, the two were married in 1869. They maintained homes in both the United States and Ireland, dividing their time between the two countries.[72]

In 1874 John and Cornelia Adair decided to go to the western prairies and try their luck at the then-popular sport of hunting buffalo. They were aided by General Phillip H. Sheridan who offered a military escort. The trip to the Great Plains whetted the interest of the Adairs and they returned to Denver in 1875 to begin a brokerage house.[73]

With the aid of George Thatcher, a mutual friend of both men, Clayton brought Goodnight and Adair together in 1877. They were not long in concluding a partnership agreement in which Adair agreed to furnish the necessary capital while Goodnight assumed the role of ranch manager.[74] The following specific conditions were also included:

1. Goodnight's salary was to be $2,500 per year.
2. Goodnight was to devote his time to the ranch exclusively.
3. The brand was to be the JA (for John Adair).
4. An accounting of all transactions was to be made every two months.
5. Goodnight was to neither give nor endorse any notes.
6. The agreement should be for five years.
7. In the event of losses, Adair had the right to terminate the agreement.
8. All assets were to be sold in the event of termination.

[71] *Ibid.*, pp. 17-23. Burton gives a good summary of the history of the Adair family as well as a biographical sketch of Cornelia Ritchie Adair, John Adair's wife.

[72] *Ibid.*, p. 20.

[73] Cornelia Adair, *My Diary, August 30th to November 5th, 1874* (Bath: Tyson and Co., Ltd., Printers and Stationers, 1918), p. 67.

[74] Burton, *History of the JA Ranch*, p. 26.

9. Adair's investment, plus ten percent interest, was to be repaid.
10. Adair was to receive two-thirds of net worth, Goodnight, one-third, in event of dissolution.
11. The number of cattle would be limited to 15,000 head.
12. All purchases made by Goodnight to be made with cash in hand.
13. All salaries and expenses to be charged to current proceeds.
14. The total land purchase should not exceed 25,000 acres.[75]

With cash available, Goodnight approached Gunter, Munson, and Summerfield on the subject of the purchase of land. The first price offered was high—a full dollar and a quarter per acre. Gunter, *et al*, knew about Adair's involvement in the ranch and was trying his best to get a high price. Negotiations continued and the amount agreed upon was finalized at seventy-five cents per acre—still a high price to pay, according to Goodnight. A stipulation in the contract enabled Goodnight to get most of the land he desired. He explained his maneuvering in this way:

> I had to get it through them or take my chances, and I wanted that canyon. I got them down to six bits an acre and closed for twelve thousand acres, provided they would let me set the compass and they would run it; and that is where the Old Crazy Quilt comes in. I took all the good land and all the water I could get and under the contract they were to designate twelve thousand acres more that I was to take the next year at my option. Well, I scattered that all over the Palo Duro Canyon; every good ranch in the country, every place a man was liable to look, I took.[76]

Gunter objected to the taking of scattered tracts of land but could not prevent it.

Soon after their partnership agreement had been signed, Goodnight and Adair, with their wives, made ready to head for the Palo Duro. They began the four-hundred mile trip from Trinidad, Colorado, with "a number of cowboy recruits . . . four loads of freight, and a hundred head of high-grade Durham bulls."

[75] The agreement was signed on June 18, 1877. Timothy Dwight Hobart Papers, Panhandle-Plains Historical Society. Located in the Panhandle-Plains Historical Museum, Canyon, Texas.

[76] Burton, *History of the JA Ranch*, p. 33.

Despite imagined Indian raiders by Mrs. Goodnight and jokes by
cowboys about starting a ranch with nothing but bulls, the party
finally arrived and were greeted by a company of cavalry from
Fort Dodge, which the government had sent out as an escort for
the Adairs.[77] Satisfied with the ranch and the competency of
Goodnight, the Adairs soon returned to Colorado.

Although Charles Goodnight had been exasperated with his
wife when she saw imagined Indians, the fall of 1878 brought a
real crisis situation with reservation Indians which Goodnight
handled in his usual level-headed manner. A large group of
Comanches and Kiowas left the reservation near Fort Sill, Oklahoma Territory, and headed for Texas to hunt buffalo. Remem-
bering the excellent camping and hunting areas in the Palo Duro
Canyon, they set a course for it. Upon their arrival, however, they
found not only that the buffalo were gone, but that the spot was
filled with Goodnight cattle. Hungry and disappointed, the Indians were not long in slaughtering JA cows.[78]

Line riders quickly sent word of the Indians' arrival to ranch
headquarters. Goodnight rode immediately to the Indian camp to
seek a solution to the problem. He asked for the chief, or *principál*,
and was met by Quanah Parker, the leader of the Comanches who
attacked the Adobe Walls trading post four years earlier. The two
men agreed to meet the following morning to make a treaty.[79]

Just before noon, the Indians arrived at the Goodnight ranch
house. Their party consisted of "ten or twelve of the old heads and
a few of the young ones. Eight or ten of the outstanding braves
were selected as 'inquisitors.' They formed a circle and . . . [Good-
night] and the interpreter . . . were in the middle."[80] The Indians
did their best to discredit Goodnight, trying to determine if he was
a *Tejano* by questioning his knowledge of the landmarks to the
north and west. Finally satisfied that the rancher was not a
Texan and that he was telling the truth, the Comanches and
Kiowas reluctantly agreed to Goodnight's offer of two beeves a
day until buffalo were found.[81]

Because he was uncertain how long the peace would last, Goodnight sent cowboy Frank Mitchell to Fort Elliot to report the

[77] *Ibid.*, p. 31.

[78] Haley, *Goodnight*, p. 306.

[79] *Ibid.*, p. 307.

[80] *Ibid.*

[81] *Ibid.*, p. 308.

Indian foray. By December 29, Lieutenant A. M. Patch left with a detachment of cavalry for the Palo Duro. The troops stayed until mid-January before returning to Fort Elliot and reporting that there were "sixty-four Comanches under Quanah, and sixty-seven Kiowas under Tapadeah" camped on the JA. Although the Indians did not become hostile, they were content with the ration agreed to in the "treaty" with Goodnight. The arrival of Captain Nicholas Nolan and a detachment of 10th Cavalry finally provided sufficient incentive for the Indians to return to the reservation.[82]

Although the Adair-Goodnight agreement called for the purchase of twenty-five thousand acres of land within the first five years, Goodnight had Adair's tacit permission to buy almost all land within the Palo Duro Canyon area, provided it could be purchased at a low price.[83] By 1882, the year the original contract expired, the JA's land holdings had expanded to 93,629 acres.[84] Goodnight paid a variety of prices for the various blocks of land:

> I bought land anywhere and everywhere I could get it provided I could get it right. I paid different prices for it. Some land cost me twenty-cents per acre, some twenty-five, some thirty and some thirty-five cents per acre. The largest amount I ever bought at one time was one hundred and seventy thousand acres at twenty cents per acre.[85]

In 1882 the JA Ranch had a herd of 27,870 cattle with a combined value of $557,400. Counting land value estimated at $150,000, horses and mules, and personal property, the assets of the JA Ranch totaled $717,981.[86] By 1884 land available in the Panhandle to the Goodnight-Adair partnership totaled over 668,000 acres. Of this amount, 333,000 acres were owned outright by the ranch, 39,688 acres were leased from the railroad, 200,000 acres were unleased school land, 25,000 acres were private lands leased inside the pasture, and 60,000 acres were vacant land.[87]

The original 1,600 cattle brought to the Palo Duro Canyon by

[82] *Ibid.*, pp. 308-310.

[83] Burton, *History of the JA Ranch*, p. 37.

[84] *Ibid.*

[85] *Ibid.*

[86] *Ibid.*, p. 39.

[87] *Ibid.*, p. 49.

Goodnight were principally purebred Durham. The herd was increased in 1877 with the addition of 3,000 more of the same breed which were purchased at sixteen dollars per head. Despite the efforts to build a purebred Durham herd, Goodnight soon discovered that "Durham cattle were not suited to this country and they began to decrease." Consequently, Goodnight began to change to Herefords as the main breeding stock for the JA. In 1882, 3,000 head of the "white-faces" were purchased from the nearby Shoe-Bar Ranch.[88] The new herd peaked in the years 1887 and 1888 when nearly 29,000 calves were branded. In 1887 alone, 16,060 calves were marked for the JA, many of which were born within the walls of the Palo Duro Canyon.[89]

Other major problems were encountered in Goodnight's attempts to raise purebred cattle. Cattle being trailed through the Panhandle markets from south and north-central Texas ranches carried with them a deadly disease dubbed "Texas Fever." Chance infestation of a fine herd of 1,000 cattle owned by Mrs. Goodnight and her brother, Sam Dyer, caused the loss of all but twenty-five head. A similar situation occurred on the Matador Ranch, south of the JA, where 500 cattle died. To prevent the further spread of the disease, carried by ticks, Goodnight and O. H. Nelson, manager of the Shoe-Bar Ranch, elected to enforce a quarantine. The forty-five miles between the two ranches were patrolled by three men carrying Winchester rifles. Paid the then-high wage of seventy-five dollars per month, they were charged with watching for passing trail herds and nesters with South Texas cattle. They also kept a close watch for possible rustlers. The "Winchester Quarantine" was effective.[90]

The continuing problem of keeping nesters off of the JA range, including Palo Duro Canyon, was tied closely to the existence of approximately 200,000 acres of unleased school land within the ranch's pastures. Goodnight, as well as most other cattlemen in the area, realized that the day of the free range was rapidly coming to an end. Goodnight knew that lands must be leased or purchased from the State of Texas. With this in mind, Panhandle

[88] *Ibid.*, p. 60. See Haley, *Goodnight*, for an excellent discussion of the first Herefords in the Panhandle.

[89] *Ibid.*, p. 61.

[90] The Winchester Quarantine was a serious business with Goodnight. In August 1881, he advised old friend George T. Reynolds that if he brought cattle through his ranch, he "would not pass through . . . in good health." Haley, *Goodnight*, pp. 361-362. Also, see Burton, *A History of the JA Ranch*, pp. 90-91.

cattlemen sent a lawyer to Austin in 1881 to assure the Legislature "that they wanted to pay for the lands they were using 'in order to hold possession and not be subjected to intrusion.'" They hoped for an act that would provide for the leasing of public lands.[91]

The result, The Land Board Act of 1883, was not what Goodnight and many other ranchers had bargained for. It provided for leasing, but with competitive bidding and a minimum bid of four cents per acre. In addition, the act allowed the sale, again through competitive bidding, of as much as seven sections of land to an individual. To Goodnight and some other ranchers, the most objectionable part of the new law was the prohibition of enclosure, or fencing of state-owned lands.[92]

By 1886, Goodnight was convinced that the 1883 law would soon cause the end of large ranching in the Panhandle. Too, the railroads had already moved into neighboring Carson County and scores of settlers had already filed on adjacent state-owned lands. To fight the provisions of the law, Goodnight and other cattlemen went to the Legislature for repeal or, at least, modification of the Land Board Act of 1883, although prospects of any relief were dismal.[93]

When the time came for competitive bidding on leases in the Texas Panhandle, ranchers bid the legal four cents per acre for the land within their range and did not attempt to lease property already preempted by their neighbors. This action thwarted the desires of the State Land Board, which had expected competition for the lands as well as a higher price. Miffed, the Land Board declared that "the law to the contrary, notwithstanding—it would lease no more land for less than eight cents an acre; that it might refuse to lease watered lands 'for any reason . . . good and sufficient'; that sales should be made only to actual settlers; and that no watered lands should be sold."[94]

Goodnight was convinced that the only answer to the problem was to sell the JA before settlers came in on a wholesale basis and made it impossible to run an efficient cattle ranch. Writing to

[91] Haley, *Goodnight*, pp. 383-401, outlines the history of the lease fight.

[92] *Ibid.* Also, see "Four Section Act" in Walter Prescott Webb, ed. *The Handbook of Texas* (2 vols., Austin: Texas State Historical Association, 1952), Vol. I, p. 638.

[93] Burton, *History of the JA Ranch*, pp. 92-97.

[94] Haley, *Goodnight*, p. 385.

William Maguay, an associate of Mrs. Adair, Goodnight outlined his thinking:

> We hope to get something through [the Legislature]. We will leave no stone unturned to this end. If I fail it will not be for the want of effort. If we can succeed in a satisfactory way it will not be so urgent to sell. At the same time I feel that the tide is against us and I think we had better get out of the current as soon as possible. I have made up my mind to do this [sell the ranch] and I shall never stop till I accomplish it.
>
> I am not so anxious to quit the cattle business as a business, neither am I so tired of running the business. I am simply alarmed at the condition things are getting in. I am too old to be broke with debts hanging over me.[95]

The issue was taken to the courts by the cattlemen in an effort to force the State Land Board into compliance with the law. The ensuing fight resulted in Goodnight being treated by many Texans as the villain in the affair. He was referred to as a "bullionaire" and accused as the "usurper of children's grass" because of the school lands involved in the litigation.[96] The Board finally lost the court trial and the law was eventually repealed by the Texas Legislature.

Regardless of the statements to the contrary that were made during the lawsuit, few settlers ever tried to settle within the boundaries of the JA and the Palo Duro Canyon before 1887.[97] In that year, a new land act was passed that provided for the purchase by individuals of as much as four sections of grazing land at one dollar per acre or one section of farming land for two dollars per acre.[98] This legislation sparked an influx of small ranchers into the area. It was not until 1900, however, that farmers appeared in the Palo Duro Canyon area and settled on state lands.[99]

Goodnight sold his remaining portion of the ranch between 1888 and 1890 and moved to Goodnight, a nearby town begun by

[95] Charles Goodnight to William Maguay, Letter, December 29, 1886, in JA Ranch Records, "Letter Press Copy Book." Located in the Archive of the Panhandle-Plains Historical Museum, Canyon, Texas.

[96] Haley, *Goodnight*, p. 383.

[97] Burton, *History of the JA Ranch*, p. 95.

[98] See "Four Section Act" in Webb, ed., *Handbook*, Vol. I, p. 638.

[99] Burton, *History of the JA Ranch*, pp. 95-96.

the cattleman himself.[100] There he operated a small ranch. But the tremendous influence of Charles Goodnight would always be strongly felt on the destiny of the Palo Duro Canyon.

Many settlers filed on lands with the JA and the Palo Duro Canyon, built houses on dugouts, and began the legally pre-scribed three-year residency requirement to gain title. By 1901, JA managers were involved in an effort to purchase or exchange lands for property outside the main JA range. Within 13 years, all land within the ranch boundaries had been acquired with the exception of one eight-section block.[101]

The Gunter, Munson, and Summerfield interests from whom Goodnight and Adair had purchased the JA continued to be active in the Palo Duro Canyon area. They owned alternate sec-tions of land, primarily in Randall County, and, after purchasing the cabin and ranching interests of Leigh Dyer, operated under the Crescent G and GMS brands. A brother-in-law of Charles Goodnight, Dyer constructed his ranch headquarters in 1877 near the confluence of the Palo Duro and Tierra Blanca creeks. By 1881, the Gunter, Munson, Summerfield interests fenced 240 sec-tions of land in one pasture.[102]

The next year, Summerfield sold his interest in the ranch to Jule Gunter, the brother of his partner Jot Gunter. The new owner had been using the T-Anchor brand in other ranching operations and the Gunter brothers, with Munson, also adopted it for the Randall County enterprise.

The brothers were not to continue the three-way agreement long, however, as they sold their interest to William Munson in 1883. It is likely that Munson clearly saw the changes in state land ownership policy and felt that he should also sell at the first opportunity. When the British-owned Cedar Valley Land Com-pany expressed an interest in the T-Anchor, Munson was not long in completing a contract of sale. In 1885 the ranch, the brand,

---

[100] *Ibid.*, p. 109. Interestingly, Albert Bierstadt, the famous American western artist, was at one time considered to be a prime prospect to purchase the JA. See Charles Goodnight to John Adair, Letter, October 24, 1886, "Letter Press Copy Book."

[101] Burton, *History of the JA Ranch*, p. 97.

[102] The best study to date of the T-Anchor Ranch is C. Boone McClure, "A His-tory of Randall County and the T-Anchor Ranch," Unpublished Master's Thesis, The University of Texas, 1930. Copy located in the Archives of the Panhandle-Plains Historical Museum, Canyon, Texas.

25,000 cattle, and 325 horses were sold for $800,000. The ranch ceased operation in 1895.[103]

After 1900, the size of ranches along the Palo Duro continued to decrease. Small tracts, once parts of the JA and the T-Anchor as well as other ranches farther down the canyon, were purchased by newly arrived cattlemen and farmers. Pastures once open were fenced and cross-fenced to provide for better grass conservation, more selective breeding, and efficient general ranch operation. Although much of the JA continues as an active cattle ranch still operated by Adair heirs, T-Anchor land has been divided and subdivided time and time again, and no semblance of the operation remains today.[104]

Without question, the Palo Duro Canyon contributed much to the history of Texas and the Panhandle and to the world-wide stereotype of Texas. The explorer, the Indian, the buffalo hunter, the soldier, the cowman, and the farmer are all an integral part of that image. Perhaps most of all, however, the Palo Duro Canyon became almost a synonym for the freedom once associated with the unfenced open range.

[103] Ernest Archambeau, "The T-Anchor Log Cabin Dedication," October 25, 1975, Typescript in the Archives of the Panhandle-Plains Historical Museum, Canyon, Texas. Also, see T-Anchor Ranch Records and the Munson Papers located in the Archives of the Panhandle-Plains Historical Museum.

[104] *Ibid.*

Quanah Parker, War Chief of the Kwahadi (Antelope) Comanches. (Photo courtesy of Mrs. James S. Kone.)

Charles Goodnight, 1836-1929. (Photo courtesy of Historic Research Center.
Panhandle-Plains Historical Museum.)

A PARK FOR THE PANHANDLE: THE ACQUISITION AND DEVELOPMENT OF PALO DURO CANYON STATE PARK

Peter L. Petersen
Professor of History
West Texas State University

The dream of a park in Palo Duro Canyon dates almost from the beginning of Anglo settlement of the Texas Panhandle. The strikingly beautiful topography of the canyon, with its rugged terrain and bright hues, offered a vivid contrast to the subdued surrounding landscape. Protected from the seemingly ever-present wind by steep walls, several locations on the canyon floor soon became favorite gathering spots for many early Panhandle residents. The attraction of the Palo Duro was readily apparent to area developers. Considerable advantage would accrue to the community nearest to any park in the canyon, and thus one of the first actions of the Canyon City Commercial Club following its organization in December 1906, was the passage of a resolution asking for the establishment of a national park on the upper end of Palo Duro Canyon.[1]

In response to this petition and others from surrounding communities, on January 6, 1908, Congressman John H. Stephens of Wichita Falls introduced a bill calling for "the purchase of a national forest reserve and park in the state of Texas, to be known as 'The Palo Duro Canyon National Forest Reserve and Park.'"[2] Stephens' bill died in the Agriculture Committee of the House, but backers of the proposal continued to press for Congressional action. During the next few years the idea of a national park in the canyon gained impressive additional support with endorsements from groups as diverse as the Texas Federation of Women's Clubs and the Red River Improvement Association. Many Texas politicians, including Representative Hatton W. Summers and Senator Morris Sheppard, joined the campaign. Stephens reintroduced his bill in 1911 and again four years later.

[1] Mrs. Clyde W. Warwick, *The Randall County Story* (Hereford, Texas: Pioneer Book Publishers, 1969), 47, 271-275.

[2] U. S., Congress, House, H. R. 11749, 60th Cong., 1st Sess., 6 January 1908, *Congressional Record*, 42: 480.

By 1917, however, he was forced to publicly acknowledge that passage anytime in the near future was unlikely.[3]

The Stephens' proposal had several strikes against it. Many non-Texans viewed the bill as just another raid on the federal treasury, a not unexpected view considering the widely-held opinion that park appropriations, in the words of one historian, "smacked too much of the pork barrel."[4] And although the administration of Theodore Roosevelt had done much to awaken the nation to the need for conservation of natural resources, aesthetic considerations, such as the preservation of natural beauty, often received short shrift in Washington.[5] Perhaps for this reason, Stephens had sought to combine in his proposal the essentially preservation function of a national park with the more utilitarian role of a national forest. But in so doing, he thrust the Palo Duro project into the frontlines of the bitter bureaucratic warfare between the Forest Service in the Department of Agriculture and the National Park Service which had been created in the Department of the Interior in 1916.[6] Finally, as if these obstacles were not enough, there remained the problem of Texas lands. Texas retained control of its public lands when it entered the Union and these lands had passed quickly into the hands of private owners. To establish a national park in Texas, therefore, involved something different from the manner in which parks were established in many other western states—it required the purchase of park land from private owners rather than simply reserving part of the public domain. The question of how to convert a portion of Palo Duro Canyon from private to public ownership, in fact, was a problem that would plague park boosters until well after World War II.

During the early 1920's many supporters of a park in the Pan-

[3] Amarillo *Daily News*, October 8, May 5, 1912, February 17, October 8, 1916; U. S., Congress, House, 64th Cong., 2nd Sess., 9 February 1917, *Congressional Record*, 54, no. 6: 304-308.

[4] John Ise, *Our National Park Policy: A Critical History* (Baltimore: Johns Hopkins Press, 1961), 40. See also, Paul Herman Buck, *The Evolution of the National Park System of the United States* (Washington: Government Printing Office, 1946), and Freeman Tilden, *The State Parks: Their Meaning in American Life* (New York: Alfred A. Knopf, 1962).

[5] Donald C. Swain, *Federal Conservation Policy 1921-1933* (Berkeley: University of California Press, 1963), 5, 123-128.

[6] John R. Jameson, "The Quest for a National Park in Texas," *West Texas Historical Association Yearbook*, L (1974), 47-48.

handle turned to Austin for help, but the obstacles there were almost as great as in Washington. Not only did Texas lack a national park, but until 1923 it did not have a single state park. In that year, Governor Pat Neff successfully urged the Thirty-Eighth State Legislature to create the Texas Park Board which, although it lacked funding, was empowered to accept donations of small parcels of land to be used as state parks. Among those appointed to the first State Park Board was Phebe Warner of Clarendon, an outspoken advocate of a park somewhere in Palo Duro Canyon. She soon recruited to the Palo Duro cause David E. Colp, the first Chairman of the State Park Board. In late 1924, Colp and Warner, along with several Amarillo civic leaders, escorted Governor Neff on a tour of the upper end of the canyon. The Governor was properly impressed, describing the scenery as "equal to that of Colorado."[7]

Colp obviously agreed and was already applying his considerable promotional abilities to plan for a park. At first he suggested the individuals owning land in the canyon should donate part of their holdings to the state. Since the only compensation Colp could offer was the promise of a memorial plaque at the park gate bearing the donor's names, there was no great rush by Palo Duro landowners to contribute. Taking a somewhat different track, Colp next endorsed a plan to create a "scenic highway" through the canyon, promising to use convict labor for the road construction. Once again, however, the question of land ownership proved to be a stumbling block. Colp had hoped that landowners would at least give the state a right-of-way for the highway. Although several owners indicated a willingness to have a road built across their land, apparently none was willing to deed the land to the state and therefore convicts could not be used by the State Park

[7]Phebe K. Warner, "Palo Duro Park," *Fort Worth Star-Telegram*, March 2, 1922; "Texas First Park Board Accepts 15 Sites," *San Antonio Express*, March 21, 1924, clippings from both newspapers in Phebe K. Warner Papers, Panhandle-Plains Historical Museum, Canyon, Texas (hereafter PPHM); William J. Lawson, "The Texas State Park System," *Texas Geographic Magazine*, II (December 1938), 1-3; Amarillo *Daily News*, November 14, 1924; Raymond Brooks, "The Birth of Texas' Great State Parks," Austin *American-Statesman*, February 19, 1966, as cited in Ross A. Maxwell, *Geologic and Historic Guide to the State Parks of Texas* (Austin, Bureau of Economic Geology, 1970), 1-2.

Board to build what amounted to a road on private land.[8] It was apparent by the mid-1920's, then, that the creation of a state park in the Palo Duro was dependent upon a sizable appropriation by the Texas Legislature—an event which seemed unlikely given the legislators' parsimonious attitude toward the entire state park concept.

Yet the park was a dream that died hard. Henry Ford and other automobile manufacturers were rapidly putting the nation on wheels while paved roads were beginning to link major western cities. The result was a surge of tourists, a source of potential income which virtually every local booster organization sought to tap. With one of the routes westward crossing the Panhandle, a park in the canyon would be a tremendous asset for the region. "Can you begin to estimate the clean cash Amarillo and the adjacent towns will miss," Warner asked, "if we refuse longer to provide a recreational center in the center of the Panhandle of Texas to serve the hundreds of thousands of people who cross the continent every year and who would stop and spend a day or week or month in the Palo Duro Canyon if such a thing were made possible?"[9]

Sustained by thoughts of tourist dollars pouring into local coffers, residents of the Panhandle continued to press for their park. By 1929, an organization called the Palo Duro Park Association, comprised of representatives from 15 Panhandle counties, was holding regular strategy sessions. Considerable confusion remained over how best to proceed. Suggestions offered included acquisition of canyon land by individual counties; creation of a park "district" with all Panhandle counties contributing to the effort; the construction of a scenic drive through much of the canyon; circumvention of the Congress by getting the President to declare Palo Duro a "national monument"; and another appeal to the Texas Legislature for assistance. Although there was no apparent consensus as to which proposal held the

[8] Amarillo *Daily News*, August 30, October 18, 19, 1924. Colp's initial enthusiasm for land donations cooled noticeably after a few months; many of the original 51 gifts to the state either proved unsuited for a park or required additional development, something legislators were unwilling to fund. Consequently, the Park Board was forced to return several parcels to their donors. See Tilden, *The State Parks*, 20-21.

[9] Phebe K. Warner, "Phebe K. Warner tells How New Palo Duro Park Would Climax Fortunate 'Breaks' for Section," undated clipping [ca. 1929] in Warner Papers, PPHM; Earl Pomeroy, *In Search of the Golden West: The Tourist in Western America* (New York: Alfred A. Knopf, 1957), 125-131.

most promise, park backers did agree that there should be an all-out campaign to advertise the glories of Palo Duro Canyon.[10]

Ironically, access to the canyon was becoming more difficult. The publicity campaign had attracted ever larger numbers of visitors who wished to view "The Scenic Wonder of Texas." Unfortunately, many of these people paid little heed to the fact that the Palo Duro Canyon was still private property. Area ranchers complained frequently of strangers tearing down fences, frightening, and even occasionally killing, livestock while making general nuisances of themselves. Eventually most ranchers closed their pastures, thus making the canyon virtually inaccessible.[11]

If the campaign to establish a park was to gather additional momentum, something had to be done that would allow large numbers of people to view the canyon without constantly infringing upon the property rights of the area ranchers. Members of the Canyon Chamber of Commerce, assisted by their counterparts in Amarillo, finally secured permission from several ranchers for an automobile excursion by the public to the west rim of the canyon on Sunday, July 13, 1930. The success of this venture—nearly 8,000 participants—led to the scheduling of a similar event for the first Sunday in November. A massive advertising campaign along with a warm Indian summer day brought over 10,000 motorists to view such famous attractions as the Lighthouse. Boy Scouts, National Guardsmen, and seven State Highway Troopers assisted local officials in directing traffic. White cloth streamers were tied to shrubbery to mark the trail across the ranchland, though this proved unnecessary as cars were almost bumper to bumper.[12]

The excursions of 1930 were a milestone in the campaign for a park. They revealed a great public interest in Palo Duro Canyon and confirmed its potential as a tourist attraction. The Canyon Chamber of Commerce was now convinced that it could wait no longer for state or federal legislation. Perhaps the opening of a small portion of the canyon to the public on a regular basis would generate enough enthusiasm that some governmental agency would be forced to act. Finally, and perhaps of greatest signifi-

[10] Amarillo *Daily News*, April 16, 10, November 8, 10, 26, 1929.

[11] Fred A. Emery to John K. Boyce and Guy A. Carlander, December 6, 1944, Guy A. Carlander Papers, PPHM.

[12] Amarillo *Daily News*, July 10, 12, November 3, 1930.

cance, the excursions had attracted the support of Fred A. Emery,
a resident of Chicago and an officer in the Byers Brothers Livestock Commission Company of Kansas City which had an
interest in approximately 25 sections of canyon land.

Eager to see a park created on this land, Emery helped arrange
an agreement with the Canyon Chamber of Commerce which
would allow free use of Section 101, Block 6, I. & G. N. Railway
Surveys, for a period of two years beginning April 13, 1931
(Section 101 is 13 miles directly east of the City of Canyon and
today serves as the location for the entrance to Palo Duro State
Park). The Randall County Commisioners then constructed a
three mile stretch of dirt road linking Section 101 with the existing highway running east of Canyon.[13]

The grand opening of "Palo Duro Park" was Sunday, May 17,
1931. As had happened with the excursions of the previous year,
the opening day crowds exceeded expectations with more than
25,000 sightseers from 14 states attending the ceremonies. It was,
according to the *Canyon News*, the "greatest triumph in the
history of 25 years of agitation for a state park in the Palo Duro
Canyons...." J. B. Elliston, president of the Canyon Chamber of
Commerce, described the opening as a "great step" toward the
creation of a state park. "It has been proved on the days the
canyons have been opened to the public and at the opening of the
park Sunday," Elliston said, "that a state park is needed and
earnestly desired. All we have to do is stay in there and fight."[14]

By this time, however, not only had the worsening Great Depression resulted in a legislative attitude of extreme economy in
the area of appropriations but Palo Duro had gained a rival in the
drive for a major park in Texas. By the early 1930's, a campaign
was well underway to establish a park in the Big Bend area along
the border with Mexico. In May 1933, the Forty-Third Legislature
passed a bill creating Texas Canyons State Park on 15 sections of
land near three canyons on the Rio Grande—Boquillas, Santa
Elena, and Mariscal. Later in the year, the Legislature increased
the size of this park by adding 150,000 acres of unsold public free
school land. The same bill resulted in changing the name of the
park from "Texas Canyons" to "Big Bend." Big Bend's promot-
ers, though pleased by this action, were not totally satisfied and

[13] *Ibid.*, July 10, 1931.

[14] *Ibid.*, May 13, 18, 1931; *Canyon News*, May 21, 1931.

immediately began a campaign to gain national park status. What made Big Bend so attractive, in addition to its rugged scenic beauty, was the incredibly low cost of land acquisition. Literally tens of thousands of acres were available at a cost of no more than one cent per acre. Compared to widely quoted asking prices of $10 to $25 per acre for Palo Duro land, the advantages of Big Bend were especially obvious during a period a economic retrenchment.[15]

Meanwhile, Fred A. Emery had acquired title to more than 15,000 acres in Randall and Armstrong counties commonly known as the "B. S. Arnold Ranch." Working closely with Emery, State Park Board Chairman D. E. Colp determined that 14,466.15 acres of Emery's land, almost all of it in Palo Duro Canyon, would answer the calls for a park in the region. There remained, of course, the perennial problem of how to acquire this land without a cash outlay. After a series of conferences, however, Colp and Emery finally came up with an ingenious plan to overcome the obstacle which had delayed the creation of a park for now almost 25 years. They decided to approach the newly-established Reconstruction Finance Corporation—a major agency in the efforts of both President Hoover and Congress to combat the depression—with a request for a loan to the Texas State Park Board, the money to be used for the development of Palo Duro Park. Income from park operations would then be used not only to repay the loan, but also to purchase the park. The R. F. C. appeared to be interested and in early January 1933, officials of the National Park Service were invited by all parties to examine the proposal. After a preliminary investigation, two National Park Service representatives called upon Emery and Colp to drop their plans for the construction of a large hotel, golf course, swimming pool, and similar resort appurtenances. Further negotiations resulted in a more modest plan involving several individual cabins scattered throughout the park. Total development cost was estimated to be $120,000 and a loan of that amount was subsequently requested from the R. F. C. Apparently skeptical about the legality of the scheme, the R. F. C. then asked that the Texas Legislature approve the use of anticipated park revenues as a means of repaying the loan. The desired enabling act quickly passed both houses

[15] See R. M. Wagstaff, "Beginnings of the Big Bend Park," *The West Texas Historical Association Yearbook*, XLIV (October 1968), 3-14; Ronnie C. Tylor, *The Big Bend: A History of the Last Texas Frontier* (Washington, D. C.: National Park Service, 1975).

and was signed by Governor Miriam A. Ferguson on May 29, 1933.[16]

By this time, however, other events were moving rapidly in the direction of eliminating the need for the R. F. C. loan. On March 31, 1933, only 27 days after his inauguration, President Franklin D. Roosevelt had signed a measure establishing an agency called Emergency Conservation Work (ECW), more popularly known as the Civilian Conservation Corps (CCC). The aim of this new agency was to put unemployed youth to work on a variety of reclamation projects—to bring together "two wasted resources," as John A. Salmond has written, "the young men and the land, in an attempt to save both."[17] Roosevelt immediately gave the CCC the assignment of having 250,000 youths at work by early summer. If this goal was to be met, great dispatch would be required of numerous governmental agencies. The Department of Labor had the responsibility of selecting the enrollees, but often delegated this function to local relief agencies. The Army was given the duty of training and transporting the new recruits, and providing for their physical well-being once camps had been established, while the Forest Service and the National Park Service selected the actual projects. This latter task proved to be particularly difficult as depression-ridden states and communities clamored for their "fair share" of the federal program.[18]

Not unexpectedly, officials of the National Park Service saw Palo Duro Canyon as a likely site for one of the anticipated 1,300 initial CCC projects. Herbert Evision of the Park Service requested that Colp and Emery hold their R. F. C. loan in abeyance until it could be determined whether the desired park could be built by the CCC. At the same time, many residents of the Panhandle became increasingly excited about the work relief such a project would provide. Soon estimates were circulating that as many as 4,000 men could be put to work building a scenic highway through the

[16] Emery to Boyce and Carlander, December 6, 1944, Carlander Papers, PPHM; *Canyon News*, May 18, June 1, 1933.

[17] John A. Salmond, *The Civilian Conservation Corps, 1933-1942: A New Deal Case Study* (Durham, N. C.: Duke University Press, 1967), 41. See also, Franklin D. Roosevelt's message to the Congress, March 21, 1933, in Edgar B. Nixon (ed.), *Franklin D. Roosevelt and Conservation, 1911-1945* (Washington: Government Printing Office, 1957), I, 143-144.

[18] Roosevelt to the Secretaries of the Interior and Agriculture and the Director of Emergency Conservation Work, May 3, 1933, in Nixon (ed.), *Franklin D. Roosevelt and Conservation*, I, 161-162. For a description of the CCC's hurried mobilization, see Salmond, *The Civilian Conservation Corps*, 26-45.

canyon. Within a few weeks a massive campaign to persuade the federal government to locate several CCC camps in the Palo Duro Canyon was well underway. Success was apparently achieved on June 1, when President Roosevelt signed a document allocating four CCC companies of 200 men each to Palo Duro Canyon. "It was simply a case of enlisting the support of everyone in a position to help," said T. E. Johnson, chairman of the Palo Duro Park Association. "Through the West Texas Chamber of Commerce, the State Park Board, the citizens committees of Claude, Canyon and other cities, Congressman Marvin Jones of Amarillo, Senator Tom Connally of Texas, and our own James O. Guleke of Amarillo, the program was worked out, submitted to federal authorities and approval obtained."[19]

The joy which greeted the news from Washington proved short-lived. Within a few days, that always aggravating question of land ownership threatened once more to dash the hopes of those who had long worked for a park in the Palo Duro. Both the National Park Service and the Texas Relief Commission continued to express concern about the actual ownership of the proposed park. Neither agency wanted to become involved in building improvements on what might turn out to be private land and thus demanded clear proof that the Texas State Park Board did indeed own the land. At this point, a truly remarkable arrangement was reached between Fred Emery and David E. Colp. The State Park Board agreed to purchase 14,466.15 acres from Emery at a price of $25 per acre by assuming first liens on the land held by two Scottish mortgage companies and then giving Emery a vendor's lien for the balance. But before the contract could be signed, representatives of the National Park Service and the CCC, after touring the area of the proposed park, requested the addition of 637 acres, consisting of Section 101 on the west rim and the site of the original "Palo Duro Park." Emery and Colp were agreeable and the park size was therefore increased to 15,103.85 acres. Total purchase price was $377,586.25 with $263,887.96 of that amount owed to Emery. The first liens at 6-1/2 percent interest were due to mature November 1, 1942, while the vendor's lien carried a 6 percent interest rate and was due July 28, 1948.[20]

Since the only cash involved in the entire transaction was a

[19] Amarillo *Daily News*, June 2, 1933; *Canyon News*, June 8, 1933.

[20] The Warranty Deed was recorded on September 20, 1933 in the *Deed Records of Randall County*, Vol. 69, 347-360; Emery to Boyce and Carlander, December 6, 1944, Carlander Papers, PPHM.

token $10.00 paid to Emery, some type of payment plan had to be negotiated. Under the terms of this contract, the Texas Park Board agreed to service the debts by pledging 50 percent of the gross income or revenue derived from park entrance and gate receipts (the contract specified a minimum entrance fee of 20 cents per adult, 10 cents for children under 14, and 35 cents for each auto), 20 percent of all concession income, and all net receipts from oil, gas and mineral leases, and from agricultural or livestock operations on park land.[21]

The Texas Relief Commission remained skeptical; only after a petition was signed by many of the Panhandle area's leading citizens saying that they approved of the purchase and repayment scheme did the Commissioners finally give their authorization on June 29. Since the following day was the deadline for authorities to approve CCC projects in Texas, there is considerable truth to T. E. Johnson's comment that "the park was just saved by the skin of its teeth."[22]

With the land question apparently resolved, the way finally had been cleared for the CCC to begin work on the Palo Duro project. The Army quickly began preparations for the establishment of a multi-company encampment on the northwest rim of the canyon. The site lacked water, and had neither electricity nor telephone service. The water problem was solved by laying a line of used oil field pipe nearly three miles to a well on the Finke ranch. Much of this pipe and the tools required for its assembly were provided by Canyon businessman and civic leader Clarence Thompson. Within a few weeks, a telephone line was strung on the fence posts beside the road to Canyon, thus provided a communications link between the camp and the nearest town. But electricity, other than that eventually provided by several undependable portable generators, did not come to Palo Duro Canyon State Park until well after the CCC had completed its work.[23]

The first company of approximately 200 CCC men arrived in Amarillo late in the evening of July 11, 1933, from Fort Sill, Oklahoma. The men remained on their train until the following morning when they were transported to the canyon in cars and trucks furnished by local residents. Later in the day, two more companies reached Amarillo, this contingent from Fort Sam Hous-

[21] Copies of these documents are in the Carlander Papers, PPHM.

[22] Amarillo *Globe*, June 30, 1933.

[23] Walter J. Caserta to the author, October 15, 1977; Amarillo *Globe-News*, May 30, 1954.

ton. Once again, local residents provided the transportation for the final leg of their journey. Just as the second group approached the canyon, a line of thunderstorms moved into the region. A heavy squall swept across the campsite, grounding every tent erected by the first arrivals and causing minor injuries to six enrollees. Undaunted, the men continued to set camps and by nightfall a "tent city" of more than 600 men had been established.[24]

Although President Roosevelt's primary goal in calling for the creation of the CCC had been to provide meaningful work for unemployed youth, the three companies assigned to the Palo Duro were filled with middle-aged men—all veterans of World War I. The decision to allow a limited number of jobless veterans to join the CCC was related to the problems caused by the so-called "bonus marchers." In 1932 and again in May of the following year, several thousand veterans had descended upon the nation's capital in an effort to secure early payment of a bonus which was not to come due until 1945. The routing of the marchers from Washington on July 28, 1932, by an Army force commanded by General Douglas MacArthur was a political mistake Roosevelt was determined not to see repeated by his administration. In response to a letter from General Frank T. Hines, head of the Veterans Administration, Roosevelt issued an executive order on May 11, 1933, allowing veterans to constitute up to 10 percent of the initial 250,000 CCC enrollees. Within a few days, Roosevelt had persuaded most of the bonus marchers to enlist in the conservation Army.[25] It was from the ranks of these unemployed veterans of World War I, more than a few of them also veterans of the two bonus marches, that came the men who were to begin building Palo Duro State Park. Although each man had his own reason for enlisting, few would have disagreed with their colleague Raymond Rigsby's contention that being in the CCC and

[24] Amarillo *Globe*, July 12, 1933; *Canyon News*, July 13, 1933.

[25] For two recent accounts of the bonus marchers, see Roger Daniels, *The Bonus March: An Episode of the Great Depression* (Westport, Conn.: Greenwood Press, Inc., 1971); and Donald J. Lisio, *The President and Protest: Hoover, Conspiracy, and the Bonus Riot* (Columbia: University of Missouri Press, 1974). See also, Salmond, *The Civilian Conservation Corps*, 35-36.

working on Palo Duro Canyon State Park "was better than walking the streets and doing nothing."[26]

Throughout the remainder of July, most of the enrollees worked under Army supervision to complete their camp. Mess halls and latrines were built for each company along with a toolshed and blacksmith and auto repair shops. A National Park Service Headquarters was established and, of course, a flagpole erected. The encampment itself soon became a tourist attraction with as many as 75 visitors a day. Canyon citizens provided the enrollees with a wide variety of entertainment including a concert by the Buffalo Band of West Texas Teachers College, while local ministers preached at Sunday services. Soon the veterans were electing "Queens" and "Sweethearts" from among their many visitors.[27]

While Army personnel directed camp refinements, the more than 30 National Park Service employees assigned to the project were busily mapping park construction plans. The first major undertaking would be the building of a road to the floor of the canyon. Although a logical beginning, the road project also answered National Park Service directives that the CCC be assigned work that could be performed with hand tools. By early August, several hundred men were at work with picks, shovels and wheelbarrows carving a winding road down the steep canyon wall.[28] Where rock obstacles were encountered, blasting holes were drilled. Even this arduous task was done by hand with one man turning the heavy drill bit as his partner lifted and then dropped it. Shortly after Labor Day, the powder men set off a huge blast which left no shortage of work for the pick and shovel crews. With the aid of literally tons of dynamite, the CCC men soon constructed a rough trail to the bottom that could be traversed by trucks. The formal opening of the nearly one and a half mile rim-to-bottom road was observed on November 26, 1933, in ceremonies sponsored by the Canyon Chamber of Commerce. Nearly 6,000 people watched as Congressman Marvin Jones removed a

[26] Interview with Raymond Rigsby, October 27, 1977. A resident of Quanah, married and the father of two children, Rigsby was 37 when he joined the CCC in 1937. Although it is difficult to generalize, there is some evidence to indicate that most members of one company came from the Houston-Beaumont area while residents of San Antonio dominated the ranks of another company.

[27] *Canyon News*, July 20, July 27, August 17, 1933; Caserta to the author, October 15, 1977.

[28] *Canyon News*, August 3, 1933; Caserta to the author, October 15, 1977; Rigsby interview, October 27, 1977.

symbolic barrier from the pathway. Because of continued construction, tourists would find their access to the canyon floor limited to Sundays for the next several months,[29] but the building of a road down the side of the canyon in less than six months was an achievement which would have been difficult if not impossible without the labor of the Civilian Conservation Corps.

There had been considerable concern in the Panhandle that once the Palo Duro road was completed, the CCC camps would be moved to other locations. Such fears were allayed in October when the federal government announced through Congressman Jones that not only would the three companies remain at Palo Duro for the winter but a fourth company of veterans would be moved there from Colorado.[30] Many of the veterans were from South Texas and were naturally apprehensive about spending a Panhandle winter living in a tent. Thus reenlistment rates began to plummet, the companies falling to about 60 percent of authorized strength. To counteract dropping enlistments, contracts were quickly let for the construction of wooden barracks. More than 100 area carpenters were soon at work erecting a dozen buildings. By mid-November the veterans were able to abandon their tents for more comfortable shelter. This move came none too soon for many of them, as unseasonably cold weather had already forced some vets to spray the north side of their tents with fire hoses in the hope that a coating of ice would block the biting wind.[31] On December 4, an additional 157 veterans arrived from Sargent, Colorado, to take up winter quarters at the Palo Duro. Thus 1933 ended with four CCC companies—1821, 1824, 1828, and 1829—with approximately 140 men each assigned to the project.

With early 1934 enlistments expected to increase the total number of CCC enrollees to well over 800 men, it was clear that additional work was needed to keep everyone busy. Soon plans were underway to extend the entrance road along the canyon floor to a location near the southeastern park boundary where a camping area was to be developed. Several crossings of the meandering Prairie Dog Town Fork of the Red River were involved and thus either bridges or concrete water-crossings would have to be

[29] *Canyon News*, November 16, 23, 1933; Amarillo *Globe*, November 27, 1933.

[30] *Canyon News*, October 12, 1933.

[31] *Ibid.*, November 9, 16, 1933; Amarillo *Globe-News*, November 19, December 5, 1933; Caserta to the author, October 15, 1977.

constructed. In addition, as soon as the weather improved, workers were to begin clearing and marking a large number of hiking trails leading away from the main road. By far the most ambitious project, however, was the construction of a large building quickly named El Coronado Lodge in honor of the Spanish explorer.[32]

Guy Carlander, an Amarillo architect who would play a major role in the history of the park for the next 20 years, was hired to draw up plans for the lodge and several smaller buildings to be constructed at different locations in the canyon. Obviously, the lodge was the major project, and at one point Carlander apparently envisioned a multi-story building with an attached observation tower. Eventually, however, a more modest plan for a single-story structure was approved. In January 1934, a large crew of workers began preparing a construction site on the north rim of Timbercreek Canyon. A great deal of blasting and rock removal was necessary before work could begin on the actual foundation of the lodge. Thus it was not until May 12 that cornerstone laying ceremonies were held with State Park Board Chairman Colp doing the honors.[33] Even though two of the CCC companies were withdrawn from Palo Duro and assigned to Temple and Troy, Texas, in late April, work on the lodge and other projects proceeded rapidly throughout the summer.[34]

More than 7,000 people attended the formal park opening on July 4, 1934. Nearly all stayed for a "performance" by the Leonard Stroud Rodeo on the canyon floor sponsored by the Texas State Park Board. Although newspaper editors, politicians, and civic leaders labeled the opening a "grand success," nagging doubts about the financial future of the park remained. With the park now open daily, attendance improved, but was still no where near the 100,000 annual visitors Colp had once predicted. Records reveal that for the entire year of 1934, 33,465 people entered the park. Gross income from gate receipts, concessions, and pasture rentals amounted to $6,426, of which $3,243.37 was applied by the

---

[32] *Canyon News*, December 21, 1933.

[33] Guy Carlander to [?] Henderson, January 1, 1934, Carlander Papers, PPHM; *Canyon News*, February 15, 1934; Amarillo *Globe-News*, February 25, March 4, April 29, May 13, 1934.

[34] For descriptions of the CCC work, see "El Coronado Lodge," *The Windy Rim*, I, No. 8 [1934], 2; and Roland E. Lee, "Historical Sketch of the Laying of the Pipe to Cedar Spring," an unpublished one-page manuscript dated May 12, 1934. Copies of both items in the Carlander Papers, PPHM.

State Park Board to the park's indebtedness. But this amount fell far short of the more than $40,000 needed annually to fully service the debt.[35] Clearly, the land problem was far from being solved.

Perhaps no one worried more about the future of Palo Duro Canyon State Park than did Conrad Wirth. As Assistant Director of the National Park Service, Wirth had followed the development of the park with a great deal of interest. While there can be little doubt that Wirth was supportive of the park in the Palo Duro for the people of the Panhandle, the failure of the State of Texas to secure a clear title to the property disturbed him. The federal government was spending several hundred thousand dollars to build improvements on land that might revert to its original owners, a prospect the National Park Service leader did not find at all pleasing. In September 1934, Wirth informed several Panhandle civic leaders who had been involved in boosting the park that unless the land title matter was resolved, he would recommend the withdrawal of the two remaining CCC companies and the termination of all construction at the park. Eventually, after the intercession of Congressman Marvin Jones and several telegrams between Washington, Amarillo, and Austin, a compromise was agreed upon whereby Emery furnished the State Park Board with a release from all liens on a total of 120 acres, specifically the land on which the park entrance, El Coronado Lodge, and the campgrounds were being built, plus a 100 foot right-of-way for the park road.[36]

With the land question again at least temporarily resolved, the way was now open for continued develpment of park facilities. Throughout the remainder of 1934 and into 1935, work progressed rapidly on the lodge while further refinements were made on the canyon road. In addition, four cabins were constructed at the "Cow Camp" camping grounds at the lower end of the park along with a latrine near the newly-built first water crossing. With native stone from a rock quarry in the park as the major building component, these construction projects continued the initial emphasis on utilizing as much hand labor as possible.

[35] *Canyon News*, May 24, July 5, 1934; Amarillo *Globe*, July 5, 1934. Statistics on park attendance and income may be found in the Carlander Papers, PPHM.

[36] Carlander to D. E. Colp, September 20, 1934; Colp to Carlander, September 25, 1934; Carlander to Colp, September 25, 1934; Emery to Boyce and Carlander, December 6, 1944, all in Carlander Papers, PPHM. The release was filed at the Randall County Courthouse on November 30, 1934.

Photo on left: Fred A. Emery, the Chicagoan from whom the land for Palo Duro Canyon State Park was eventually acquired. (Photo courtesy of the Panhandle-Plains Historical Museum.) Photo on right is of Amarillo architect Guy Carlander, who played a major role in the acquisition and development of the park. (Photo courtesy of Mrs. Guy Carlander.)

Members of the Civilian Conservation Corps contingent of World War I veterans assigned to the Palo Duro project eating "chow" next to their tents in the summer of 1933. (Photo courtesy of the Panhandle-Plains Historical Museum.)

CCC men using hand tools to construct the canyon road in 1933. (Photo courtesy of the author.)

The road to the canyon floor as it looked shortly after its official opening in late 1933. (Photo courtesy of the Panhandle-Plains Historical Museum.)

CCC men on break from their labors pose for a photographer on the canyon rim. (Photo courtesy of the Panhandle-Plains Historical Museum.)

By 1934 barracks and mess halls for the CCC enrollees had replaced the original "tent city." (Photo courtesy of Walter J. Caserta.)

National Park Service employees, Army personnel, and CCC enrollees in front of the headquarters building in 1935. Project Superintendent E. A. Kingsley is fifth from the right; Walter J. Caserta of the National Park Service is fifth from the left. (Photo courtesy of Walter J. Caserta.)

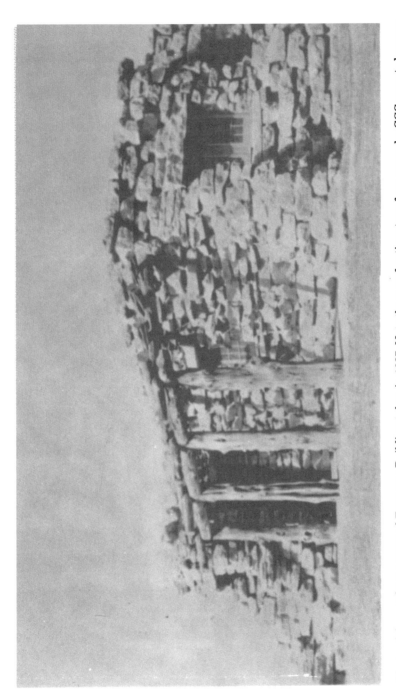

Photo of the newly-constructed Entrance Building taken in 1937. Note the use of native stone from a nearby CCC operated quarry. (Photo courtesy of Walter J. Caserta.)

A stone chimney from the recreation hall, standing like a solitary sentry, marks the location of the giant CCC encampment. (Photo courtesy of Wayne Hughes.)

In April 1934, the composition of the CCC companies at Palo Duro underwent the first of a series of major changes which would occur during the next two years. In assigning veterans to the project, the Army had paid little attention to racial matters. But now, for reasons apparently unrelated to the Palo Duro experience, it was announced that the approximate 60 black enrollees at work in the canyon would be reassigned to Sweetwater and the two veteran companies would become "all white." Three months later, the two veteran companies were reassigned, one moving to a soil erosion project north of Amarillo and the other to a similar camp near Memphis. To replace the departing veterans, the Army and the National Park Service sent two all black companies from East Texas.[37]

The transition from an integrated project to one that was all white and then to one that was all black in the span of four months produced considerable confusion and occasional consternation among Panhandle residents. One outraged Amarillo civic leader complained that he could not "conceive [of] such an indignity to Randall County citizens" and urged Congressman Jones to "stop" the assignment of the Negro companies to Palo Duro Canyon. But Clyde Warwick, the Iowa-born editor of the *Canyon News*, reminded his readers that "the Negroes who have been at the Palo Duro Park in the past have been the best workers, obedient in every phase of work and happy in the pursuit of their labors." Although there may have been no connection between events, many people believed that it was not coincidental that shortly after the black companies arrived, a caravan of white-robed Ku Klux Klan members visited Canyon and paraded around the square in their cars.[38]

The assignment of the black companies created many new problems for the National Park Service and Army personnel at the camp. Whereas the veterans—both black and white—had knowledge of barracks life and military discipline before joining the CCC, and because of their age, naturally brought with them considerable work experience, these new companies consisted largely of young, raw recruits with little work experience or military discipline. Walter J. Caserta, a Senior Foreman-Landscape Architect employed by the National Park Service, recalls that the assignment of several hundred young blacks to the project was

[37] *Canyon News*, April 18, 25, August 15, 29, 1935.

[38] J. O. Guleke to Marvin Jones, August 14, 1935, copy in Carlander Papers, PPHM; *Canyon News*, August 15, October 3, 1935.

"quite an experience for all concerned." Caserta remembers the new arrivals as "nice, good, clean, hardy and good working." And thus within a few weeks, the men were hard at work continuing the projects begun by the veterans.[39]

Yet problems remained. Many of the blacks disliked the Panhandle weather and longed for the more familiar climate of their homes in East Texas. Others complained about the lack of social opportunities. There were no blacks in Canyon and the Negro population of Amarillo was relatively small. Nor did the surrounding communities do much to make them welcome. Gone were the Queen contests, band concerts, and other entertainment which had greeted the first CCC men two years earlier. In part, this can be explained by a natural decline of interest and enthusiasm, the presence of CCC workers in the canyon was no longer new or exciting, but the basic reason was obviously racial. Consequently, the blacks felt themselves to be isolated and ignored, and some alleged that their assignment to Palo Duro Canyon made them little more than federal prisoners. There is considerable truth to this complaint, as Texas Park Director Colp had once described the Palo Duro as "ideal" for Negroes because it was located so far from any town.[40]

Consequently, reenlistments declined and in 1936, one of the companies was disbanded. Even so, tension continued to grow and in late summer of 1936, the remaining blacks went on strike. Although few details of what happened have ever been made public, for a period of several hours supervisory personnel and leaders of the striking CCC company, both heavily armed with shovels, pick and axe handles, confronted each other. Eventually, the explosive situation was defused, an agreement reached, and the strikers went back to work. Apparently, however, they had made their point. In mid-October, 1936, it was announced that all blacks at Palo Duro would be reassigned to projects downstate and that a company of young whites would be sent from Bonham to take their place.[41]

With the arrival of Company 894 from Bonham, the Palo Duro became one of the few projects in the United States to have had all

[39] Caserta to the author, October 15, 1977.

[40] *Ibid.; Canyon News,* August 15, 1935. See also, John A. Salmond, "The Civilian Conservation Corps and the Negro," *Journal American History,* LII (June 1965), 75-88; and Charles Johnson, "The Army, the Negro, and the Civilian Conservation Corps," *Military Affairs,* XXXVI (October 1972), 82-88.

[41] *Canyon News,* October 22, 1936; Caserta to the author, October 15, 1977.

three types of companies: veterans; blacks; and now the so-called "Juniors." Although young, members of 894 were well-experienced in park construction, having already built Bonham State Park. They immediately began work on finishing the lodge and entrance building and soon were building additional cabins along the canyon rim as well as more concrete water crossings.[42] These new arrivals were talented and enthusiastic workers. Given enough time, they would be able to complete all the construction begun by their predecessors. The only question was whether they would have the time, as once again the National Park Service was voicing reservations about the land situation.

There had been a three day meeting in Amarillo in mid-August 1935, involving representatives of the National Park Service, D. E. Colp of the State Park Board, and various Amarillo and Canyon civic leaders. At that time, Conrad Wirth and several other N. P. S. people again expressed their concern. "I am not at all disappointed in the Palo Duro," Wirth said, "but certain things must take place before the National Park Service will feel free to continue its development." Pointing to the fact that the park actually consisted of only 120 acres of lien-free land, Wirth observed that he knew of no other 120 acre park in the United States where so much work had been done. When asked if the National Park Service would halt all CCC activity at the park unless the Texas Legislature moved quickly to secure clear title to the entire 15,000 acres, Wirth refused to answer. But those in attendance left the meeting with the clear impression that unless something was done soon, the National Park Service would withdraw from the Palo Duro project.[43]

The attitude of the State Park Board was little better. Early in January 1936, Board Chairman David Colp, long one of the park's most enthusiastic supporters, died of pneumonia in a hospital at Temple. Although Colp's successor, former Governor Pat Neff, expressed support for continued operation of a park in the Palo Duro, Panhandle residents feared that the Board would soon lose interest in the park. Events seemed to bear out that prediction and within a few months, Canyon newspaperman Clyde Warwick would be claiming that "the State Park Board

[42] Author's interviews with George Melton, December 21, 1975; Pete Stansill, August 24, 1977; and W. Clyde Johnson, September 21, 1977.

[43] *Canyon News*, August 22, 1935; James O. Guleke to Marvin Jones, August 16, 1935, copy in the Carlander Papers, PPHM.

does not care a hill of beans about Palo Duro Park. . . ."44

In late September 1936, the State Park Board announced that it had entered into a five year contract with a Fort Worth corporation to operate all the concessions at Palo Duro State Park. In effect, the Palo Duro State Park Corporation would operate the park in return for a percentage of park income. As W. T. Taylor, spokesman for the corporation, explained upon his arrival in Canyon, "We are here to co-operate with the people of Canyon to popularize the Palo Duro, and to make it an attractive place so that more people will come." Attendance during 1937 did improve over 1936, increasing from slightly more than 33,100 to 43,000, though it is impossible to tell whether this was due to Taylor's efforts or to a decline in the severe dust storms which had struck the Panhandle in 1935-1936. In any case, the increased attendance and corresponding improved income still fell far short of meeting the financial obligations of the park. The debt continued to mount and by late 1937 unpaid interest had added nearly $100,000 to initial purchase price of $377,586.25.45

With no solution to the park's problems in sight, the National Park Service announced that all CCC work at the Palo Duro would cease on December 15, 1937, and that Company 894 would be assigned to a soil conservation camp north of Amarillo. In making the announcement, W. F. Ayres, inspector of the National Park Service, expressed hope that the shut-down would be only temporary. But he warned that work on the park would not be resumed until the National Park Service had "positive proof" that the State of Texas owned the land upon which work was being done. Twelve months later, when the National Park Service began to dismantle the barracks and other camp buildings, the *Canyon News* reported that representatives of the federal government now believed the situation was "hopeless" and that there was almost no chance of the CCC ever returning to the Palo Duro.46

During the next few years, attempts to rectify the situation met with little success. A petition drive in 1939 resulted in some 2,500 people requesting that the park "be designated, authorized and

---

44 *Canyon News*, January 16, 30, 1936, August 19, 1937.

45 *Ibid.*, October 1, 8, 1936. A copy of the contract between the Texas State Park Board and the Palo Duro Canyon State Park Corporation is in the Carlander Papers, PPHM.

46 W. F. Ayers to Walter J. Caserta, November 26, 1937, copy furnished the author by Caserta; *Canyon News*, December 2, 16, 1937, December 22, 1938.

taken over by the National authorities for the creation of a
National park or monument under the jurisdiction, development
and control of the National Park Service." But leaders of the
National Park Service told Marvin Jones that they would not
purchase the land, although they were willing to administer the
area as a National Monument if the State of Texas would buy the
park outright and then "donate" it to the federal government, a
prospect that to say the least seemed highly unlikely.[47] At one
point, the Hereford Chamber of Commerce unsuccessfully urged
the city of Amarillo to purchase and operate the park. But given
the continued unspectacular attendance—only 28,381 people in
1939—Amarillo city commissioners were very reluctant to get
that deeply involved in the park business.[48]

The coming of World War II only added to the woes of the finan-
cially-troubled park. Gasoline rationing cut sharply into both
tourism and local pleasure driving; consequently fewer people
visited the park in 1942 than in any year since its opening. The
decline in visitors, food rationing, and "the scarcity of help"
finally resulted in the closing of El Coronado Lodge by Frank
Miller, who had taken over the operation of park concessions in
1940.[49] The park's indebtedness continued to mount until by early
1945 it had reached a total of $579,851.11—roughly $38 per acre![50]

As the end of the war approached, the future of Palo Duro State
Park once again became a matter of concern for Panhandle residents. Early in 1945, the Amarillo Chamber of Commerce
launched an all-out drive to rescue the recreation area. The first
line of action was another attempt to secure an appropriation
from the Texas Legislature to rid the park of its indebtedness. To
have any chance of passage, an appropriation bill of this sort had
to have the enthusiastic support of area politicians, particularly
State Senator Grady Hazlewood. But Hazlewood believed that

[47] A copy of this petition is in Emery to Boyce and Carlander, December 6, 1944;
Jones to Carlander, January 6, 1940. Apparently the National Park Service believed the land in Palo Duro State Park to be worth no more than eight dollars an
acre whereas the lien holders were asking for more than twenty-five dollars an
acre. Jones to Carlander, November 28, 1938, Carlander Papers, PPHM.

[48] Amarillo *Times*, May 26, 1940.

[49] "Palo Duro Canyon State Park Statement of Operations for the Year 1943;
Emery to Boyce and Carlander, December 6, 1944, both in Carlander Papers,
PPHM.

[50] Frank D. Quinn to Grady Hazlewood, March 1, 1945, Hazlewood Papers,
PPHM.

the debt of $38 per acre was more than twice the actual value of
the land and was thus reluctant to support the request when the
Forty-Ninth Legislature convened in January 1945. After a few
weeks, the lienholder did express a willingness to settle for a
smaller amount, but as Hazlewood explained in a letter to Congressman Eugene Worley, the compromise offer came too late:

> At the beginning of the session Mr. Emery would not knock a
> single dollar. Of course the beginning of the session is the
> proper time to introduce an appropriation bill. Some six
> weeks later he agreed to knock off $100,000 and not a cent
> more. That still left the land at about $32 an acre. Now, at the
> last moment he has agreed to cut it down to $300,000. Well, of
> course, I am not a magician and have no supernatural
> powers, and it would be utterly and absolutely impossible to
> ever get the required 2/3 vote necessary to introduce an ap-
> propriation bill like that now at this late date.[51]

Following the failure of the Forty-Ninth Legislature to act on a
land-purchase appropriation for Palo Duro Park, a game of cat and
mouse ensued between Emery, the Texas State Park Board, and
park boosters in the Panhandle. Pointing to the fact that the first
mortgages on the land were scheduled to come due before the next
regular session of the Legislature (originally scheduled to ma-
ture on November 1, 1942, the notes had been extended because of
the war), Emery began to warn of foreclosure. The State Park
Board responded with a reminder that it held clear title to the 120
acres on which stood El Coronado Lodge, the entrance, and the
stone cabins and campgrounds. Meanwhile, rumors spread that
in the event of a foreclosure sale, some unspecified group would
attempt to acquire the remaining acres of the park by payment of
an amount equal to the first liens. In an effort to protect several
sizable loans to Emery, the Commerce Trust Company of Kansas
City then purchased these deeds of trust from the two Scottish
companies which had held them for more than two decades.[52]
    The Palo Duro Park Committee of the Amarillo Chamber of
Commerce found the situation so hopeless that by December

[51] Hazlewood to Eugene Worley, April 3, 1945, Hazlewood Papers, PPHM. See
also Rex Baxter to Bryle Elliston, February 27, 1945, and a memo prepared by
Baxter entitled "Report on the Status of Palo Duro Park" addressed to John
Boyce, Ross Rogers, and Guy Carlander, March 8, 1945, Carlander Papers, PPHM.

[52] Amarillo *Globe*, February 22, 1945; E. H. Pugsley to Frank D. Quinn, May 15,
1945; Pugsley to Rex B. Baxter, November 23, 1945; Emery to Pat Flynn, November 23, 1945, all in Carlander Papers, PPHM.

1945, it was reduced to begging anyone in the Panhandle who had "any plan or suggestion which might result in saving" the park to come forward. Several suggestions were made, the most promising of which, at least in the eyes of many, was the proposal that a local political entity acquire title to the land by issuing $300,000 in revenue bonds which would be retired through park receipts. The Commerce Trust Company and Fred Emery expressed interest in the idea, but despite a strenuous campaign by Carlander and others, the cities of Canyon and Amarillo, Randall County, and West Texas State College, all declined to become directly involved in the scheme.[53]

Thus by early Spring, 1946, reports of imminent foreclosure began appearing in local newspapers. On April 30, for example, the *Amarillo Times*, quoting "unimpeachable sources," said that the park would be put up for public auction on June 4. Although the fourth came and went without the sale, later in June, notices of sale were posted at the Randall County Courthouse; the park would be offered to the highest bidder on July 2. Whether Emery actually intended to go through with the threatened foreclosure is unclear, because on June 28, he called Carlander to announce that the sale had been cancelled. The Texas State Park Board, he reported, was "interested in working out a new deal." The deal, which was signed in mid-August, involved an agreement whereby the notes on the park land were extended until September 1, 1947, with a reduction in the interest rate to three per cent per annum. It was also agreed that Emery and his creditors would settle for $300,000.00 and that the Park Board would seek authorization from the Fiftieth Legislature to issue bonds in that amount payable from future park revenues.[54]

Shortly after the Fiftieth Legislature convened in early 1947, Senator Grady Hazlewood and Representative Blake Timmons of Amarillo introduced a bill empowering the Texas State Park Board to enter into a Trust Indenture ". . . mortgaging and encumbering the land and properties, the revenue and income" of Palo Duro State Park to secure payment of $300,000.00 in bonds. The legislation met with little opposition, passing the House without a

[53] *Canyon News*, December 6, 1945, May 30, 1946; Amarillo *Times*, May 22, June 7, 1946; C. C. Small to Carlander, June 1, 1946; Small to S. B. Whittenburg, June 1, 1946, both in the Carlander Papers, PPHM.

[54] Amarillo *Times*, April 30, 1946; *Canyon News*, June 27, August 22, 1946; memorandum on telephone call from Emery to Carlander, June 28, 1946, Carlander Papers, PPHM.

dissenting vote, and was signed by Governor Beauford Jester late in March.[55]

A few weeks later, the Texas State Park Board entered into a Trust Indenture with the American National Bank of Austin as Trustee providing for the issue of $150,000 Series A (150 $1,000 bonds) and $150,000 Series B Bonds (150 $1,000 bonds) bearing three percent interest and payable from revenues of the park (90 percent of the admission fees; 20 percent of gross concessions income; and 100 percent of grazing rentals). The first $12,000 of the above income had to go for repayment of the bonds. The next $2,000 was assigned to park maintenance. Any revenue in excess of this mandated $14,000 was to be divided equally between prepayment of the bonds and park improvements.[56]

News of the bond sale was greeted with sighs of relief throughout the Panhandle. In expressing his satisfaction, Virgil Patterson, president of the Amarillo Chamber of Commerce, said, "Now that the ownership question has been settled the chamber will appoint a committee to assist the state parks board in every way." The goal of Patterson and Palo Duro supporters was to insure sufficient attendance to meet the park's continued financial obligations. A minimum of maintenance had been conducted in the decade since the CCC left the Palo Duro and park facilities, especially the road, were in bad need of repairs. In some quarters it was feared that park revenues would remain inadequate unless the state appropriated a sizable sum for a major park refurbishment.[57] But little help was forthcoming from Austin, and once again Panhandle residents realized that continued operation of a public recreation area in Palo Duro Canyon was primarily their responsibility.

Fortunately, events would soon lighten what had once seemed to be a nearly impossible burden. By the late 1940's, growing national affluence and additional leisure time had created new interest in recreation and travel. The arrival of Amarillo newspaperman and promoter John McCarty to take over operation of the park concessions in 1949, insured that Palo Duro would re-

[55] Article 6077j, *Vernon's Annotated Civil Statutes, Texas; House Journal,* 50th Texas Legislature (March 20, 1947), 1005-1009; *Canyon News,* March 31, 1947.

[56] Texas Parks and Wildlife Department office memorandum entitled "Entrance Fees to Palo Duro Canyon State Park," from E. B. Camiade to J. R. Singleton, April 3, 1968, in R. C. Hauser to Duane F. Guy, October 6, 1977.

[57] Amarillo *Globe,* August 14, 1947; Amarillo *Times,* March 11, 1949.

ceive its share of the tourist dollar. During his five year tenure, McCarty brought buffalo, deer, and longhorn cattle to the park; arranged for a "treasure hunt" where visitors scoured the canyon looking for fake coins dropped from an airplane (grand prizes included a horse, a trip to Rio de Janeiro, and a new car), and had trips to the Palo Duro given as prizes on the very popular national radio shows, *Queen for a Day*, and *Bride and Groom*.[58] The success of these and other promotional activities was clearly reflected in increased attendance and income. Annual park revenue soared from $23,001 in the twelve month period following May 15, 1948 to over $107,000 just 10 years later. This money provided for badly needed improvements which in turn brought even more people to the park. It also provided for rapid payment of the park bonds. Although all of the bonds had a maturity date of 1982, through pre-payment the Series B Bonds were retired by 1960 and the Series A completely paid off six years later.[59] After more than a half century of struggle, the dream of an unemcumbered park in Palo Duro Canyon had finally become a reality.

Justifiably proud of their achievement, many Panhandle residents nevertheless felt a slight tinge of bitterness as they thought about their lengthy battle for the park. Senator Grady Hazlewood spoke for many of his neighbors when he recounted the Palo Duro story in 1953. During the 13 years he had been in the Senate, Hazlewood told members of the State Park Board, the people of the Panhandle had "been ignored and overlooked just about as many times as possible in many respects." Palo Duro Canyon State Park was a case in point.

> I was a member of the Senate when the Legislature voted one and a half million dollars to buy Big Bend State Park. Session after session I saw Palo Duro State Park get $250.00 for maintenance, although it contained 15,000 acres, while other state parks received anywhere up to $1,500.00, and some more. I introduced an appropriation bill to buy Palo Duro State Park, but with no success. Finally the Legislature very "generously" agreed to let us have this park if we would pay for it outselves. I know of no other state park in Texas that has

[58] John L. McCarty, "An Important Report to you," [ca. August 1949], Carlander Papers, PPHM; McCarty to Hazlewood, June 26, 1953, Hazlewood Papers, PPHM; Amarillo *Globe-News*, May 30, 1954.

[59] Texas Parks and Wildlife Department office memorandum entitled "Entrance Fees to Palo Duro Canyon State Park," from E. B. Camiade to J. R. Singleton, April 3, 1968, in R. C. Hauser to Duane F. Guy, October 6, 1977.

been paid for by the people of the local area. . . . When it is paid
for by our local efforts it will belong to all of Texas—not us.[60]

Hazlewood was certainly correct in emphasizing the role "local
efforts" had played in creating the park. From the resolution
adopted by the Canyon City Commercial Club in 1906 to the promotional activities of area chambers of commerce in the 1960's,
civic leaders, newspaper editors, regional politicians, and public-
spirited individuals, such as Phebe Warner, James O. Guleke,
Clarence Thompson, Guy Carlender, and scores of others, had
contributed innumerable hours to the park project. At the same
time, however, one should not overlook the very important contributions of non-Panhandle people. D. E. Colp, for example,
made numerous trips from Austin to Amarillo over the dirt and
gravel roads which then linked the two cities, always without pay
and often without even reimbursement for the gas and oil con-
sumed by his ancient car. National Park Service personnel from
across the nation, such as Walter Caserta of New Orleans, who
helped design the water crossings, did much to shape the park
during the crucial years 1933-1937. And even today, more than 40
years after their departure, almost everywhere one looks a person
can see the handiwork of hundreds of CCC men—veterans of the
Great War from Houston and San Antonio, East Texas blacks,
and "Juniors" from Bonham. Without their labor, the park would
never have been built. Truly, then, the park was a cooperative
effort involving several levels of government and many, many
people. All who visited it today owe a great debt to those who
struggled so long to make the beauty of Palo Duro Canyon accessible to the public.

[60] Hazlewood to Frank D. Quinn, July 13, 1953, Hazlewood Papers, PPHM.

PHOTO COURTESY OF TEXAS PANHANDLE HERITAGE FOUNDATION

AN AMPHITHEATER FOR THE PANHANDLE

Duane F. Guy
Professor of History
West Texas State University

With the completion of a two-lane road into the canyon and camping and picnic facilities, Palo Duro State Park began to take on a new character. While access to the canyon floor was easier and facilities for visitors' conveniences were added, the rustic beauty, charm, and splendor of the canyon remained. The visitors to the park were still able to view the effects of millions of years of wind and water erosion virtually untouched by human hands. The existence of the canyon and the creation of the state park remained a relatively well-guarded secret for the first few years after its opening.

The lack of publicity beyond the area immediately surrounding the canyon was only one of the reasons for the comparatively small number of visitors to the park. The Great Depression was still the dominating factor in American life and caused people to be concerned first with day-to-day existence. Little time or money was left to devote to travel and recreation. The economy began to improve toward the end of the 1930's, but an equally serious set of circumstances were ominously at work which, in a short time, created the greatest holocaust in modern history—World War II. During the war years, the attentions of the people were fixed on battlefields throughout the world and little attention was given to the further development of the park or its use. With the onset of gasoline and tire rationing, travel was curtailed to essential trips, leaving little for excursions for pleasure.

With the end of war, the number of visitors to the park increased rapidly as more and more people took to the highways, seemingly determined to make up for lost time. Only twelve miles from a major north-south highway, Palo Duro State Park was ideally located to attract tourists from all directions. In addition, efforts were being made to publicize the park to attract additional visitors and overnight campers. Facilities were gradually increased so that by the close of the 1950's it had become a convenient and popular site for visitors. Not only are the cross-country travelers who view the canyon for the first time struck with the suddenness and immensity of the great gash which breaks the monotony of the plains, but longtime residents of the region, regardless of how often they visit the canyon, still feel a certain amount of amazement that something so magnificient and majestic is in their region. Legally that part of the canyon which is the state park belongs to all the people of the state of Texas; however, to the residents of the Panhandle, it is "their" canyon. In 1934, appropriations of $50,000.00 had been requested from the state legislature to construct a theater on the site "as a memorial to Charles Goodnight and other pioneers of the plains."[1] The appropriation was never made and apparently no further effort was made and the idea was dropped. This early effort therefore had no effect on the efforts of those who revived the idea many years later.

This pride of the people of the Panhandle in their canyon accounts, to a considerable degree, for the success of a dream of a small number of dedicated and determined individuals. Often the origin of a particular idea or dream is difficult to locate precisely. In the case of the musical drama "TEXAS," the exact time and place can be easily identified. It occurred in July 1960, when Ples and Margaret Harper were having dinner with William and Margaret Moore. The conversation centered that evening upon certain interests that the four people had in common. The first was the existence of Palo Duro Canyon, about which little was known outside the confines of the Panhandle. Also of concern was the fact that relatively few visitors to the canyon were present during the most spectacular part of the day—when the rays of the setting sun strike the red cliffs on the eastern side bringing out all the vividness and beauty of the canyon.

These four also had a deep sense of history and a feeling of admiration and respect for the early pioneers of the Panhandle. While none of the four were professional historians, they all shared a feeling for the past and felt the need to portray the history of the Panhandle in such a way as to make it come alive and to instill into the present generation an appreciation of the hardships which the early settlers had to endure.

Of equal concern was a basic economic problem. The City of Canyon consistently experienced a significant reduction of revenues as West Texas State University ended its spring semester. There was also the problem of providing opportunities for speech, drama, and music students enrolled for the summer sessions. The opportunities for providing practical experiences for them were seriously curtailed during the summer months.[2]

[1] *Amarillo News*, November 24, 1934.

[2] Interview with Margaret Harper by author, March 3, 1977. Transcript in Archives, Panhandle-Plains Historical Museum.

During the course of the conversation, mention was made of an article which had appeared in the July 1960, issue of *Reader's Digest* entitled "His Theater is as Big as All Outdoors," by Allan Rankin. Before the evening was over, Margaret Harper had agreed to write a letter to Paul Green in which she pointed out that the geography and history of the Panhandle of Texas would provide the ideal setting for a symphonic drama.[3] In less than a week a reply was received from Paul Green indicating his willingness to meet and discuss the project.

The rapid and favorable reply from such a noted playwright came as a shock. It was "... like inviting the President to dinner and having him say he'd come."[4] The elation felt over the response was somewhat tempered by the necessity of raising enough money to pay the travel expenses of Green and John Parker, the business manager of "The Lost Colony." It was estimated that it would cost about $750 to bring the two to Canyon. The raising of this money was undertaken by the Harpers, Moores, Avent W. Lair, President of the Canyon Rotary Club, Winifred Lair, then President of the Music Arts Club of Canyon, and Joe Gidden, who became President of the Chamber of Commerce on January 1, 1961.

During the period the money was being raised, material on the history of the Panhandle of Texas was being sent to Green. As he began to delve into the history of the region, he came to the realization that there was no one figure around whom he could build a plot. There was no historical personage such as Jefferson or Washington or Benjamin Franklin. Instead Green saw the history of the Panhandle as a struggle "... of man against nature, of man conquering."[5]

The "man conquering" theme is central to many of Green's works. As a young man he worked on his father's farm in eastern North Carolina. He worked the cotton and corn and cut timber with his brothers and Negro farm hands. During these formative years he grew to love and respect the wonders of nature. This love and respect for nature appears in many of his plays and perhaps was a factor in his choosing the outdoor theater as a setting for his dramas.

During these years he "pondered a lot on the nature of this land

[3] Margaret Harper to Paul Green, July 3, 1960.

[4] Harper Interview, March 3, 1977.

[5] Interview with Paul Green by Judy Speer, July 19, 1974. Transcript in Archives, Panhandle-Plains Historical Museum.

of ours—our nation, America . . .—where we're going."[6] He, like many others of his generation, were caught up in the idealism and dreams of President Woodrow Wilson. When the United States declared war on Germany in 1917, Green enlisted in the Army ". . . under his fervor and the power of his speeches." With the end of the war he returned to the University of North Carolina to complete his studies and wrote plays. He studied philosophy at Chapel Hill and at Cornell.[7] His study of philosophy led him to study Greek civilization and inevitably to the question—why was their civilization so great, perhaps the greatest the world has ever seen. His conclusion was that the Greek playwright played a significant role in creating their civilization. One fact "that stuck out strong all the way through was that all this subject matter in all their plays that people witnessed . . . had to do with legends, historical characters . . . subject matter taken right out of the life and history of the Greek people."[8]

As Green pondered over his theory that civilizations are built upon what the people believe in, are concerned with, and are fed with spiritually, he became convinced that a great civilization cannot be built on cheap thoughts, sensations, and sensualism.[9] This was the same theory and basic belief of those who were dreaming, organizing, and working to create a living monument to those "conquering men" of the Panhandle. Even before the hard, tedious, and frequently frustrating work of bringing the idea to fruition began, a basic concept had already emerged. "In these times it is fitting to turn our attention to a great statement of American faith, so beautifully and forcefully presented that our young people can see the past forces which must guide our present directions."[10]

With this concept as the motivating force, a small group of Canyon citizens met to pursue the possibilities of creating some type of organization to make the dream a reality. It was this group that raised the necessary funds to bring Green and Parker to Canyon in April 1961. Green and Dr. Ples Harper spent many hours exploring the canyon looking for a possible site to build an amphi-

[6] *Ibid.*

[7] *Ibid.*

[8] *Ibid.*

[9] *Ibid.*

[10] Newsletter of Panhandle Heritage Foundation, undated.

theater. Green's first impression was ". . . nature's really cut up out here."[11]

A barbecue dinner was given during his first visit, attended by those who had contributed to finance Green's trip to Canyon. The evening was either "cold as blazes and the wind blowing"[12] or "it was a beautiful night,"[13] depending on the eye of the beholder or his memory. With the canyon wall as a backdrop and silhouetted against a blazing bonfire, Green painted a word-picture of what he saw and what could be done in the way of a drama. Already familiar with sound and light productions elsewhere, he could visualize how the canyon could be the setting for such a production. He described Indian smoke-signals rising from the top of the cliffs and the canyon echoing with sound and music.

By the end of the evening the group was aware of the potential of the canyon as a site for a production. However, they also came away from the meeting with mixed emotions about the project. While most could appreciate what could be done and were inspired by the presentation, there were many skeptics. The skepticism ranged from "Who in hell is gonna drive thirty miles into the canyon to see a play?" to how to raise what appeared initially to be a staggering sum of money.

There were however, many in the group who were convinced that, even though there would be many problems and obstacles to overcome, efforts should be made to investigate the possibilities of producing a drama and constructing an amphitheater. Consequently, an organizational meeting was held on May 7, 1961, in the Randall County Courthouse. The object of the first meeting was to "acquaint the area of the desire to construct an amphitheater in Palo Duro State Park and there to present a historical drama each summer."[14] It was decided to form a nonprofit organization and issue revenue bonds to partially finance the venture.

Joe Gidden, then President of the Canyon Chamber of Commerce, presided over the meeting. He informed the small gathering that it would cost approximately $120,000 to construct the theater and put on the first production. It was expected that this sum would be sufficient to build the bowl with concrete risers and

[11] Green Interview, July 19, 1974.

[12] *Ibid.*

[13] Harper Interview, March 3, 1977.

[14] Minutes of first meeting of Panhandle Heritage Foundation, May 7, 1961. Revenue bonds were never issued.

a stage, purchase props, costumes, lights, and sound equipment, and pay a small sum to those preparing the drama.[15] Gidden predicted that there would be 1,500 people in the theater every night watching the drama of early pioneers. "Now that's what they're doing on the east coast and there's no reason we can't do it out there."[16]

Election of officers for the still nonexistent organization was held at the first meeting. Those elected were Margaret Harper, President; Pete Cowart, Vice-President; Jerry LaGrone, Treasurer; and Dorothy Neblett, Secretary. These four and Raymond Raillard, William A. Moore, and Avent Lair constituted the first Board of Directors. They were to serve for the organizational period of six months. Two other decisions were also made at the first meeting, both of which proved to be very wise.

The first was to use the City of Canyon as sort of a testing ground for the idea. In the days and weeks following the meeting, person to person contact was made with the citizens of Canyon. Each was given an explanation of what was planned and was asked to contribute to the project. The reaction of those contacted indicated that, though skeptical, citizens would support the idea.

The other was that if a project of such proportions was to succeed, support from the entire Panhandle area was essential. At the first meeting a list of all the counties of the Panhandle was made and each person in attendance was asked if he knew someone in each of the counties. Every person at the first meeting was assigned a county or community to contact and given the responsibility of bringing someone to the next meeting, which was scheduled for June 6. A small brochure, which included a short description of the proposed project, was printed and distributed. This brochure and the personal contacts made resulted in having representatives from 12 communities at the June sixth meeting.

Those attending this meeting did so for various reasons and many had reservations about the project. Those responsible for calling the meeting knew, however, that they had an invaluable asset working in their favor—"Panhandle Pride." While the term is nebulous and difficult to define precisely, it is nevertheless a

[15] Interview with Raymond Raillard by author, February 23, 1977. Transcript in Archives, Panhandle-Plains Historical Museum.

[16] *Ibid.*

potent force which can and has been utilized by people of vision and determination. To many the area is bleak, barren, and monotonous. To longtime residents, however, it is an area of fertile soil, vast open spaces, and in its own way a land of beauty and majesty. The unbroken landscape is perhaps the reason why Palo Duro Canyon seems to have such a fascination to the residents of the Panhandle. It is the one feature in the area with which many can call their own, regardless of how far away they live from it.

Those in attendance were not only aware of this feeling but were also wise enough to recognize how important it would be to the success of the enterprise. It was only natural, therefore, that when a name for the new organization was being discussed, this feeling for local and area pride would be important. Consequently the name "The Texas Panhandle Heritage Foundation, Incorporated" was readily adopted and the procedures for obtaining a state charter were begun.

While the legal process of incorporating was underway, the more immediate and pressing problem was to begin the fund-raising campaign. Members of the original Board of Directors traveled many miles to talk about, describe, and "sell" the idea to many communities in the Panhandle. Much support and enthusiasm was thus generated for the project, and it soon became obvious that "Panhandle Pride" was going to be an important factor in its ultimate success. Perhaps the most important and, in many ways crucial, meeting was held with the Fine Arts Council of the Amarillo Chamber of Commerce. Largely as a result of this meeting several well-known individuals became interested and enthusiastically supported the proposed project. Soon thereafter a "Functioning Board" was created to further the plans and organization.

In the meantime the local fund-raising efforts had met with limited but sufficient success to enable the organizers to begin to develop plans and construct a model of the amphitheater. While interest and enthusiasm was building in the Panhandle, the next step was to convince the Texas State Parks Board to permit the construction of a theater in the canyon. In October, 1961, an agreement was made with the Board and permission was granted to construct the theater.

Shortly before the legal process had been completed, on September 1, 1961, the Texas Panhandle Heritage Foundation was formally incorporated. Two months later the first Board of Directors met as an incorporated body to push forward with added enthusiasm and encouragement. Even though all signs were positive and the project seemed to be moving ahead rapidly, there was still the nagging problem of raising sufficient funds to begin and complete the building of the theater. As it became obvious that the dream of a few had not only the potential, but also the distinct possibility of becoming a reality, it became necessary to begin to think in terms of specific figures.

While preliminary estimates had been made no definite amount could yet be established. Being unwilling to be deterred by such technicalities, the decision was made to launch a campaign to obtain "seed" money. "Join now, decide later, and finish in December."[17] Within 10 days $10,000 had been raised in Canyon, a sum sufficient to establish an office—a chair and a small table placed in the corner of the office of the Canyon Chamber of Commerce—and employ Edith Eckhart as the first paid employee.

In the meantime the persistent efforts of the instigators of the project were beginning to pay dividends in several ways. At the November 1961 Board Meeting it was decided that the time had come to take more definitive steps toward moving ahead with the fund-raising campaign. It was at this meeting that Paul Green, who was still actively engaged in researching the history of the area, suggested that the organization request financial assistance from the state.[18] The Texas Parks and Wildlife Commission did construct the restrooms in 1963, and the following year a special appropriation from the Legislature provided for the construction of the concessions building and the dressing rooms.

Having the determination to see the projects become a reality and having the means to do so are frequently two different things. While the first was present in abundance, the latter seemed, at first glance, woefully lacking and would have daunted, frustrated, and discouraged many in pursuing the idea further. Fortunately for the future of the project, those present at this meeting were unable to see the improbability of completing so large an undertaking. It was therefore decided that ". . . we should move, and how we should move, and . . . how much."[19]

The next move was to present the plans to the Amarillo Area Foundation. The Foundation, seeing the possibilities and potential of the proposal, became a vigorous and enthusiastic supporter. The Foundation agreed to endorse the project and act as

[17] Harper Interview, March 3, 1977.

[18] *Ibid.*

[19] *Ibid.*

the agency to supervise the collection and expenditures of funds. It was then suggested that future efforts must be on a much larger scale then previously envisioned and the whole operation must be of such a scope to match the size and grandeur of the canyon itself. Consequently, a new goal of $300,000 was established and a professional fund-raising campaign firm was consulted.

Two committees were then created to start the fund-raising campaign in earnest. The first was a Development Committee which included all the original Board Members plus others throughout the area which gave a broad base to the campaign. Lawrence Hagy served as chairman of this committee and through his untiring efforts the idea was beginning to attract more attention throughout the area. At the same time a fund-raising committee was set up with Wales Madden, Jr., as chairman. Under his direction and individual efforts approximately one-half of the original goal was raised within a relatively short time.

At the same time the original fund-raising campaign was proceeding by contacting individuals in all the counties of the Panhandle. This campaign had two objectives—the first to obtain financial support, the second to acquaint the area with the concept of preserving the long and proud heritage of the Panhandle. While the first objective met with considerable success, it was the second which in many ways proved the most important and long-lasting. It was during this person-to-person contact period that there began to emerge into the open that latent force which, though it may be undefinable, typifies the area. It is the willingness of the people of the area to help their neighbors during times of adversity and share with their good fortunes. It is a feeling of uniqueness, brought about by years of struggling to overcome or at least cope with the elements of nature. It is also due partly to the fact that the Panhandle is a semi-isolated part of the State of Texas. Although the lands of the area were used to pay for the construction of the Capitol Building of the state, had sustained countless thousands of cattle, had produced millions of tons of agricultural products and had produced a sizable amount of revenue for the state, this area was, for many years, looked upon almost as a stepchild of the more populated areas of the state. It is partly because of these two factors that there developed over the years a feeling of unity and oneness among the citizens of the Panhandle.

It was this same feeling that played a vital part in bringing the proposal to fruition. The reaction of many of those contacted was

"I'm glad you thought of this, it will be something for the Panhandle."[20] With this attitude so frequently expressed, it became apparent that the production would belong to the citizens of the Panhandle.

Further confidence that the citizens of the area would support the project became apparent when it was decided to sell memberships in the Panhandle Heritage Foundation. This campaign to sell memberships was begun on the assumption that, sometime in the future, there would be a theater constructed, a script written, and a drama of some sort produced. The only visible evidence that could be used to sell the memberships was an architect's drawing, a model of the proposed theater and, probably most important, the enthusiasm of those involved.

By September 1962, approximately one-half of the amount needed was available. It was then that the future of the whole project hung in the balance. The options open were, at best, extremely limited. The first was to acknowledge that the proposal was beyond the local resources and thus admit that it must be abandoned. There is no evidence that this option was ever considered or even admitted. The other option was to use the money that was available and begin construction.

Following the advice of Cal Farley, who advised the founders to " . . . go as far as you can with the money that you have,"[21] a contract for the construction of the bowl was awarded in September 1962. By the early part of 1963, the concrete bowl and the concrete risers, the side stages, and the elevated main stage had been completed. The main stage was constructed of packed and rolled caliche. The audience sat on the concrete risers. Numbers were stenciled on the risers so each person had his own reserved piece of concrete for the evening. The parking lot had also been leveled, and a thin layer of caliche had been spread over the area.

Both the stage and parking area had certain disadvantages. During dry, hot, and windy periods, it required very little traffic to turn the red clay to a fine powder which was soon distributed over the entire area by the wind. When it rained, the same red clay was converted to a slippery, sticky sea of mud.

The first uses of the concrete bowl were an Easter sunrise service on April 14, 1963, and the dedication of the county plaques a week later. The theater remained virtually unused for over a year after these initial services. Even though the bowl itself remained

[20] Raillard Interview, February 23, 1977.

[21] Harper Interview, March 3, 1977.

empty, efforts to further the project continued. It became more and more obvious that a production of some magnitude, which would demonstrate the potential of the theater, was essential. It was therefore decided to invite Robert Nail and his production "Fandangle," a famous Western show given most years in Albany, Texas, to the canyon. The invitation was accepted, and it was decided that the show would be presented three evenings. Nail spent a month in Canyon preparing for the production, using local talent in all but the leading roles. Four days before the scheduled first performance the lead actors and singers came from Albany to rehearse and put the entire show together.

Tickets for the show had been sold in sufficient quantities to fill the theater all three nights. Two days before opening night an ominous sign appeared—rain. The day of the opening night was clear, however, and it was with a great deal of excitement that the first live performance in the new theater was anticipated. It was a beautiful evening as the audience, crews, and performers gathered. The show began and continued for all of 20 minutes when a "sudden summer thunderstorm" struck as only a Panhandle storm can strike. The rain came down in torrents. Within minutes the stage and parking lot were a sea of red mud. The audience had no alternative but to slip and slide their way to their cars as no other shelter was available.

While the first performance had a somewhat disquieting opening, the performers looked forward to the second night. The second night had an even shorter run than the first—only 15 minutes elapsed between the opening and a cloudburst. The third night had an even less auspicious beginning as the cloudburst came 10 minutes after the opening.

While the original agreement was for three performances, everyone involved was determined to put on the show. Arrangements were made to use the auditorium of the Canyon High School for Sunday evening. However, on that day the weather cleared and it was decided that once more they would try to perform in the canyon. By late in the afternoon it appeared that the weather would cooperate, so an intensive radio and television campaign was begun telling everyone who had tickets to come to the theater to see the show. By opening time it was obvious that finally the clouds were going to stay away. The evening was perfect and the show was concluded.

Even though "Fandangle" was performed only once, the response was such that any doubts about the validity of the idea of producing a show in the canyon were removed. That the site was correct for beauty and acoustics had been proven. That people would "drive thirty miles to see a show" was established. There was still, however, a major obstacle between the dream and the reality.

The major obstacle was still insufficient funds to complete the necessary additions to the theater. A contribution had been made by the Bivins family of Amarillo, Texas, to purchase sound and light equipment. It had already been determined exactly what was needed as a portable sound system had previously been set up in the theater and tested. The equipment had not, as of then, been purchased for the simple reason that there was no building in which to install it.

It was not until the Board of Directors meeting in November 1964, that the solution to this problem presented itself. After a rather lengthy discussion Pete Gilvin of the Gilvin and Terrill Construction Company, who had recently accepted a position on the Board, said: "Oh, why don't I just build you a light and sound building, if the architects will draw one that I can build with my bridge building machinery. I'll just go out there and do it."[22] He also agreed to have the parking lot paved. By the following spring it had been done, and the sound and light equipment had been purchased. Joe Batson supervised the purchasing of the equipment and did much of the work of installation, so by the spring of 1965 enough of the theater had been completed to permit the planning and preparation for a performance for that summer.

Somewhat independently of each other, Margaret Harper and Rosa Cowart began writing scenes for a performance. When they compared their ideas, they found that what each had done complimented the other. From these rather tentative beginnings, they soon concluded that a variety show with a common theme followed by a sound and light production would prove the feasibility of a much larger production and also demonstrate the near perfect acoustics of the theater. Nationwide publicity had been given to the show even before it opened. A group of travel writers had visited the canyon a few days before opening night and were given a demonstration of the sound and light equipment.

"Thundering Sounds of the West" opened on June 17, and continued until September 6, 1965. The show consisted of a series of variety acts, which were different each night depending upon which act was available. The cast was composed of 30 to 40 per-

[22] Harper Interview, March 3, 1977.

formers who were paid $5 for each performance. It was also agreed that when the audience was one thousand or more their salaries would be doubled for that performance. The cast became very adept at counting the audience, yet never missing a line or cue. By closing night 36,000 people had seen the show.

The response to the first production was so encouraging that the Board Members turned their full attention and efforts to presenting the type of production they had first talked of in 1960. Contact with Paul Green had been consistently maintained throughout this period. His six years of research and investigation of the character and mood of Panhandle history had begun to produce a rather clear concept of the type of story he wanted to tell. The one thing he sought above all else was to make the production as simple and down-to-earth as possible.[23]

The storyline, which in many ways is common to all of Green's plays, comes from his own beliefs and admiration of those elements which created the mood and character of not only the early settlers of the Panhandle of Texas, but also the entire nation.[24] The intent of his story is clearly and consistently stated— "man conquering the difficulty of nature, learning how to rule over this land, make it behave."[25] "Man is by nature a doer. He's active—he wants to build, he wants to make something, to do something."[26] Not only does man conquer, he also refuses to be conquered by either the elements or other men.

It is this theme that Green uses to portray the never-ending struggle of the early settlers of the Panhandle. The tragedies, sorrows, defeats, and frustrations are a vital and integral part of the story. The characters are never portrayed as greater-than-life, but rather as individuals who are trying to cope and survive in a harsh and often unyielding environment. Even the Indians, who returned for a brief visit to land which they had once claimed, are portrayed neither as wretched, deceitful barbarians nor as the "noble savage." Rather they are depicted as a proud people who, while admitting and accepting their defeat, still retain their dignity and self-respect. At no point during the entire production does the author create a hateful or disreputable villain. Antagonisms and violence are present, yet it is an antagonism based

[23] *The Canyon News,* June 30, 1966.

[24] *Ibid.*

[25] *Ibid.*

[26] *Ibid.*

on differing principles and violence produced by natural elements over which the characters have no control.

The storyline is that which provides continuity and holds the production together. There are, however, two other ingredients of the production which are essential—music and dancing. The selection of the music was based on the idea that the author was "... trying to give the people what you might call 'folk' or cowboy singing."[27] Once the selections had been made, the arrangements were done by Royal Brantley, Associate Professor of Music at West Texas State University, and Isaac Van Grove who had been conductor of the Chicago Opera Company, composed for the Ruth Graham Dancers, and had worked with Paul Green on other shows.

The musical arrangements of these two complemented and were complemented by the dance routines, the third dimension of the production. The choreography is the product of the expertise of Neil Hess, one of the noted choreographers of the country. Raging prairie fires, waltzes, and old-fashioned hoedowns are interjected into the production in a manner that makes each sequence a vital part of the story.

By early spring of 1966 the various parts of the production were beginning to fall into place. Auditions were being conducted by Raymond Raillard, Executive Vice-President of the Texas Panhandle Heritage Foundation. He traveled extensively throughout the Panhandle and adjoining areas with a small tape recorder interviewing potential actors and singers. Neil Hess was auditioning dancers and working out the various routines to be used. William and Margaret Moore, the directors, had been working with Green on the play and by June were ready to begin rehearsals. The scenery, props, costumes, and hundreds of small details and problems were being taken care of, and on June 30, 1966, the first dress rehearsal was held.

The following night, July 1, 1966, witnessed the culmination of six years of hard work, dreams, frustrations, disappointments overcome and skeptics silenced, when a lone horseman appeared on the edge of the canyon bearing the Texas flag. His appearance signaled the opening of the production "TEXAS."

In the two months of July and August of 1966 over 60,000 people saw the production. Each year the attendance has shown a steady increase as news of the production has spread throughout the nation and many parts of the world. On July 12, 1978 the one

[27] *Canyon News,* June 30, 1966.

millionth person entered the theater to witness the musical drama which clearly demonstrates that man is a doer and a builder.

ROAD LOG FROM CANYON, TEXAS, THROUGH PALO DURO CANYON STATE PARK

This Road Log begins at the Panhandle-Plains Historical Museum, located one block east of the junction of Interstate 27 (U. S. 87) and State Highway 217 (Palo Duro Drive), on the north side of the highway. The log continues to Palo Duro Canyon State Park, located 12 miles east on Highway 217, winds along Park Road 5 through the bottom of the canyon, and retraces for a short distance toward the City of Canyon once again.

The authoritative and interesting log will give both newcomers and seasonal rockhounds alike an in-depth look at the geology, geography, and history of a most interesting region.

The reader is referred to the map, chart, and illustrations found in the article "Geology of Palo Duro Canyon State Park."

Mileage between points	Cumulative Mileage	
	0.00	North side of State Highway 217 in front of Panhandle-Plains Historical Museum. The historical marker, left, reads:

THE CHARLES GOODNIGHT MEMORIAL TRAIL

"The highway from this museum to Palo Duro Canyon State Park is the approximate course used by Charles Goodnight, outstanding Texas cowman and trail blazer, when he trailed 1,600 cattle from Colorado to found the first ranch on the Staked Plains of Texas in 1876.

He entered precipitous Palo Duro Canyon by way of old Comanche Indian trail, drove thousands of buffalo from the present park area, and established his home ranch a few miles farther down the canyon.

Goodnight was born in Illinois March 5, 1836. At the age of nine he rode bareback to Texas behind a covered wagon driven by his parents. He hunted with Caddo Indians beyond the frontier at 14; guided Texas rangers fighting Comanche and Kiowas at 25; blazed cattle trails about 2,000 miles long with Oliver Loving at 30.

In partnership with John G. Adair, he expanded the original Palo Duro Ranch into the giant JA and other holdings of more than a million acres and 100,000 cattle. He preserved buffalo, founded a college, encouraged settlement of the plains and led in a long fight for law and order.

This foremost plainsman died March 22, 1929, and was buried at Goodnight, Texas."

0.10	0.10	Old Administration Building, West Texas State University, at left.
0.10	0.20	The modern building on the corner at left is the WTSU Science Center.
0.45	0.65	Building on the left was the armory of Company F of the 36th Division, Texas National Guard. The historical marker near the armory records:

SITE OF AN EARLY BARBED WIRE FENCE IN THE PANHANDLE

"In the latter 1800's, when fencing was needed in the tree-less Texas Panhandle, the solution proved to be barbed wire. Joseph F. Glidden of Illinois devised and by 1876 was manu-facturing (with I. L. Ellwood) the first really practical barbed wire on the market. H. B. Sanborn was sent to Texas as their agent, and remained to become a builder of the Panhandle.

Wanting free access to water and grass, ranchers at first resisted fencing. Cowboys disliked it, as fewer range riders were needed on fenced lands. Old timers grew bitter, because of blocked trails—herds had to be hauled rather than driven to market.

Yet newcomers wanted fencing, in order to have use of land purchased for ranching. Merchants and City-builders wanted fences, to assure settlement.

The T-Anchor, owned by Jot Gunter and Wm. B. Munson, real estate investors of Grayson County, built a line fence on this site in 1881, enclosing a 240,000-acre horse pasture. Also built in this area, by popular subscription, was a "drift" fence to hold cattle back from wandering south in blue northers and blizzards.

Barbed wire gradually came into general use. It saved the cattle industry, because improvements in breeding and feed-ing were possible on fenced ranges."

0.30	0.95	Ahead and downhill we see the road cross Tierra Blanca Creek and rise eastward over a series of terraces up to the High Plains surface.

0.45	1.40	Center of the bridge over Tierra Blanca Creek.
0.45	1.85	Climbing onto the 1st terrace above the floodplain.
0.50	2.35	Climbing onto the 2nd terrace.
0.60	2.95	Climbing onto the High Plains surface.
0.20	3.15	Entrance, south side of road, to Warren Hereford Ranch. Good view south and west of the Canyon Pleistocene lake basin. Note well developed caliche in road cut.

The ancient lake basin, so well displayed from this vantage point, presumably was breached and drained by the headward erosion of the Prairie Dog Town Fork of the Red River. It is not certain whether these terraces are stream terraces or wave-cut benches, or some combination of both.

One interpretation is that they are wave-cut terraces and that their position on the north and east flanks of the basin, together with the much steeper basin margins along those flanks, indicates that the prevailing wind during the Pleistocene was as it is today, i.e. from southwest to the northeast. The south and west margins of the basin slope very gently, whereas the north flank and the east flank, our present location, are much steeper. Furthermore, the more common occurrence of fossilized remains of horses, camels, elephants, sloths, and other Ice Age mammals to the southwest suggests that broad mud flats, in which the mammals became mired as they searched for prey, lay in that direction.

Much, if not most, of the lake sediments have been removed following
the breaching of the basin, and in at
least one place (near the University
Farm and just south of the overpass
to Hunsley Hills) erosion has exposed
a knob of Triassic rocks, which must
have been an island or a small shoal
in the ancient lake.

As an aside, it is interesting to re-
member that horses and camels first
evolved in North America but became
extinct here while they flourished in
the Old World. They only returned to
the New World when man brought
them. The Spanish brought the horse
to Mexico in the 1500's; the plains
Indians were using horses by the
early eighteenth century. The U. S.
Army, late in the nineteenth century,
imported camels for use in the arid
southwest. The army sergeants were
no match for the cantankerous camels,
however, and the camels eventually
ran wild. All are dead now.

0.20	3.35	Drainage at right (south) is westward into the old lake basin.
0.75	4.10	Flashing orange light at junction with Farm Road 1541. Amarillo is about 12 miles to left.
0.30	4.40	Two historical markers at right. Their narratives are as follows:

FRANCISCO VASQUEZ DE CORONADO
on the Texas Plains

"On April 22, 1540, Francisco Vasquez de Coronado (1510-
1544) set out from Culiacan (in present Sinaloa, Mexico) with
an expedition of 1500 men to search for seven golden cities
reported far to the north. Coronado entered the present
United States in Arizona and proceeded northeast to the Rio
Grande pueblos in New Mexico where he spent the winter of

1540-1541. On April 23, 1941, Coronado left the Rio Grande, travelling eastward to seek the golden City of Quivira.

A native guide called "El Turco" led the conquistadores aimlessly across the arid plains in an attempt to get them lost. On May 29, 1541, with supplies depleted, Coronado entered Palo Duro Canyon, where wild fruit and water abounded. While in the canyon Coronado discovered the guide's betrayal. On June 2, Coronado selected 30 men and started northward in quest of Quivira. The rest of the expedition, under command of Tristan de Arellano, remained in the canyon for 12 weeks before returning to the Rio Grande. According to legend, Frey Juan de Padilla conducted a feast of Thanksgiving for the group while in Palo Duro Canyon.

In 1542, after failing to find the seven cities of gold, Coronado returned to Mexico a broken man."

LOS CIBOLEROS
(New Mexican Buffalo Hunters)

"For centuries Pueblo Indians of present New Mexico trekked to the plains to hunt buffalo to supplement their diet of beans and corn. After acquiring horses from the Spanish in the 18th century, the annual trips were made more easily and with greater success. By the 19th century, the Ciboleros (from "Cibolo"—Spanish for buffalo) became very important, providing food for the growing New Mexican population and hides for the rich Santa Fe-Chihuahua trade.

Cibolero expeditions included as many as 150 people. The daring cazadores (hunters), picturesque in leather jackets and flat straw hats, rode into herds armed only with lances, killing 8 to 25 bison each in one foray, and depending on the speed, agility, and skill of their horses for safety. Others, including occasional women and children, cut meat into strips for drying and cured the hides for tanning. With their carts laden with fruits of the hunt, the Ciboleros returned to New Mexico and a heroes welcome.

The plains Indians, protecting their hunting grounds, maintained constant warfare against the Ciboleros throughout the 19th century, but the colorful lancers survived until Anglo-American hunters decimated the great buffalo herds in the late 1870's."

| 0.75 | 5.15 | To right (south) note rolling topography. The High Plains definitely are "plains," not "planes." |

1.00	6.15	St. Paul Lutheran Cemetery to right (south).
0.10	6.25	To left (north) is a typical forest of the High Plains.
0.30	6.55	A pocket-sized example of a High Plains playa. These dot the High Plains with a density of about one per square mile. Most are larger than this one; a few are smaller. In places they are aligned, suggesting a basic structural control. In other places they are oriented, i.e. they are elliptical and with their long axes parallel to sub-parallel. Study has shown that wave action produced by a prevailing south-west to northeast wind will cause elongation of a circular basin in a direction perpendicular, i.e. north-west-southeast, to the prevailing wind direction. Most of the basins are deflation wind excavated depressions; they have dunes along their downwind margins. Others may be related to deepseated desiccation dehydration fissures, solution of gypsum in the Triassic beds, and it is not impossible that one or two may be meteorite impact depressions. It has been suggested that great herds of buffalo milling around or wallowing in a concentrated area may have been the initial cause of some of these interesting depressions but this seems unlikely. Numerous small depressions a foot or so deep and 50-100 feet in diameter are scattered across the High Plains but whether or not any of these has been enlarged by buffalo to form a typical playa is uncertain.

During wet periods or following exceptionally heavy rains, these playas become playa lakes. Unfortunately, they have floors of very low permeability clay, and the runoff that they trap evaporates rapidly. Infiltration of water below the playa bottom is negligible, although a number of studies and experiments have evaluated various methods of aquifer recharge through playas (Buckthal and Underwood, 1977).

Just beyond this playa on the right is a much smaller and younger one.

0.80	7.35	Windmill reminds us of a form of energy that is abundant on the High Plains but which, thus far, has been utilized to a minimal extent.
0.85	8.20	Crossing the large-diameter water line of the Lake Meredith water distribution system, which carries water for municipalities as far south as Lamesa, more than 150 miles from here. The line at this point is eight feet in diameter.
0.50	8.70	Surface slopes gently eastward and southeastward toward Palo Duro Canyon.
0.05	8.75	Drainage to right (south) represents the upper reaches of a major tributary to Palo Duro drainage, Timbercreek.
0.20	8.95	At right (south), spreader dam across channel, an effort to control erosion and to conserve runoff. Downstream from dam, note vertical banks of channel. In this area, you can see clearly that grass plays much the same role in landscape evolution and control that a thin resistant layer of rock would play. Here also, and in many other areas in the region, the process of "piping" is important in the widening of channels. That is, water percolates downward along desiccation fissures or along burrows or roots and rootlets and emerges on

the free face of the bank of a channel. Grain by grain removal of the unconsolidated material widens the channel by undercutting its banks. This is a major process in the arid and semi-arid southwest.

0.15	9.10	Shallow drainage channel crosses under road and meanders toward Timbercreek Canyon. Mesquite trees, unfortunately great water hogs, abound. By the way, old-timers in the region agree that the mesquite never blooms until *after* the last freeze.
1.05	10.15	Marshall ranch house. Immediately beyond, road right (south) to Sunday Canyon development, an area of weekend and permanent residences with beautiful views of Palo Duro Canyon.
0.10	10.25	Headward reaches of Timbercreek Canyon to right (south). Note the thick caliche "caprock" of the Ogallala (Pliocene), much thicker here than where we see it along our drive into the canyon. The underlying Trujillo Formation (Upper Triassic) of the Dockum Group has been eroded into several totem pole-like pinnacles. A luxuriant growth of cottonwoods and junipers covers the canyon floor.
0.20	10.45	Good view right (south) of Timbercreek Canyon and the caliche of the Ogallala caprock. Note the hummocky character of the caliche, giving it a grossly "algal" appearance. With no limestone beds in the surface and near-surface stratigraphic section, you may well wonder about the source of the calcite in the caliche. There are two: abundant calcareous cement in underlying rock and calcareous windblown dust from New Mexico, where limestone outcrops are

widespread. The red beds of the upper part of the Trujillo contrast with the lighter color of the overlying Ogallala.

0.40	10.85	Elkins Ranch entrance left (north); good view of Palo Duro Canyon trending generally southeast. Ahead on the right is Six Gun Territory and just beyond, the Canyon Country Trading Post.
0.10	10.95	Entrance to Palo Duro Canyon State Park; beginning of Park Road 5. Stonework at entrance and office beautifully done in the 1930's by the men of the Civilian Conservation Corps (the "CCC"). The rock is the resistant sandstone of the Triassic Trujillo Formation.

Palo Duro Canyon State Park, established in 1931, covers slightly more than 15,000 acres, only a small part of the much larger Palo Duro Canyon which extends far to the southeast. In this area, the Canyon is 600-800 feet deep; elevation at the rim is about 3,500 feet. Palo Duro, in Spanish, means "hard wood" and refers to the junipers in the canyon from which the Indians were fond of fashioning their bows and arrows.

0.15	11.10	Historical marker at left; the narrative reads:

THE OLD JA RANCH

"In 1876, veteran Texas cattleman Charles Goodnight entered Palo Duro Canyon by way of an old Comanche Indian trail near here, to establish the first ranch in this area.
In 1877, Goodnight in partnership with Englishman John Adair moved farther down the canyon to lay out headquarters of the JA Ranch. This pioneer venture became one of the

greatest cattle operations in the world, taking in more than a million acres of land and grazing 101,023 head of cattle.

Goodnight had become acquainted with the Palo Duro as a scout and guide for Texas Rangers during the Civil War. He knew that the canyon, fenced in by the overhanging caprocks, was an ideal spot for a ranch; it furnished water and shelter in the winter and the adjacent plains provided ideal grazing in the summer.

Upper division of this ranch (the Park area) was reserved for the pure bred, or JA Herd. The vast lower end of the JA was ranged by the Longhorns—gradually being improved by better blood.

In 1887 the Goodnight-Adair partnership was ended. Adair retained the JA, which in the hands of his heirs, is still one of the great ranches of Texas."

0.15	11.25	Fenced pasture to left contains a few head of the famous Texas Longhorn steer, not always visible from the road. They are magnificent animals that are all but extinct now. During the halcyon days of the nineteenth century cattle industry, an estimated 10 million head of Texas Longhorns were driven up the Goodnight-Loving, Chisholm, or other trails to Abilene, Kansas.
		In 1956 and 1957, the Aoudad or Barbary Sheep were introduced into Palo Duro Canyon by the Texas Parks and Wildlife Department. These wary, skittish animals have thrived in the rugged back country of the canyon and have increased in number to the point where they are hunted during a short season each year.
		Sometime ago, just ahead on the right, a herd of 15 mule deer were seen grazing just a few yards off the road.
0.50	11.75	Cliffside residences of some of the Park employees at right. These dwellings also are made of the resistant sandstone of the Trujillo.

0.10	11.85	Sharp turn right to Interpretive Center.

0.10   11.95   Interpretive Center. From the terrace, or from its several canyon-side picture windows, you can see the sequence of rock units clearly distinguished by their contrasting color and weathering characteristics. Extending upward from the canyon floor for 150 feet or so is the brick-red Quartermaster Formation of Late Permian age. Directly in front of us, in the middle distance, are the Spanish Skirts, a bluff on the flank of Timber Mesa. There, the red and white striped claystone of the Quartermaster is overlain by the maroon and lavender claystone of the Tecovas. These striking colors, together with the ruffled appearance created on the lower slopes by small gullies, give the appearance of the flaring skirts of a Spanish dancer. Just to the right of the Spanish Skirts is Catarina Cave, a feature that owes its origin more to "piping" than to solution.

Unconformably overlying the Quartermaster Formation is the Dockum Group of Late Triassic age. The Dockum consists of the Tecovas Formation (average thickness 120 feet) below and the Trujillo Formation (average thickness 200 feet) above. The Tecovas, the variegated claystone overlying the Quartermaster, has few resistant beds and is largely a slope-former. Near the top is a distinctive clean white fine-grained quartz "sugar sand" up to 40 feet thick.

The Ogallala Formation (Pliocene and 20-40 feet thick) is the light-colored unit overlying the Dockum

Group, and the unconformity separating the two represents about 190
million years. The caliche caprock
at the top of the Ogallala is clearly
visible. Not evident at this range is
the basal member of the Ogallala, the
so-called "Potter Gravel," which contains pebbles of igneous, metamorphic, and sedimentary rocks derived
from the rising Rocky Mountains to
the west. Also in this basal unit of the
Ogallala are waterworn, reworked
shells of the pelecypod *Gryphaea*
testifying to the presence in the area
at one time of rocks of Cretaceous age.
The blanket of sand, silt, and gravel
spread eastward by streams during
the late Miocene and early Pliocene
was deposited on an uneven surface
of Permian, Triassic and, in places,
Cretaceous, rocks. Today, as the
water table in the Ogallala drops,
those farms and ranches overlying
buried valleys may have 40-50 years
of irrigation water remaining whereas those overlying buried hills may be
without irrigation water in 15-20
years.

Incising the Ogallala in places are
late Pliocene and Pleistocene lake
basins, many of them completely
filled with sediments. As you scan the
upper part of the section in the canyon walls, these lake sediments are
distinctively whiter than the surrounding Ogallala. The uppermost
material, the unnamed cover sand, is
largely eolian sand deposited widely
over the High Plains and in places is
as young as yesterday.

From this vantage point you can see
the well-developed three-level effect
in the canyon: (1) the broad canyon
floor; (2) the broad mesas capped by
the resistant sandstone of the Tru-

jillo Formation; and (3) the upper-most High Plains surface. Also from this point, you can see The Light-house, an erosional pinnacle of the Trujillo Formation and a well-known landmark. It is in a rather inacces-sible location about three miles up Little Sunday Canyon from the junc-ture with Palo Duro.

Stratigraphically, Palo Duro Canyon can be placed at the top of the Grand Canyon in Arizona, i.e. the Quarter-master Formation, the lowest and oldest unit exposed widely in Palo Duro is about the same age as the Coconino Sandstone, the rock unit that forms the rim of much of the Grand Canyon.

0.10	12.05	Park Road 5.
0.65	12.70	Longhorn steer pasture to left; chimney and fireplace mark the site of old ranch house.
0.15	12.85	Begin descent down steep grade; use low gear. At this point on the left can be seen a bed of greenish-gray sand that has yielded fossil horse teeth of early Pleistocene age. In the brown sand nearby, the remains of a large land tortoise were found. These sediments are believed to have been deposited in and on the margin of a Pleistocene lake.
0.10	12.95	In distance, below horizon, Lighthouse can be seen. Ogallala caliche caprock to right and left along road.
0.15	13.10	At sharp curve left, "Potter Gravel" at base of Ogallala visible overlying uppermost formation of the Dockum Group, the Trujillo.

0.10   13.20   Broad bench (mesa) supported by the
                                     resistant sandstone of the Trujillo. To
                                     left, mudstone and sandstone of the
                                     upper Trujillo.

                                     Here the resistant cross-bedded sand-
                                     stone of the Trujillo may be examined
                                     at close range. In this zone, there are
                                     abundant spherical to sub-spherical
                                     concretions weathering out of the
                                     Trujillo. Three-dimensional perspec-
                                     tives of some of the cross beds are
                                     available, and joints and their effect
                                     on weathering are especially well dis-
                                     played.

                                     A quick run up slope across the road
                                     will bring you to the "Potter Gravel"
                                     at the base of the Ogallala and to the
                                     silicified (opalized) siltstone just
                                     above. Unfortunately, no precious
                                     opal is recorded from Palo Duro Can-
                                     yon.

0.05   13.25   Good view of the main part of Palo
                                     Duro Canyon. The drainage here is
                                     the Prairie Dog Town Fork of the Red
                                     River.

                                     To right, the Trujillo Formation rep-
                                     resenting channel and floodplain de-
                                     posits of streams flowing southeast
                                     to northwest. WTSU faculty and stu-
                                     dents have studied the transverse
                                     braid bars well developed in this part
                                     of the Trujillo and concluded that
                                     much of this material was deposited
                                     in the distal (lower) parts of a braided
                                     stream system (Asquith and others,
                                     1973; Asquith and Cramer, 1975, p.
                                     657-661).

                                     Across the Canyon in the wall the
                                     stratigraphic section is easily distin-
                                     guished: the brick-red claystone of the
                                     Quartermaster Formation at the
                                     base; the variegated claystone of the

Tecovas and the overlying mudstone and resistant sandstone of the Trujillo; lighter colored Ogallala with the resistant caliche caprock at the top; the whole capped by young cover sand.

0.20   13.45   At right, a slump block of the fine-grained quartz "sugar sand" of the upper Tecovas; note the distinctive box-work of "honey comb" weathered surface.

0.20   13.65   Sharp turn left.

0.10   13.75   Sharp turn right. Straight ahead in slump block is good view of contrast in color and lithology of Quartermaster and overlying Tecovas.

0.15   13.90   Outcrop of Quartermaster at right.

0.05   13.95   Canyon floor; stables at left.

0.05   14.00   Palo Duro Pioneer Amphitheater to right. The prominent cliff is the backdrop for the musical drama "Texas," which features a company of 80 actors and singers. Approximately a million people have seen this delightful program during the years it has been staged, to date.

0.30   14.30   Goodnight Trading Post to left. For many years, the trading post was housed in the building now used as the Interpretive Center.

0.15   14.45   At right is the two-mile, narrow-gauge Sad Monkey Railroad, named for the face of a sad monkey visible in the resistant Trujillo Sandstone that caps Triassic Peak, overlooking the train station. Lower slopes of the peak have several pedestal rocks.

0.15	14.60	Bridge over Timbercreek. Please note as you glance about during the drive through the park that the Quartermaster Formation dips gently first one way, then another. These are not necessarily slump blocks; most commonly these dips represent the presence of folds produced by the expansion of anhydrite as it converted to gypsum during the process of hydration.
0.10	14.70	At right is turnoff to parking area for Catarina Cave, which can be reached by following an easy trail several hundred yards westward. As mentioned earlier, the cave is not a true solution feature for the most part. It is an example of a feature that was produced by grain-by-grain removal of material by "piping" rather than removal by solution.
		Several rock shelters are visible high under the resistant Trujillo sandstone that caps Timber Mesa to the south.
0.25	14.95	Cliffs ahead have Ogallala on skyline, with Trujillo, Tecovas, and Quartermaster below. Prominent layer at 11:30 o'clock is massive, resistant sandstone of the Trujillo. At 3 o'clock across the canyon, is the distinct contact between the Quartermaster and the overlying Tecovas Formation.
0.15	15.10	Entrance to Hackberry campground at left; old windmill and tank at right.
		Trailer dump station ahead on left.
0.05	15.15	Rest rooms and water fountain at left.

0.05	15.20	Hackberry campground to right and left. Good outcrop of Quartermaster just upstream to left.
0.05	15.25	Water Crossing (WC) No. 1. In late August 1968, following heavy rain in the drainage basin of the Prairie Dog Town Fork of the Red River, water rose 11 feet above this low-water bridge. This is an example of the one in 50-year or one in 100-year flood that seems to occur at much shorter intervals.
0.05	15.30	Replica of pioneer dugout to right; Quartermaster Formation in hillside to left.
0.10	15.40	Paved road right to picnic area and rest rooms.
0.20	15.60	Short, unpaved side road to right just before bridge; convenient parking place from which to reach Velloso Dome, about 350 yards distant.

To reach Velloso Dome, walk west a few yards, cross main channel of Prairie Dog Town Fork of Red River, continue west to channel of Sunday Creek; walk upstream 300 yards or so to outcrop of massive gypsum of the Cloud Chief.

The massive gypsum that crops out in Velloso Dome is the Cloud Chief Gypsum that immediately underlies the Quartermaster Formation. Velloso Dome, exposed over only a few acres, has structural relief of a few tens of feet. It was named by Fandrich (1966, p. 25) who suggested that it was the result of the hydration of anhydrite to gypsum. Especially noteworthy are the small-scale folds and faults that were produced probably during the volume adjustment of the anhydrite as it converted to gypsum during hydration.

0.15	15.75	Capitol Peak at 2:45 o'clock. There the Quartermaster is overlain by the Tecovas.
0.10	15.85	The skyline at left is formed by the Ogallala, which constitutes the upper part of precipitous Fortress Cliff.
0.30	16.15	Just beyond sign for WC No. 2, good view at 10 o'clock of Fortress Cliff; Trujillo overlain by Ogallala.
0.05	16.20	WC No. 2. Quartermaster downstream to left with Fortress Cliff beyond; Capitol Peak upstream to the right.
0.10	16.30	Loop road (alternate Park Road 5) enters from right; continue straight ahead.
0.05	16.35	Good view to left of Fortress Cliff and complex lateral changes in Trujillo. The caliche caprock of the Ogallala is well developed. In nearground, Tecovas overlies Quartermaster.
0.20	16.55	WC No. 3. Fortress Cliff in view upstream to left; Quartermaster Formation downstream to right.
0.30	16.85	WC No. 4. Quartermaster Formation in sight downstream to left.
0.05	16.90	To right, Fortress Cliff camping area, with shelters.
0.15	17.05	At 9 o'clock, prominent hill of Quartermaster with hill of Tecovas beyond; backdrop is formed by Fortress Cliff. At the base of the cliff near the southeast end, there is an area of springs and lush vegetation.

0.10	17.15	WC No. 5. Quartermaster in view upstream to left and downstream to right. During occasional flash floods, people may be stranded for several hours between these water crossings. During the flash flood of 28-29 August 1968, no lives were lost, but helicopters were used to evacuate stranded park visitors. One pickup camper was washed downstream.
		On the left just beyond WC No. 5, there are numerous large blocks of Trujillo sandstone, some of which are as large as a small house. This area is aptly named the "Rock Garden."
0.15	17.30	Sunflower campground road to right.
0.20	17.50	Sunflower campground road to right.
0.05	17.55	Note large Trujillo boulders at left with well-developed cross beds.
0.20	17.75	Dirt road to right.
0.15	17.90	Cottonwood picnic area to right, with drinking fountain, rest rooms. The 1968 flood deposited about a foot and a half of sand and silt over this area, inundating picnic tables and benches. Cone-shaped areas of turbulence around some of the cottonwoods prevented deposition until the stage of declining current, when sand and silt with inward dipping cross beds filled in the symmetrical cone-shaped void. Six weeks later, the gentle etching and erosive action of wind had revealed the eroded upper ends of the cross beds as concentric rings around the tree trunks. These structures have been described by Underwood and Lambert (1974). These quaquaversal inward dipping (centroclinal) cross beds have since been identified in ancient rocks in Wales and in Poland.

0.25	18.15	Cactus camping area to right.
0.10	18.25	Good view dead ahead of Quartermaster-Tecovas contact. That unconformity has a temporal value of about 30-40-million years.
0.20	18.45	Paved road right to day camping area with rest rooms.
0.05	18.50	Paved road left to Mesquite ("Rock Garden") camping area with trailer hookups. A well-worn trail leads up the slopes of the east canyon wall to the left, which exposes a beautiful section of Tecovas.
0.05	18.55	Paved road right to day camping area.
0.25	18.80	Circle; proceed around to historical marker on south side.
0.05	18.85	Historical marker, which reads:

BATTLE OF PALO DURO CANYON — 28 September 1874

"One of the most significant battles of 1874-75 Indian campaign: columns of troops converging from five directions harassed Indians on Panhandle Plains for over six months. The 4th Cavalry under Col. Ranald S. Mackenzie, moving north from Ft. Concho, tracked a large band of Indians to their secret canyon camp.

Moving silently at dawn down a perilous path on the south rim, the first troops reached the floor of the canyon before the aroused camp fled. Some of the warriors took up positions on the canyon walls from which they fired on the troops, seeking to give their families time to escape. Realizing his tactical disadvantage, Mackenzie ordered the Indian camp and supplies burned and withdrew taking along 1400 captured horses (1000 of which he later destroyed).

The cavalry suffered no casualties in the fight and only four Indian dead were counted. Having lost half their horses as well as all their supplies and shelter, the Indians drifted back to their reservations at Ft. Sill and Ft. Reno."

0.10	18.95	Turn right on Alternate Park Road 5.

0.05   19.00   Barren Tecovas slopes to left, 9-10
                         o'clock, are deadly. A wise precaution
                         is:

                                 Avoid slopes without vegetation,
                                       especially if you are
                                       wearing sneakers.

                         These barren slopes, usually fairly
                         steep, develop on mudstone or clay-
                         stone. Because of abundant calcite in
                         the rocks, evaporation and resulting
                         precipitation on the surface of calcite
                         creates a "case hardened" effect.
                         Thus, although the slope looks like it
                         consists of soft rock, in fact it is very
                         difficult to obtain a hold, especially if
                         you are sliding.

                         The very real danger is that unwary
                         and inexperienced visitors playing
                         carelessly on these slopes may begin
                         to slide, and once they begin moving
                         downslope, it is almost impossible to
                         dig in for a handhold or foothold. The
                         crucial factor is that the typical mud-
                         stone slope ends in a 20-40 foot verti-
                         cal drop entirely sufficient to break
                         necks, backs, legs, and arms and to
                         cause fatal concussions. It is sadden-
                         ing to report that almost every year
                         someone loses his life in the canyon.

0.10   19.10   WC No. 6. Good view downstream to
                         left of the entire section, Quarter-
                         master to Ogallala; the caliche cap-
                         rock is well developed.

0.45   19.55   At 9 o'clock an area pockmarked with
                         openings enlarged by piping.

                         At 10:30 o'clock, the deadly Devil's
                         Slide; it has taken several lives.

0.25	19.80	Paved road right to Juniper trailer area; look left and back to north slope of Devil's Slide; note vertical drop at base of steep slope.
0.15	19.95	At 9 o'clock, Quartermaster-Tecovas contact which also is visible in hillside ahead.
0.35	20.30	Good view ahead and across canyon of Fortress Cliff.
0.30	20.60	Outcrops of red siltstone of Quartermaster to left and right; thin seams are satin spar gypsum. Note also the varied dip of the Quartermaster.
0.05	20.65	Pseudo-karst or "false solution caves" at left.
0.30	20.95	Fortress Cliff, 1-2 o'clock.
0.20	21.15	Good view of Capitol Peak ahead; main part of Palo Duro Canyon at 2 o'clock.
0.15	21.30	At 9 o'clock, another good view of Quartermaster-Tecovas unconformity (an apparent disconformity).
0.10	21.40	A typical outcrop of the lower part of the Quartermaster that features the converging-diverging horizontal to sub-horizontal seams of satin spar gypsum within the brick-red claystone of the Upper Permian Quartermaster Formation.
		The Quartermaster is abundant with interesting sedimentary structures. Some of its characteristic features are reduction halos and reduction zones. Pseudomorphs or "false forms" after halite (salt) crystals ("hopper crystals") are common on the underside of some beds.

0.15	21.55	End of Alternate Park Road 5 (loop road); turn left.
0.10	21.65	WC No. 2. Capitol Peak upstream to left.
0.60	22.25	Left, parking area for day camping.
0.20	22.45	Park Road 5; turn left.
0.05	22.50	Replica of old dugout to left.
0.10	22.60	WC No. 1 and Hackberry campground. Downstream and around the bend a large slump block of Quartermaster has partially blocked the channel of the Prairie Dog Town Fork of the Red River. This is a good example of a process that plays a major role in widening the canyon. Eolian transport, slope wash, and creep all are processes that operate to move material, but the episodic and catastrophic processes like slump and rock slide are those which produce the dramatic and significant changes.
0.10	22.70	Rest rooms and water fountain at the right.
0.05	22.75	Trailer dump station; just beyond paved road right to Hackberry campground.
		Old windmill and tank to left.
0.25	23.00	Sad Monkey at summit of Triassic Peak, straight ahead.
0.15	23.15	Unpaved road left to Catarina Cave parking area.
0.10	23.25	Stone bridge over Timbercreek.

0.15	23.40	Sad Monkey Railroad; just behind the station is a cactus garden, a partly shaded green lawn, and a water fountain.
0.15	23.55	Goodnight Trading Post.
0.30	23.85	Palo Duro Pioneer Amphitheater; turn left.
0.05	23.90	Northwest side of parking area.

From this vantage point it is possible to obtain a good view of pedestal rocks and of the Tecovas and Trujillo formations. The nature trail that leads downslope from the rim ends near here. You may wish to spend a few minutes looking at the amphitheater where "Texas" is staged and at the adjoining facilities. This summer, from June 15-August 20, "Texas" was given nightly, except Sundays. The show averages only about three "rainouts" per summer.

0.10	24.00	Exit amphitheater parking area onto Park Road 5; turn left.
0.05	24.05	Stables at right.
0.40	24.45	"Sugar sand" of the Tecovas to left; road climbs past resistant sandstone of the Trujillo.
0.45	24.90	Bench on mesa capped by sandstone of the Trujillo.
0.40	25.30	High Plains surface; good view of Palo Duro at left, showing the three-level or "balcony" topography.
0.75	26.05	Road left to Interpretative Center.
0.80	26.85	Park entrance and headquarters.

0.15	27.00	Entrance to Palo Duro Canyon State Park. Sign: Canyon - 12 miles; Amarillo - 24 miles.
0.75	27.75	Headward reaches of Timbercreek Canyon, at left.
0.40	28.15	Road left to Sunday Canyon. To right and left in this area you may see incipient channels tributary to Palo Duro.

Because a volcanic ash bed (Pearlette Type "O") dated at 600,000 years clearly has been incised by part of the canyon system, we can say that the development of Palo Duro Canyon has been accomplished over a span of 600,000 years. But in the area of the incipient channels far upstream from the main canyon, the canyon system may be as young (or as old) as the last heavy rain.

3.00	31.15	Lake Meredith water line heading south to Lamesa; Amarillo skyline to right.
0.90	32.05	Relatively young playa to left (south).
0.50	32.55	Playa lake.

Seeing this playa again, we are reminded of the possible role of buffalo in the formation of High Plains playas. We may be more inclined to accept the thesis that buffalo left their imprint on the plains surface when we consider the size of some of the herds. A single herd, sighted near the Arkansas River in 1871, was estimated at ". . . not less than four million head" (Rathjen, 1973, p. 146).

2.65	35.20	Intersection, Texas 217 with Farm Road 1541. Turn left (north), to Amarillo; straight ahead four miles to Canyon.

INDEX